McDougal Littell
Wordskills

SO-BEC-820

Purple Level

James E. Coomber
Concordia College
Moorhead, Minnesota

Howard D. Peet
North Dakota State University
Fargo, North Dakota

McDougal Littell
A HOUGHTON MIFFLIN COMPANY
Evanston, Illinois • Boston • Dallas

IMPORTANT: No part of this book may be reproduced or transmitted in any form or by any means, electronic or mechanical, including photo-copying, recording, or by any information storage and retrieval system, without permission in writing from the Publisher.

ISBN-13: 978-0-395-97990-7   ISBN-10: 0-395-97990-0

Copyright © 2000 by McDougal, Littell & Company
Box 1667, Evanston, Illinois 60204
All rights reserved. Printed in the United States of America.

13 14 15 16 17-DWI-09 08 07 06

CONTENTS

To the Student

Why study vocabulary? Increasing the number of words that you know helps you read, write, and speak better. You'll understand more of what you read with less reliance on the dictionary, and you'll be able to express yourself more accurately. This doesn't mean using twenty-dollar words to amaze others. It just means using the right words to say exactly what you mean.

How to Use This Book

You may notice something unusual about this vocabulary book. Definitions are not given with the word lists. Instead, you are given something more powerful—strategies for determining the meanings of words yourself. You'll find this information in Strategies for Unlocking Word Meaning (pages 1-12). Then, in the following units, you will master new words using a five-step process:

1. First you will infer the word's meaning through context clues.
2. Second you will refine your understanding by studying the word's use in a reading selection.
3. Then your understanding will be reinforced through a variety of exercises.
4. Next you will relate the word to other words in the same family.
5. Finally you will use the word in writing and speaking.

The words in this book are ones you are likely to encounter in your reading. Some you may already know; others may be completely unfamiliar. As you study these words, try to move them into your "active vocabulary." This means that you understand the words well enough to use them in your speaking and writing.

A Personal Vocabulary-Building Program

You can apply the vocabulary skills in this book to learning any new words that you encounter. Here are several tips that will help you:

1. Keep a vocabulary notebook. Jot down the new words you encounter. Record the essential information for each word: correct spelling, part of speech, pronunciation, definition.
2. Review the words in your notebook. Take a few minutes each day to study them. Set a realistic goal of learning a certain number of new words per week.
3. Study the words actively. Active study means that you use as many senses as possible in studying the word. Say the word. Listen to yourself say it. See the word in your mind's eye. Then make sure you use the word as soon as possible in conversation or in writing. A rule of thumb is that if you use a word twice, it is yours.
4. Invent your own memory devices. Try to associate the word with other similar words you know. Create a mental image that relates to the word and helps you remember its meaning. One student remembered the meaning of the word *pretentious*, "showy, flaunting," by picturing a small boy playing make-believe, *pretending* to be a king.

There is one final reason for studying vocabulary, one that we hope you discover for yourself as you use this book: Words are fascinating! They are as surprising and alive and insightful as the people who use them.

Special Unit: Strategies for Unlocking Word Meaning

What happens when you encounter an unfamiliar word in your reading? If you have a dictionary at hand, you can look up the word. If you don't have a dictionary, you still have two excellent strategies that can help you make sense of the word: **context clues** and **word parts analysis.** You will be using these strategies in every unit of this book. With practice, you can master these strategies and improve your reading skills.

Part A   Determining a Word's Meaning from Context

Skilled readers often use context clues to determine a word's meaning. **Context** refers to the words or sentences before or after a certain word that help clarify what the word means. There are several types of context clues you can look for, including **definition and restatement, example, comparison, contrast**, and **cause and effect**.

Definition and Restatement

Sometimes a writer will directly define a word, especially if the word is a technical term that may be unfamiliar to readers. Here is an example:

The doctor used a *sphygmomanometer*, an instrument that measures blood pressure.

Through the use of a definition as the context clue, the meaning of *sphygmomanometer* becomes obvious. More often, a writer will restate the meaning in a less precise form than a dictionary definition, as in the following:

During the emergency, the pilot *jettisoned* his surplus fuel; in other words, he threw the fuel overboard to lighten the plane.

Definition and restatement are often signaled by punctuation (note the comma in the first example) and by key words and phrases, such as *in other words* in the example above.

Words Signaling Definition and Restatement		
which is	or	also known as
that is	in other words	also called

Example

The context in which a word appears may include one or more **examples** that unlock the meaning of an unfamiliar word, as in the following sentence:.

The zoologist's research involved several types of *lepidoptera*, including butterflies and moths.

Although the word *lepidoptera* is not fully defined through the context in which it appears, the two examples, *butterflies* and *moths*, reveal a great deal of information about the meaning of *lepidoptera,* a group of insects with broad wings whose larvae are caterpillars.

The example clue may be signaled by punctuation such as the comma in the example sentence above. Certain words and phrases may also signal examples.

Words Signaling Examples		
like	for instance	this
including	especially	these
such as	other	these include
for example		

Comparison

Another type of context clue is **comparison.** The writer makes a comparison between what is referred to by the word in question and something that is more familiar. By noting the similarities between the things described, you can get an idea of the meaning of the unfamiliar word.

Similar to the other members of the hog family, the *peccary* forages for roots with its snout and tusks.

Although you may not know exactly what a *peccary* is from this sentence, you at least know it is in the pig family and that it has a snout and tusks. Comparisons are often signaled by these key words:

Words Signaling Comparisons		
like	resembling	also
as	likewise	identical
in the same way	similarity	related
similar to		

Contrast

Context may also help reveal the meaning of a word through **contrast,** as in this example:

Rather than adopt the *penurious* spending habits of her parents, Jane was generous with her money.

In this example the structure of the sentence indicates to us that *penurious* is the opposite of the word *generous.* The words *Rather than* imply a contrast, not a similarity. The following key words and phrases signal contrasts:

Words Signaling Contrasts		
but	on the other hand	dissimilar
although	unlike	different
on the contrary	in contrast to	however
rather than		

Cause and Effect

Another type of context clue is **cause and effect**. The cause of an action or event may be stated using an unfamiliar word. If, however, the effect of that action is stated in familiar terms, it can help you understand the unfamiliar word. Consider the following example:

Keisha was *emaciated* as a result of losing weight during her long illness.

In this sentence, the cause—a long illness leads to the effect—losing weight. Therefore, *emaciated* must mean "made unnaturally thin." Certain key words and phrases may signal cause and effect:

Words Signaling Cause and Effect		
because	consequently	when
since	therefore	as a result

Inference from General Context

Often the clues to the meaning of an unfamiliar word are not as obvious as those used in the preceding examples. You will need to **infer**, or draw a conclusion about, the word's meaning. In some cases, the entire sentence may suggest or hint at the meaning of the word. When no specific clues are given, read the whole sentence carefully to get some sense of the meaning of the word. Consider this example:

The Wolfman is a classic movie about a *lycanthrope* who grew excessively hairy whenever the moon was full.

Even though you may not know the word *lycanthrope*, you can probably guess its meaning by noting the last part of the sentence, which at least partially explains it. The words that surround *lycanthrope* suggest that it is another word for *werewolf*, notorious monster from folklore.

In some cases, information several sentences away from the unfamiliar word may unlock the meaning. Study the following example:

The doctors prescribed a strict *regimen* for Mr. Thompson following his heart attack. While he was in the hospital, he attended lectures on nutrition and physical fitness. He was given booklets to read and information to memorize. After he was released, he was instructed to watch his weight carefully, eat foods low in fat and sodium, and exercise on a regular basis.

Clues to the meaning of *regimen* are found in the last sentence. Watching his weight, eating foods low in fat and sodium, and exercising regularly are all part of the regimen, or controlled system of diet and exercise, that will help Mr. Thompson recover from his heart attack.

Sometimes the supporting details in a paragraph must be examined together to help you infer the meaning of an unfamiliar word. Look at the example below.

Her living room featured an *eclectic* mix of furnishings. The end tables were French Provincial; the sofa and easy chairs were a contemporary style; the rocking chairs were Early American; and the coffee table was homemade.

Determining Meaning from Context Look for context clues to help you determine the meaning of each italicized word. Write the definition in the blank.

1. The tightrope walker's foothold seemed very *tenuous* as he wavered back and forth in the air.

   _____

2. During her bout with measles, Pat had such *photophobia* that she closed all the draperies and turned off the lights.

   _____

3. When the *cooper* was finished working for the day, he carried all of his newly made barrels into a storage room.

   _____

4. Unfortunately, all *miscreants* are not in jail.

   _____

5. Because of its appearance, *pyrite* is known as fool's gold.

   _____

6. It seemed like a *propitious* omen for Zachary when he found the lucky penny.

   _____

7. The great dark *manse* reminded Rachel of her uncle's old manor house in Hungary.

   _____

8. One kind of deep-sea diving apparatus seen in Jacques Cousteau's films is the *bathyscaph*.

   _____

9. In order to rid the garden of weeds with trailing underground root systems, you must completely *deracinate* the plants.

   _____

10. *Colloquialisms*, such as "gimme a break" and "okay," are not acceptable in formal settings.

    _____

Number correct _____ (total 10)

Understanding Context Clues Use a dictionary to learn the meaning of any unfamiliar words in the list below. Then, for each word, write a sentence that contains a context clue related to the word's meaning. Try to use a different type of context clue for each sentence. After the sentence, name the kind of context clue you used, choosing from one of the following: **definition and restatement; example; comparison; contrast;** and **cause and effect.**

| burly | criterion | impeach | aversion | acme |

1. _____

_____

2. _____

_____

3. _____

_____

4. _____

_____

5. _____

_____

Number correct _____ (total 5)

Part B Determining Meaning Through Word Analysis

Word analysis is another way to determine a new word's meaning. If you know what each part of a word means, you can often understand the complete word.

Prefix   a word part that is added to the beginning of another word or word part
Suffix   a word part that is added to the end of another word or word part
Base word   a complete word to which a prefix and/or a suffix may be added
Root   a word part to which a prefix and/or a suffix may be added. A root cannot stand alone.

Examine the word *disrespectful*. It is made up of the prefix *dis-*, the base word *respect*, and the suffix *-ful*.

dis ("the opposite of") + respect ("to honor") + ful ("full of") disrespectful = showing a lack of respect

Now look at a word with a root instead of a base word. *Invincible* is made up of the prefix *in-* ("not"), the Latin root *vinc* ("to conquer"), and the suffix *-ible* ("having the quality of"). Therefore, something *invincible* is "incapable of being conquered."

Prefixes

The following chart contains prefixes that have only one meaning.

Prefixes That Have a Single Meaning		
Prefix	**Meaning**	**Example**
bene-	good	benefit
circum-	around	circumvent
col-, com-, cor-	with, together	collapse, compile
contra-	opposed	contradict
equi-	equal	equidistant
extra-	outside	extralegal
hemi-	half	hemisphere
hyper-	over, above	hypercritical
inter-	between, among	international
intra-	within	intracellular
intro-	into	introvert
mal-	bad	maltreat
micro-	tiny	microfilm
mid-	halfway	midday
mis-	wrong	misspell
non-	not	nonworking
post-	after in time, space	postpone
pre-	before	predawn
retro-	backward, behind	retroactive
sub-	under, below	subzero

Some prefixes have more than one meaning. Study these common prefixes listed in the following chart.

Prefixes That Have More Than One Meaning

Prefix	Meaning	Example
ab-, a-	not	abnormal
	away	absent
	up, out	arise
ad-	motion toward	adopt
	nearness to	adjoin
ante-	before, prior to	antecedent
	in front of	anteroom
anti-	against	anticensorship
	prevents, cures	antidote
	opposite, reverse	antimatter
be-	around, by	beset
	about	bemoan
de-	away from, off	derail
	down	decline
	reverse action of	defrost
dis-	lack of	distrust
	not	dishonest
	away	dispatch
em-, en-	to get into, on	embark
	to make, cause	enfeeble
	in, into	enclose
il-, im-, in-, ir-	not	immature
	in, into	investigate
pro-	in favor of	prolabor
	forward, ahead	propel
re-	again	replant
	back	repay
semi-	half	semicircle
	twice in a period	semiannual
	partly	semiconscious
super-	over and above	superhuman
	very large	supertanker
trans	across	transatlantic
	beyond	transcend
un-	not	unhappy
	reverse of	unfasten

Suffixes

Like a prefix, a suffix has a meaning that can provide a strong clue to the definition of a whole word. Suffixes can also determine the part of speech of a word. Certain suffixes make words into nouns; others create adjectives, verbs, or adverbs.

Once you know suffixes and their meanings, you can form new words by attaching suffixes to base words or roots. For instance, the suffix *-ous* ("full of") can be added to the noun *ignominy* ("shame and dishonor") to form the adjective *ignominious* ("shameful or dishonorable.") Note that the *y* from *ignominy* is changed to an *i* before the *-ous* suffix is added. For information about spelling rules for adding suffixes, see the **Spelling Handbook**, pages 207–214.

Noun suffixes, when added to a base word or root, form nouns. Become familiar with the following common noun suffixes.

Noun Suffixes That Refer to Someone Who Does Something

Suffix	Examples
-ant	commandant, occupant
-eer	auctioneer
-er,	manager
-ician	beautician, statistician
-ier	cavalier
-ist	geologist, somnambulist
-or	counselor

Noun Suffixes That Make Abstract Words

Suffix	Examples
-ance	vigilance
-ancy	vagrancy, vacancy
-ation	imagination
-cy	accuracy
-dom	freedom, kingdom
-ence	independence
-hood	womanhood, brotherhood
-ice	cowardice, prejudice
-ism	realism, federalism
-ity	sincerity
-ization	civilization
-ment	encouragement, commitment
-ness	kindness, fondness
-ship	ownership, worship
-sion	decision
-tude	gratitude, solitude
-ty	frailty

Adjective suffixes, when added to a base word or root, create adjectives—words that are used to modify nouns and pronouns.

Adjective Suffixes		
Suffix	**Meaning**	**Example**
-able	able to	readable
-acious	full of	vivacious
-al	relating to	musical
-ant	relating to	triumphant
-ful	full of	harmful
-ible	able to	convertible
-ic	pertaining to or like	heroic
-ical	pertaining to	cyclical
-ish	pertaining to or like	waspish
-ive	pertaining to	descriptive
-less	without	senseless
-like	like	lifelike
-ly	like	scholarly
-most	at the extreme	topmost
-ous	full of	furious
-ular	pertaining to	cellular

Verb suffixes change base words to verbs. The following chart lists four common verb suffixes.

Verb Suffixes		
Suffix	**Meaning**	**Example**
-ate	to make	activate
-en	to become	lengthen
-fy	to make	simplify
-ize	to become	crystallize

Adverb Suffixes change base words to adverbs—words that modify verbs, adjectives, and other adverbs. The following chart lists the most common adverb suffixes.

Adverb Suffixes		
Suffix	**Meaning**	**Example**
-ly, -ily	manner	quickly
-ward	towards	skyward
-wise	like	clockwise

Roots and Word Families

A word root cannot stand alone, but must be combined with other word parts. A great many roots used in our language originally came from Greek or Latin. These roots generate whole families of English words. A **word family** is a group of words with a common root. For example, all of the words in the following word family are derived from the Latin root *ten*, meaning "to hold or keep."

detention	retentive	tenant
impertinent	retinue	tenure
pertinent	tenacity	untenable

By learning word roots, you develop your vocabulary because you can recognize roots in many related words. The following two charts show some common Greek and Latin roots.

Useful Greek Roots

Root	Meaning	Examples
anthrop	human	anthropology
aster, astr	star	asterisk
auto	self, alone	automobile
bi, bio	life	biology
bibl	book	bibliography
chron	time	chronology
crac, crat	govern	democracy
dem	people	epidemic
gen	birth, race	generation
geo	earth	geoscience
gram	write	grammar
graph	write	paragraph
hydr	water	hydrogen
log	word, reason	dialogue
logy	study of	geology
meter, metr	measure	barometer
neo	new	neophyte
nom, nym	name, word, law	synonym
ortho	straight, correct	orthodontist
pan	all, entire	panorama
phil	love	philosopher
phobia	fear	claustrophobia
phon	sound	phonograph
psych	mind, soul	psychology
scope	see	telescope
soph	wise, wisdom	sophisticated
tele	far, distant	television
theo	god	theology
therm	heat	thermometer

Useful Latin Roots

Root	Meaning	Examples
capt	take, hold, seize	capture
cede, ceed, cess	go, yield, give away	proceed, recession
cred	believe	credit, creed
dic, dict	speak, say, tell	dictate, dictionary
duc, duct	lead	induce, conductor
fac, fec, fic	do, make	factory, defect, fiction
fer	carry	transfer, ferry
ject	throw, hurl	eject, inject
junct	join	junction, conjunction
miss, mit	send	dismiss, admit
mot, mov	move	motion, move
par	get ready	prepare, repair
pon, pos, posit	place, put	component, deposit
port	carry	porter, portable
puls	throb, urge	pulsate, compulsory
scrib, script	write	scribble, scripture
spec, spic	look, see	spectacle, conspicuous
stat	stand, put in a place	statue, stature
ten	stretch, hold, keep	tendon, tenant
terr	land	terrain, territory
tract	pull, move	tractor, retract
ven, vent	come	convention, event
vers, vert	turn	versatile, invert
vid, vis	see	video, vista
voc, vok	call	vocation, invoke
vol	wish	volunteer, malevolent
volv	roll	revolve, involve

Determining Word Meaning through Prefixes and Suffixes Draw lines to separate each of the following words into three parts—prefix, base word, and suffix. Determine the meaning of the prefix and suffix. Then, by adding the meanings of the prefix and suffix to the base word, write the meaning of each complete word.

1. anticlimactic _____

2. desterilize _____

3. disinclination _____

4. illiteracy _____

5. microbiologist _____

6. nonclassical _____

7. prearrangement _____

8. repurify _____

9. supernaturalism _____

10. unnavigable _____

Number correct _____ (total 10)

Determining Word Meaning Through Prefixes, Suffixes, and Roots Each of
the following words is made from combinations of roots, prefixes, and suffixes.
Use your knowledge of word parts to determine the meanings of the words and
write a definition for each. You may check your definitions in a dictionary.

1. graphology _____

2. hydrophobia _____

3. interact _____

4. introspective _____

5. motivate _____

6. pantheism _____

7. postscript _____

8. remit _____

9. tenacity _____

10. transport _____

_____

Number correct _____ (total 10)

Number correct in Unit _____ (total 35)

UNIT 1

Part A Target Words and Their Meanings

The following twenty words are the focus of the first unit. You will find them in the reading selection that follows, as well as in the exercises in this unit. Some of these words may be unfamiliar to you, but you will become better acquainted with them and better able to use them in your reading and writing. For a guide to the pronunciations provided for these words and others found in this book, refer to the **Pronunciation Key** at the end of the Glossary.

1. absurdly (əb surd′lē, ab-; -zurd′-) adv.
2. acquiesce (ak′wē es′) v.
3. ascend (ə send′) v.
4. beneficent (bə nef′ə s'nt) adj.
5. coerce (kō urs′) v.
6. conference (kän′fər əns, -frəns) n.
7. contemplate (kän′təm plāt′) v.
8. correspondent (kôr′ə spän′dənt, kär′-) n., adj.
9. distinction (dis tiŋk′ shən) n.
10. dominate (däm′ə nāt′) v.
11. enable (in ā′b'l) v.
12. fundamentally (fun′də men′t'l ē) adv.
13. impress (im′pres) n. (im pres′) v.
14. indifferent (in dif′ər ənt, -dif′rənt) adj.
15. oblige (ə blīj′, ō-) v.
16. plausible (plô′zə b'l) adj.
17. plight (plīt) n.
18. serenity (sə ren′ə tē) n.
19. shroud (shroud) v., n.
20. singular (siŋ′gyə lər) adj.

Inferring Meaning from Context

For each sentence write the letter of the word or phrase that is closest to the meaning of the word or words in italics. Use context clues to help you determine the correct answer. (For information about how context helps you understand vocabulary, see pages 1–5.)

_____ 1. After anticipating a difficult trigonometry test, the class was both surprised and pleased to find it *absurdly* simple.

a. understandably b. ridiculously c. miserably d. insultingly

_____ 2. John's sister could not believe that her parents *acquiesced in* John's decision to quit school a week before graduation.

a. opposed b. went along with c. suggested d. laughed at

_____ 3. Although Mr. Grosz's arthritis made it difficult for him to *ascend* the steps to his apartment without pain, he could go downstairs easily.

a. avoid b. go down c. approach d. go up

_____ 4. Ms. Jackson is a charitable, kind person; her most *beneficent* act was to take in her neighbors after a fire destroyed their home.

a. expensive b. difficult c. generous d. uncharacteristic

_____ 5. We did not willingly choose to sign the petition supporting the parking restrictions; we were *coerced* into signing it when threatened with the loss of our jobs.

   a. convinced   b. surprised   c. misled   d. forced

_____ 6. At half time the officials had a brief *conference* to discuss their strategy for handling the crowd during the second half of the game.

   a. argument   b. timeout   c. ruling   d. meeting

_____ 7. Before she made her final decision, Joleen seriously *contemplated* the pros and cons of buying the sports car.

   a. agreed to   b. misunderstood   c. thought about   d. rejected

_____ 8. The foreign *correspondent* for our daily newspaper files her news stories at the American embassy.

   a. accountant   b. reporter   c. informer   d. language teacher

_____ 9. It is harder to see the *distinction* between pink and rose than between black and white.

   a. difference   b. similarity   c. interference   d. intensity

_____ 10. Clara, who likes to talk, would have *dominated* the class discussion if Mr. Morales hadn't insisted that other students participate as well.

   a. controlled   b. distorted   c. evaded   d. enjoyed

_____ 11. The proceeds from the candy sale were greater than expected, *enabling* the class to take a camping trip.

   a. making it possible for   b. making it impossible for   c. making it necessary for   d. forcing

_____ 12. Although the professor's theory about the importance of vitamin C in preventing colds is *fundamentally* sound, it does not explain exactly how the vitamin works.

   a. fortunately   b. intentionally   c. basically   d. debatably

_____ 13. André is not usually moved by classical music, but he was *impressed* by the orchestra's performance of Beethoven's *Fifth Symphony*.

   a. incensed   b. made uncomfortable   c. insulted   d. strongly affected

_____ 14. To be sure that their calls are accurate and objective, referees must ignore personal biases and try to be *indifferent to* the outcome of a game.

   a. ignorant of   b. interested in   c. neutral about   d. professional about

_____ 15. The terms of this lease *oblige* the tenants to pay for any property damage that occurs while they are living in the apartment, even if it is not their fault.

   a. encourage   b. allow   c. require   d. compensate

_____ 16. Mary gave a *plausible* excuse for her lateness; nevertheless, Jane was not entirely convinced.

   a. laughably stupid   b. totally convincing   c. seemingly valid
   d. completely unbelievable

_____ 17. Trapped on a remote ledge without food or water, the mountain climbers were in a desperate *plight*.

    a. cave b. situation c. plot d. hurry

_____ 18. Somehow Alison managed to maintain her *serenity* during the fire, when everyone else was panicking.

    a. self-esteem b. peacefulness c. honesty d. indifference

_____ 19. Along the coast, fog often *shrouds* roads, seriously reducing visibility.

    a. obscures b. destroys c. improves d. detours

_____ 20. Most of the jurors thought that the defendant had been framed, but the foreman expressed a *singular* interpretation that helped them to see the situation in a very different way.

    a. musical b. common c. unique d. brief

Number correct _____ (total 20)

Part B Target Words in Reading and Literature

You should now have a general idea of the meaning of each target word. Refine your understanding by examining the shades of meaning these words have in the following excerpt.

The Open Boat

Stephen Crane

This excerpt is from Stephen Crane's "The Open Boat," the story of the crew of a ship that went down at sea. The men have weathered the night in a lifeboat, and sunrise finds them preparing for the dangerous task of rowing through the threatening waves to the Florida shore.

When the **correspondent** again opened his eyes, the sea and the sky were each of the grey hue of the dawning. Later, carmine[1] and gold were painted upon the waters. The morning appeared finally, in its splendor, with a sky of pure blue, and the sunlight flamed on the tips of the waves.

On the distant dunes were set many little black cottages, and a tall white windmill reared above them. No human, nor dog, nor bicycle appeared on the beach. The cottages might have formed a deserted village.

The voyagers scanned the shore. A **conference** was held in the boat. "Well," said the captain, "if no help is coming, we might better try to run through the surf right away. If we stay out here much longer, we will be too weak to do anything for ourselves at all." The others silently **acquiesced** in this reasoning. The boat was headed for the beach. The correspondent wondered if none ever **ascended** the tall wind-tower, and if then they never looked seaward. This tower was a giant, standing with its back to the **plight** of the ants. It represented

5

10

_____

[1] carmine: red or purplish red; crimson

15

in a degree, to the correspondent, the **serenity** of nature amid the struggles of
the individual—nature in the wind, and nature in the vision of men. She did not
seem cruel to him then, nor **beneficent,** nor treacherous, nor wise. But she was
indifferent, flatly indifferent. It is, perhaps, **plausible** that a man in this situation,
impressed with the unconcern of the universe, should see the innumerable
flaws of his life, and have them taste wickedly in his mind, and wish for another
chance. A **distinction** between right and wrong seems **absurdly** clear to him,
then, in this new ignorance of the grave-edge, and he understands that if he
were given another opportunity he would mend his conduct and his words, and
be better and brighter during an introduction or at a tea.

"Now, boys," said the captain, "she is going to swamp sure. All we can do is   25
to work her in as far as possible, and then when she swamps, pile out and
scramble for the beach. Keep cool now, and don't jump until she swamps sure."

The oiler[2] took the oars. Over his shoulders he scanned the surf. "Captain,"
he said, "I think I'd better bring her about and keep her head-on to the seas and
back her in."   30

"All right, Billie," said the captain. "Back her in." The oiler swung the boat
then, and seated in the stern, the cook and the correspondent were **obliged** to
look over their shoulders to **contemplate** the lonely and indifferent shore.

The monstrous inshore rollers heaved the boat high until the men were again
enabled to see the white sheets of water scudding[3] up the slanted beach. "We   35
won't get in very close," said the captain. Each time a man could wrest[4] his
attention from the rollers, he turned his glance toward the shore, and in the
expression of the eyes during this contemplation there was a **singular** quality.
The correspondent, observing the others, knew that they were not afraid, but
the full meaning of their glances was **shrouded**.   40

As for himself, he was too tired to grapple **fundamentally** with the fact. He
tried to **coerce** his mind into thinking of it, but the mind was **dominated** at this
time by the muscles, and the muscles said they did not care. It merely occurred
to him that if he should drown, it would be a shame.   44

---

[2] oiler: a person who oils machinery or engines
[3] scudding: moving swiftly
[4] wrest: to turn or twist; to take by force

Refining Your Understanding

For each of the following items; consider how the target word is used in the
passage. Write the letter of the word or phrase that best completes each sentence.

_____ 1. We would expect a *correspondent* (line 1) to be especially good at
a. writing   b. solving disputes   c. rowing.

_____ 2. That "The others silently *acquiesced* in this reasoning" (line 11)
indicates that the people in the boat   a. agreed   b. were looking for
their own answers   c. lacked courage.

_____ 3. When Crane talks about the "*plight* of the ants" (line 14), he is referring
to the   a. food chain in the ocean   b. incompetence of people who
tended the wind-tower   c. predicament of the men in the lifeboat.

_____ 4. The correspondent sees nature as *indifferent* (line 18) to the men in the
lifeboat, because of its   a. benign character   b. hostility   c. lack of
concern.

_____ 5. The correspondent says of the others that "the full meaning of their
glances was *shrouded*" (line 40), because   a. they were asleep   b. they
were too frightened to look at him   c. he could not tell what they felt.

Number correct _____ (total 5)

Part C   Ways to Make New Words Your Own

By now you are familiar with the target words and their meanings. This section presents a variety of reinforcement activities that will help you make these words part of your permanent vocabulary.

Using Language and Thinking Skills

Understanding Multiple Meanings Each box in this exercise contains a boldfaced word with its various definitions. Read the definitions and then the sentences that use the word. Write the letter of the definition that applies to each sentence.

---

impress
a. to mark by using pressure; to stamp (v.)
b. to affect the mind or emotions strongly (v.)
c. to fix in the memory or mind (v.)

_____ 1. I cannot *impress* upon you too strongly the importance of the fire-prevention rules.

_____ 2. Sally's courage has always *impressed* me.

_____ 3. This machine is used to *impress* patterns on large bolts of material.

---

shroud
a. a burial cloth (n.)
b. a veil or screen (n.)
c. a rope stretched from the side of a ship to the mast (n.)
d. to hide, cover, or screen (v.)

_____ 4. The strong wind tangled the sails in the *shrouds*.

_____ 5. Good card players learn to *shroud* their feelings so that they don't reveal their hands.

_____ 6. The 2,100-year-old mummy was wrapped in seven *shrouds* of linen and three of silk.

_____ 7. Alice hid her shyness behind a *shroud* of loud good humor.

> **correspondent**
> a. agreeing; matching (adj.)
> b. a letter writer (n.)
> c. a reporter who covers news events in a distant location for a magazine or newspaper

_____ 8. Events in Germany are regularly reported by the newspaper's *correspondent* in Bonn.

_____ 9. President John Adams and his wife, Abigail, were frequent *correspondents* during the Revolutionary period; their letters reveal the events and attitudes of their era.

_____ 10. In the following exercise, match the words in the first column with their *correspondent* synonyms in the second column.

Number correct _____ (total 10)

Practicing for Standardized Tests

Synonyms Write the letter of the word from each set whose meaning is closest to that of the capitalized word.

_____ 1. ABSURDLY: (A) wisely (B) humorously (C) thoughtfully (D) calmly (E) ridiculously

_____ 2. ASCEND: (A) fall (B) climb (C) force (D) slide (E) solve

_____ 3. BENEFICENT: (A) recreational (B) selfish (C) concealed (D) strange (E) charitable

_____ 4. COERCE: (A) imprison (B) release (C) understand (D) force (E) rise

_____ 5. CONTEMPLATE: (A) condemn (B) consider (C) encounter (D) agree (E) permit

_____ 6. DISTINCTION: (A) calmness (B) motivation (C) difference (D) goal (E) possibility

_____ 7. DOMINATE: (A) impress (B) abuse (C) control (D) acquiesce (E) finalize

_____ 8. OBLIGE: (A) obtain (B) compel (C) dominate (D) resent (E) discourage

_____ 9. SERENITY: (A) calmness (B) reverence (C) panic (D) laziness (E) celebration

_____ 10. SHROUD: (A) neutralize (B) sadden (C) reward (D) cover (E) dull

Number correct _____ (total 10)

Spelling and Wordplay

Crossword Puzzle Read each clue to determine what word will fit in the corresponding squares. There are several target words in the puzzle.

ACROSS

1. A meeting
9. Abbr. *Associated Press*
11. Not inner
12. A long period of time
13. Sick
14. Abbr. *Revised Standard*
15. To rise
18. Abbr. *Right*
19. A break in an electrical circuit (2 words)
20. Swine
23. Poet's word for *before*
24. Abbr. *Electrical Engineering*
26. Abbr. *Royal Naval Hospital*
27. Weeps loudly
30. A word of choice
31. Abbr. *Minnesota*
32. Abbr. *Eastern Daylight Time*
33. Time gone by
34. Abbr. *Univ. of California*
35. Ma's mate
36. Spanish *yes*
37. Lemon___ ___
38. Abbr. *Pound*
39. Abbr. *San Francisco*
40. Slang: Undercover police officer who enforces narcotics laws
42. An auction
43. Abbr. *Foot*
45. To control
49. To observe
50. Short for Edward
52. To make indebted
53. Painful
54. A negative word
55. Bundles of cotton or hay
56. Special feature
61. Calmness
62. Abbr. *Daylight Saving Time*

DOWN

1. Overseas reporters
2. To force out
3. Abbr. *New Testament*
4. Chemical symbol for iron
5. To rub out
6. Poet's word for *never*
7. To think about
8. To complete
9. Short for Albert
10. Predicament
13. To stamp into the mind
16. Burial cloth
17. To force
21. Showing no interest
22. Ridiculous
25. To make possible
28. Abbr. *On Account*
29. Abbr. *Street*
41. A small, sweet cake
42. To droop
44. Golf-ball holders
46. Abbr. *Millibar*
47. Abbr. *Illinois*
48. Chemical symbol for nickel
49. Songs for a single voice
51. To perform an act
53. Past participle of *say*
55. Abbr. *Bought*
56. Abbr. *Doctor*
57. Abbr. *U.S. Naval Seaman*
58. 7th tone of the musical scale
59. That thing
60. Abbr. *New York*

Part D Related Words

A number of words are closely related to the target words you have studied. Use your knowledge of the target words and of word parts to determine the meanings of these words. (For information about word parts analysis, see pages 6–12.) If you are unsure of any definitions, use your dictionary. Learning these related words expands your vocabulary and helps you learn the target words more thoroughly.

1. absurdity (əb sur′dətē, ab-; -zur′-) n.
2. ascent (ə sent′) n.
3. benefactor (ben′ə fak′tər) n.
4. beneficiary (ben′ə fish′ē er′ē, -fish′ər ē) adj., n.
5. benefit (ben′ə fit) n., v.
6. benevolent (bə nev′ə lənt) adj.
7. coercion (kō ur′shən, -zhən) n.
8. confer (kən fur′) v.
9. contemplation (kän′təm plā′shən) n.
10. correspond (kôr′ə spänd′, kär′-) v.
11. descend (di send′) v.
12. descendant (di send′ənt) n.
13. distinctive (dis tiŋk′tiv) adj.
14. dominant (däm′ə nənt) adj., n.
15. implausible (im plô′zə b′l) adj.
16. impression (im presh′ən) n.
17. indifference (in dif′ər əns, -dif′ rəns) n.
18. serenade (ser′ə nād′) n., v.
19. singularity (siŋ′gye lar′ə tē) n.
20. transcend (tran send′) v.

Understanding Related Words

Matching Ideas In the blank write the word that best describes the idea expressed in each sentence.

ascent   confer   correspond   distinctive   implausible
coercion   contemplation   descendant   dominant   transcend

_____ 1. Mark's math teacher, who was also the basketball coach, told the class that students would not get an A, regardless of their test scores, unless they attended every home game.

_____ 2. Jason had gotten advice from his friends and family about what school he should attend. Now he had to think everything through and make a decision.

_____ 3. Each of Marla's reasons for wanting to borrow her brother's football helmet was more unbelievable than the last. Her brother refused to acquiesce until Marla could come up with a valid reason for needing the helmet.

_____ 4. Queen Elizabeth II of England comes from a long line of monarchs who have ruled Germany and Great Britain.

_____ 5. Giving to the poor and sacrificing for others are values held by most peoples—beliefs that cross religious and cultural boundaries.

_____ 6. Ian was the winner of the Most Unusual Costume award at the party. His Loch Ness monster costume was unique.

_____ 7. In the ten years prior to their dramatic flight at Kitty Hawk, North Carolina, in 1903, the Wright brothers learned everything they could about flying.

_____ 8. Every day across the country, readers check the numbers on their lottery tickets to see if the numbers match the winning numbers in the newspapers.

_____ 9. Robert E. Lee and Ulysses S. Grant had one of the most important meetings in American history at Appomattox Court House in Virginia, where they discussed how to end the Civil War and reunite the North and South.

_____ 10. The lion is the king of beasts.

Number correct _____ (total 10)

Turn to **Doubling the Final Consonant** on pages 212–213 of the **Spelling Handbook**. Read the rule and complete the exercise provided.

Analyzing Word Parts

The Latin Prefixes ac- and as- The Latin prefix *ac-* in the target word *acquiesce* and the prefix *as-* in the target word *ascend* both mean "to." These prefixes also appear in many other English words, such as the related word *ascent* as well as the words below. Use your knowledge of these prefixes and of other word parts to match the definitions to the words listed below. Then write the letter of the correct definition in the blank. Use your dictionary if necessary.

_____ 1. accessory   a. an advancement or upward slope

_____ 2. accommodate   b. an attack

_____ 3. ascribe   c. something added as secondary

_____ 4. ascent   d. to do a favor for

_____ 5. assault   e. to attribute or give credit to

Number correct _____ (total 5)

The Latin Root bene The target word *beneficent* derives from the Latin root *bene*, meaning "well." The following words also contain the root *bene*:

benefactor   beneficial   beneficiary   benefit   benevolent

Look up the meanings of these words in your dictionary. Then complete the following sentences using the most appropriate word.

1. The new park system will _____ everyone living in the county.

2. Adam was surprised to learn that he had been named a _____ in his uncle's will.

3. Ms. Robinson is known as a _____ of the arts in our city.

4. The doctor said that aerobic exercise would be more _____ than medication in treating my asthma.

5. Mr. Argyle looks fierce, but he is really a very _____ man.

Number correct _____ (total 5)

Number correct in Unit _____ (total 65)

Word's Worth: shroud

Today one of the primary meanings of the word *shroud* is "a burial garment." However, the word itself is far from dead, and in fact, is a perfect example of how a living language grows and changes. *Shroud* originally came from the Old English verb *sker*, meaning "to cut;" the noun form of this word, *schrud*, meant "something that has been cut," especially clothing. In the sixteenth century the word came to have the more specialized meaning it has today. As a verb, *shroud* now means to hide, veil, or obscure something, and its most general meaning as a noun is anything that covers, screens, or protects. However, by some process shrouded in mystery, the noun has come to refer to several different things: a rope that runs from the side of a ship to its mast; a cord that attaches the harness of a parachute to the canopy; a fiberglass guard that protects a spacecraft from the heat of a launch; and a rib that supports a turbine or fan.

The Last Word

Writing

As the *correspondent* for your school newspaper, you have been asked to cover the town government meeting in which a bill to ban all handguns in your community is being voted on. Write your news story, describing not only the proposed legislation and the number of votes for and against it, but also capturing the emotion and drama of the event.

Speaking

Prepare a speech in which you present a *plausible* explanation for why you shouldn't have to give this speech. Be sure to make your arguments clear and convincing.

Group Discussion

A *beneficent* person does good for others. Discuss the following questions with your classmates: (1) If you could give someone, or everyone, whatever you chose, what would it be? (2) If you could be given anything at all, what would it be? (3) Would you rather be a benefactor and do good deeds or be a beneficiary and receive them? Why?

UNIT 2

Part A Target Words and Their Meanings

1. abode (ə bōd′) n.
2. alter (ôl′tər) v.
3. contamination (kən tam′ə nā′shən) n.
4. counterpart (koun′tər pärt′) n.
5. diversify (də vʉr′sə fī′) v.
6. impetuous (im pech′ oo wəs) adj.
7. initiate (i nish′ē it, -āt) adj., n.
    (i nish′ē āt′) v.
8. interaction (in′tər ak′shən) n.
9. irrecoverable (ir′i kuv′ ər ə b'l) adj.
10. irreversible (ir′i vʉr′sə b'l) adj.
11. lethal (lē′thəl) adj.
12. magnitude (mag′nə tood′, -tyood′) n.
13. millennium (mi len′ē əm) n.
14. modify (mäd′ə fī′) v.
15. radiation (rā′dē ā′shən) n.
16. relatively (rel′ə tiv lē) adv.
17. sinister (sin′is tər) adj.
18. species (spē′shēz, -sēz) n.
19. universal (yoo′nə vʉr′s′l) adj.
20. vegetation (vej′ə tā′shən) n.

Inferring Meaning from Context

For each sentence write the letter of the word or phrase that is closest to the meaning of the word or words in italics. Use context clues to help you determine the correct answer. (For information about how context helps you understand vocabulary, see pages 1–5.)

_____ 1. The Pueblo Indians of the Southwest lived in cliff dwellings, *an abode* that afforded them peace and safety.

    a. a heritage b. an advantage c. a destination d. a home

_____ 2. Mary said that she would *alter* the dress by shortening the hem and lowering the waistline.

    a. lengthen b. approximate c. change d. copy

_____ 3. The clean river Jed remembered from his childhood was now murky and choked with industrial *contamination*.

    a. pollution b. markets c. patents d. complexes

_____ 4. During World War II, Franklin D. Roosevelt, President of the United States, dealt with General Charles DeGaulle, the leader-in-exile of France. DeGaulle was Roosevelt's *counterpart*, a position similar in status.

    a. ally b. enemy c. equivalent d. role model

_____ 5. You should *diversify* your diet by eating different types of food each day, including some from each of the four basic food groups.

    a. contemplate b. stick to c. devour d. vary

_____ 6. Tina resolved to think things through carefully before acting in the future, rather than being so *impetuous* and behaving irrationally.

a. indecisive b. impulsive c. destructive d. cautious

_____ 7. To set the mood for its fiftieth-anniversary celebration, the university *initiated* the proceedings with a debate between members of the first and the most recent graduating classes.

a. started b. stopped c. interrupted d. protested

_____ 8. As they mixed the two liquids, the chemistry students didn't know what the chemical *interaction* would produce; they were surprised at the explosion that resulted.

a. change in color b. action on each other c. change in amount
d. theory

_____ 9. For years, people presumed that the remains of the *Titanic*, a luxury ship that struck an iceberg in the Atlantic in 1912 and sank in two miles of water, were *irrecoverable*, but French divers have succeeded in finding and exploring the wreckage and may begin bringing relics to the surface.

a. irretrievable b. of unknown value c. protected by law d. valuable

_____ 10. Nicole's decision to transfer schools was *irreversible*; not even her best friend could convince her to change her mind.

a. not able to be changed b. able to be changed c. able to be understood d. not able to be understood

_____ 11. The label on the cleaning fluid warned that the fluid could be *lethal* if swallowed and that it should be stored out of children's reach to prevent tragedy.

a. ineffective b. illegal c. deadly d. expensive

_____ 12. Rick thought that it would take him no more than two hours to clean out the attic, but when he saw how much needed to be done, he realized that he had greatly underestimated the *magnitude* of the job.

a. unpleasantness b. magnificence c. altitude d. size

_____ 13. The Battle of Hastings took place in 1066, early in the second *millennium* A.D.

a. century b. million years c. thousand years d. millipede

_____ 14. Because of the approaching storm, the captain *modified* the ship's course from north-northwest to due west.

a. changed b. mistook c. distributed d. continued

_____ 15. The *radiation* of heat from the potbellied stove in the middle of the room kept everyone warm.

a. spreading out b. closing off c. lack d. revelation

_____ 16. In Death Valley, California, summer temperatures commonly reach 120° F, so a summer day with a high in the 90's is *relatively* cool.

a. usually b. undeniably c. seldom d. comparatively

_____ 17. The greenish-black color of large thunderclouds is a *sinister* sign in tornado country; people should heed this warning of an impending storm and take shelter.

   a. welcome   b. colorful   c. threatening   d. heavy

_____ 18. Although horses and donkeys are members of the same family—Equidae— they are different *species* and do not produce fertile offspring.

   a. nationalities   b. sizes   c. varieties   d. color

_____ 19. A smile is *a universal* gesture—its meaning is understood anywhere.

   a. an ambiguous   b. a widespread   c. a limited   d. a logical

_____ 20. The jungle *vegetation* includes numerous tropical trees, undergrowth, and high-climbing vines.

   a. animal life   b. plant life   c. highway system   d. climate

Number correct _____ (total 20)

Part B   Target Words in Reading and Literature

You should now have a general idea of the meaning of each target word. Refine your understanding by examining the shades of meaning these words have in the following excerpt.

The Obligation to Endure

Rachel Carson

During her lifetime, biologist Rachel Carson was concerned about the use of chemicals and their effects on the natural world. In this passage from Silent Spring, *Carson focuses on the interaction between organisms and their environment—and on the ability of humanity to change the environment for the worse.*

The history of life on earth has been a history of **interaction** between living things and their surroundings. To a large extent, the physical form and the habits of the earth's **vegetation** and its animal life have been molded by the environment. Considering the whole span of earthly time, the opposite effect, in which life actually **modifies** its surroundings, has been **relatively** slight. Only   5
within the moment of time represented by the present century has one **species**—man—acquired significant power to **alter** the nature of his world.

During the past quarter century this power has not only increased to one of disturbing **magnitude,** but it has changed in character. The most alarming of all man's assaults upon the environment is the **contamination** of air, earth, rivers,   10
and sea with dangerous and even **lethal** materials. This pollution is for the most part **irrecoverable;** the chain of evil it **initiates** not only in the world that must support life but in living tissues is for the most part **irreversible.** In this now **universal** contamination of the environment, chemicals are the **sinister** and little-recognized partners of **radiation** in changing the very nature of the   15

world—the very nature of its life. Strontium 90, released through nuclear explosions into the air, comes to earth in rain, or drifts down as fallout, lodges in soil, enters into the grass or corn or wheat grown there, and in time takes up its **abode** in the bones of a human being, there to remain until his death. Similarly, chemicals sprayed on croplands or forests or gardens lie long in soil, entering [20] into living organisms, passing from one to another in a chain of poisoning and death. Or they pass mysteriously by underground streams until they emerge and, through the alchemy[1] of air and sunlight, combine into new forms that kill vegetation, sicken cattle, and work unknown harm on those who drink from once-pure wells. As Albert Schweitzer has said, "Man can hardly even [25] recognize the devils of his own creation."

It took hundreds of millions of years to produce the life that now inhabits the earth—eons[2] of time in which that developing and evolving and **diversifying** life

---

[1] alchemy: process of changing one thing into another
[2] eon: an extremely long, indefinite period of time

reached a state of adjustment and balance with its surroundings.   The
environment, rigorously shaping and directing the life it supported, contained   30
elements that were hostile as well as supporting.   Certain rocks gave out
dangerous radiation; even within the light of the sun, from which all life draws its
energy, there were short-wave radiations with power to injure.   Given not in
years but in **millennia**—life adjusts, and a balance has been reached.   For time
is the essential ingredient; but in the modern world there is no time.   35

The rapidity of change and the speed with which new situations are created
follow the **impetuous** and heedless pace of man rather than the deliberate pace
of nature.   Radiation is no longer merely the background radiation of rocks, the
bombardment of cosmic rays, the ultraviolet of the sun that have existed before
there was any life on earth; radiation is now the unnatural creation of man's   40
tampering with the atom.   The chemicals to which life is asked to make its
adjustment are no longer merely the calcium and silica and copper and all the
rest of the minerals washed out of the rocks and carried in rivers to the sea; they
are the synthetic creations of man's inventive mind, brewed in his laboratories,
and having no **counterparts** in nature.   45

Refining Your Understanding

For each of the following items, consider how the target word is used in the
passage.   Write the letter of the word or phrase that best completes each sentence.

_____ 1. The extent to which living things have modified their surroundings,
according to Ms. Carson, is "*relatively* slight" (line 5) compared to
a. the variety of living things   b. the short time that people have inhabited
the earth   c. how long the environment has modified living things.

_____ 2. That some types of pollution are *irrecoverable* (line 12) suggests that
undoing pollution's damage is   a. hopeless   b. costly   c. acceptable.

_____ 3. Ms. Carson says that strontium 90 "takes up its *abode*" in human bones
(line 19), suggesting that it   a. infects anyone the person touches   b. is
eliminated quickly if the person drinks milk   c. becomes a permanent
part of the body.

_____ 4. In contrast to people whom Ms. Carson describes as *impetuous* (line 37),
she depicts nature as   a. quicker to change   b. slower to change
c. more incomprehensible.

_____ 5. A human creation that has "no *counterparts* in nature" (line 45) would
be   a. plastic   b. gold   c. sediment

Number correct _____ (total 5)

Part C Ways to Make New Words Your Own

By now you are familiar with the target words and their meanings. This section presents a variety of reinforcement activities that will help you make these words part of your permanent vocabulary.

Using Language and Thinking Skills

Finding the Unrelated Word Write the letter of the word that is not related in meaning to the other words in the set.

_____ 1. a. remain b. alter c. change d. modify

_____ 2. a. residence b. inhabitant c. abode d. dwelling

_____ 3. a. prudent b. impetuous c. rash d. impulsive

_____ 4. a. inferior b. counterpart c. equal d. duplicate

_____ 5. a. extremely b. extensively c. relatively d. intensely

_____ 6. a. species b. item c. kind d. class

_____ 7. a. vegetation b. flora c. rock formation d. plant life

_____ 8. a. emanation b. absorption c. emission d. radiation

_____ 9. a. poisonous b. lethal c. safe d. toxic

_____ 10. a. magnitude b. size c. magnetism d. extent

Number correct _____ (total 10)

Practicing for Standardized Tests

Antonyms Write the letter of the word that is most nearly *opposite* in meaning to the capitalized word.

_____ 1. COUNTERPART: (A) equal (B) principle (C) duplicate
(D) relationship (E) opposite

_____ 2. CONTAMINATION: (A) vegetation (B) pollution (C) purification
(D) consideration (E) prevention

_____ 3. DIVERSIFY: (A) modify (B) unify (C) vary (D) improve
(E) release

_____ 4. IMPETUOUS: (A) deliberate (B) rash (C) beneficial (D) petrified
(E) important

_____ 5. INITIATE: (A) cancel (B) create (C) radiate (D) inaugurate (E) fail

_____ 6. IRREVERSIBLE: (A) irreverent (B) changeable (C) respectable
(D) hopeless (E) credible

_____ 7. LETHAL: (A) beneficial (B) contaminated (C) plausible (D) factual (E) legal

_____ 8. MODIFY: (A) diversify (B) expand (C) force (D) retain (E) alter

_____ 9. SINISTER: (A) self-contained (B) hostile (C) friendly (D) absurd (E) threatening

_____ 10. UNIVERSAL: (A) common (B) unintelligent (C) neighborly (D) singular (E) incorrect

Number correct _____ (total 10)

Spelling and Wordplay

Word Maze Find and circle each target word in this maze.

```
C R I L S P E C I E S I B L M
O E R A P M A G N I T U D E U
N L R S O I N I T I A T E D I
T A E R A T O M E D V N V I N
A T C E S A T P R V I T E V N
M I O V I L L E A T N R G E E
I V V I E T L T C I V A E R L
N E E N S E A U T N A P T S L
A L R U I R E O I O N R A I I
T Y A A H N I U O I E E T F M
I L B C O O N S N T S T I Y O
O A L A B O D E S A E N O E D
N H E D E R S I Y I R U N C I
A T I R E M N O N D P O A E F
B E L H A I B I T A E C L P Y
E L B I S R E V E R R I H S Y
```

abode
alter
contamination
counterpart
diversify
impetuous
initiate
interaction
irrecoverable
irreversible
lethal
magnitude
millennium
modify
radiation
relatively
sinister
species
universal
vegetation

30

Part D Related Words

A number of words are closely related to the target words you have studied. Use your knowledge of the target words and of word parts to determine the meanings of these words. (For information about word parts analysis, see pages 6–12.) If you are unsure of any definitions, use your dictionary. Learning these related words expands your vocabulary and helps you learn the target words more thoroughly.

1. alteration (ôl′tə rā′shən) n.
2. altercation (ôl′tər kā′shən) n.
3. contaminate (kən tàm′ə nāt′) v.
4. diverse (dī vʉrs′, də-; dī′vʉrs) adj.
5. diversification (də vʉr′sə fi kā′shən) n.
6. diversion (də vʉr′zhən, dī-) n.
7. divert (də vʉrt′) v.
8. initial (i nish′əl) adj., n., v.
9. initiation (i nish′ē ā′shən) n.
10. interact (in′tər akt′) v.
11. magnanimous (mag nan′ə məs) adj.
12. modification (mäd′ə fi kā′shən) n.
13. radiate (rā′dē āt′) v.
14. reversible (ri vʉr′sə b'l) adj.
15. universe (yōō′nə vʉrs′) n.
16. vegetate (vej′ə tāt′) v.

Understanding Related Words

Finding Examples In the blank write the word that best describes the situation.

alteration   magnanimous
altercation   radiate
contaminate   reversible
diversion   universe
initiation   vegetate

_____ 1. drawing the enemy's attention away from a sneak attack

_____ 2. changing the placement of two paragraphs to make your composition read more smoothly

_____ 3. refusing to get out of bed for a month

_____ 4. arguing about who got to a parking place first

_____ 5. forgiving your brother for borrowing your favorite cassette tape and losing it

_____ 6. energy moving out in all directions from the sun

_____ 7. receiving a pin that signifies your acceptance as a new club member

_____ 8. spilling thousands of gallons of crude oil into the ocean

_____ 9. buying a coat that can be worn with either side out

_____ 10. space and beyond

Number correct _____ (total 10)

Turn to **The Addition of Prefixes** on page 203 of the **Spelling Handbook.** Read the rule and complete the exercise provided.

Words in Action In the blank write the letter of the action that best demonstrates the meaning of the italicized related word.

_____ 1. The *initial* step in baking a pie would be

    a. assembling the ingredients.

    b. rolling out the crust.

    c. reading the recipe.

    d. mixing the ingredients.

_____ 2. If the doctor told you that your daily diet required *diversification*, you should

    a. eat less and exercise more.

    b. eat out in restaurants more.

    c. write a poem about food.

    d. eat a variety of different foods.

_____ 3. If you wanted to *interact* with someone, you would most likely

    a. take a drama class.

    b. daydream about the perfect romance.

    c. get together with a friend.

    d. write a one-act play.

_____ 4. If your friend wants to *divert* your attention from your broken leg, she might

    a. offer to drive you to the doctor's office.

    b. suggest that you read a good adventure story.

    c. tell you about how she broke her leg when she was young.

    d. ask you to describe how you were injured.

_____ 5. *Modification* of your vacation plans would mean

    a. deciding to go to a different place.

    b. collecting all your pictures from previous vacations.

    c. asking other people where they went on vacation.

    d. subscribing to a travel magazine.

Number correct _____ (total 5)

Word's Worth: *sinister*

Sinister, which entered the English language in the sixteenth century, has retained exactly the same form as its Latin ancestor, *sinister*. However, its original meaning, "on the left side," which was purely descriptive and neutral, has become laden with negative connotations in its current sense of "ominous," "evil," or "disastrous." How did such a drastic change in meaning come about? It all goes back to the ancient Roman practice of augury, or predicting the future, and the belief that the direction east was lucky and west, unlucky. When making their predictions, many augurs stood facing north, with their right sides to the east and left sides toward the unlucky west. Although the practice of augury has fallen out of fashion, left-handedness is still considered unfavorable—and for no good reason. Think of all the English expressions, such as *left-handed compliment* and *leftist*, that also have negative connotations. You never hear of someone depending on his or her *left-hand man* or trying to stay on someone's *left* side, not if that person is in his or her right mind.

Analyzing Word Parts

The Prefix *inter-* The prefix *inter-* comes from the Latin word for "between" or "among." This prefix is found in the target word *interaction*, the related word *interact*, and many other words, such as *interpreter*, *interrupt*, *interstate*, and *interview*. Be careful not to confuse *inter-* with the prefix *intra-*, which means "within." Using your knowledge of context clues and word structure, complete the following sentences with the appropriate word from the list below:

interact   interpreter   interrupt   interstate   interview

1. The _____ highway system, which consists of a series of high-speed, limited-access traffic ways that pass through every state in the country, is operated by the federal government.

2. After they send in their applications and résumés, promising job candidates are invited to come in for an _____ with the personnel director.

3. A rattlesnake happened to _____ the vaudeville show when it slithered onto the stage.

4. Since Moreni spoke only Italian and Goff spoke only English, they needed an _____ before they could exchange anything more than smiles and handshakes.

5. The newcomers refused to _____ with any of their neighbors, and, after a month, no one even knew their names.

Number correct _____ (total 5)

The Latin Root *magni* The root *magni* comes from the Latin word *magnus*, meaning "great." This root is contained in the target word *magnitude*, the related word, *magnanimous*, and many other English words, such as *magnate*, *magnificent*, and *magniloquent*. In the blank write the word from the list below that best describes the situation illustrated in the sentence. Use your dictionary if necessary.

magnanimous   magnate   magnification   magnificent   magniloquent

_____ 1. As he wiped cream pie from his face, Chet assured us that he held no grudges and joined in the laughter.

_____ 2. Clint was not really sure what he wanted to say, so he decided to distract his listeners with lengthy sentences and words that few of them would understand.

_____ 3. In addition to owning a major movie studio, Forsyth Jones also controlled the shipping industry in his region.

_____ 4. The Taj Mahal in Agra, India, a lavish tomb built by a Mogul emperor, is one of the seven wonders of the world.

_____ 5. The Kitt Peak Observatory contains an eighty-two-inch solar telescope, the world's largest and most powerful.

Number correct _____ (total 5)

Number correct in Unit _____ (total 70)

The Last Word

Writing

Rachel Carson's book *Silent Spring* led to the restriction of the use of DDT, an insecticide that is a lethal environmental contaminant. Write a short research paper describing several toxic chemicals being used today, how and why they are used, and the *contamination* problems they create. Finally, discuss the pros and cons of eliminating the use of these chemicals.

Speaking

Without energy from the sun, life on earth would not be possible. However, solar *radiation* also has harmful effects that can be fatal. Do research to discover the various types of radiation given off by the sun and how we can protect ourselves from the dangers they pose. Present your findings in a report to the class.

Group Discussion

Human societies differ greatly in almost every aspect—the type of work that is done, who does it, the obligations people have to each other, the meaning they assign to nature and their own place in it, and their basic outlook on life. Despite these vast differences, however, there are aspects of human behavior and beliefs that are *universal*. As a class, discuss what some of these *universals* might be.

UNIT 3

Part A Target Words and Their Meanings

1. acculturation (ə kul′chə rā′shən) n.
2. ameliorate (ə mēl′yə rāt′) v.
3. articulate (är tik′yə lit) adj. (-lāt′) v.
4. aspiration (asp′ə rā′shən) n.
5. attainment (ə tān′mənt) n.
6. category (kat′ə gôr′ē) n.
7. consensus (kən sen′səs) n.
8. economic (ē′kə näm′ik, ek′ə-) adj.
9. ethnicity (eth nis′ə tē) n.
10. heritage (her′ə tij) n.
11. inequality (in′i kwäl′ə tē, -kwôl′-) n.
12. interpretation (in tʉr′prə tā′shən) n.
13. median (mē′dē ən) adj., n.
14. mobilize (mō′bə līz′) v.
15. mundane (mun dān′, mun′dān) adj.
16. rectify (rek′tə fī′) v.
17. segment (seg′mənt) n. (-ment) v.
18. tactic (tak′tik) n.
19. unify (yoo′nə fī′) v.
20. vociferous (vō sif′ər əs) adj.

Inferring Meaning from Context

For each sentence write the letter of the word or phrase that is closest to the meaning of the word or words in italics. Use context clues to help you.

_____ 1. If immigrants make no attempt to learn the language of their new home, they will never achieve *acculturation* and acceptance into that society.
  a. financial gain   b. mental growth   c. physical growth
  d. cultural adaptation

_____ 2. Martin Luther King, Jr., attempted to *ameliorate* the unequal economic and social conditions of American blacks by staging a nonviolent protest against racial discrimination.
  a. legalize   b. define   c. ignore   d. improve

_____ 3. If you can't *articulate* your ideas so others can understand them, it may be because the ideas are unclear in your own mind.
  a. clearly express   b. deny   c. research   d. envision

_____ 4. Because Matt's *aspiration* is to be a professional photographer, he built a darkroom in his basement and takes pictures at every opportunity.
  a. distinction   b. acquiescence   c. ambition   d. inspiration

_____ 5. Luck has less to do with the *attainment* of success than does hard work.
  a. envy   b. achievement   c. questioning   d. contemplation

_____ 6. All of the job applicants could be classified into two *categories*—those with teaching experience and those who had never taught.
  a. sides   b. groups   c. locations   d. schools

35

_____ 7. We did not reach *a consensus;* many people opposed our proposal.
　　　a. an argument　b. a conversion　c. a recount　d. an agreement

_____ 8. The governor called a special session of the legislature to deal with pressing *economic* matters such as pay raises and financial investments.
　　　a. money　b. personal　c. reluctant　d. ecologic

_____ 9. The international food festival, a showcase of *ethnicity*, offered Greek gyros served alongside Chinese egg rolls and fried rice.
　　　a. cultural affiliation　b. vegetarian tendencies
　　　c. religious beliefs　d. indigestion

_____ 10. Attitudes and basic personality traits are as much a part of an individual's *heritage* as are physical characteristics.
　　　a. beneficence　b. plight　c. habitation　d. inheritance

_____ 11. The firm denied any discrimination in its hiring practices, yet there was blatant *inequality* in the numbers of minorities in high-paying positions.
　　　a. unevenness　b. loss　c. misunderstanding　d. mistrust

_____ 12. Ira's *interpretation of* the poem was quite different from Monica's, but each analysis was well supported and valid.
　　　a. explanation of　b. reading of　c. interest in　d. confusion about

_____ 13. After pricing cars, our family decided against both the most and the least expensive models and instead chose one with *a median* price.
　　　a. a secondhand　b. an intermediate　c. a low　d. a mismarked

_____ 14. Paramedics must *mobilize* quickly to respond to any emergency.
　　　a. train　b. dismiss　c. ready　d. detain

_____ 15. Jean escaped from the *mundane* world of chores and homework by writing about an imaginary planet.
　　　a. unrealistic　b. everyday　c. municipal　d. articulate

_____ 16. Henry tried to *rectify* his mistake of breaking the glass vase by apologizing to his host and offering to replace the vase.
　　　a. compound　b. ignore　c. record　d. correct

_____ 17. Max memorized his long speech by *segmenting* it into smaller parts.
　　　a. uniting　b. separating　c. blending　d. mapping

_____ 18. After our team lost five games, the coach devised new defensive *tactics*.
　　　a. uniforms　b. impressions　c. strategies　d. orders

_____ 19. The governor tried to *unify* the differing factions of state senate.
　　　a. undo　b. usurp　c. unite　d. confuse

_____ 20. Madge was so *vociferous* in her support of the team that the cheerleading coach asked her to lead the pep rally.
　　　a. shy　b. intelligent　c. loud and enthusiastic　d. tactful

Number correct _____ (total 20)

36

Part B Target Words in Reading and Literature

You should now have a general idea of the meaning of each target word. Refine your understanding by examining the shades of meaning these words have in the following excerpt.

The Chicanos

Matt S. Meier and Feliciano Rivera

In the following excerpt from the conclusion to The Chicanos: A History of Mexican Americans, *Matt S. Meier and Feliciano Rivera discuss the common goals and conflicting strategies of today's Chicanos. This diverse group of Mexican Americans faces many problems in achieving social and political equality but is united in its insistence on change.*

Today Mexican Americans are still **segmented** into many groups, each with its own **interpretation** of what the Mexican American is and where he is going. The Chicano community continues divided, with **unifying** elements of **ethnicity** and cultural **heritage** frequently being sidetracked by such **mundane** issues as **economic** position, social status, and professional **attainment.** Differences of opinion concerning means to the achievement of civil and political rights continue to plague the Chicano movement; however, conflicts within its leadership usually concern **tactics,** not goals. A broad **consensus** exists among Mexican Americans that they want many specific sociopolitical and economic benefits that other Americans enjoy.

5

10

Mexican American citizens today still face many problems. Health conditions within their communities are still poor, and health services continue to be inadequate; in housing, the picture is similar, although there has been some improvement. In education, Chicanos are still treated as second class in too many areas, and public schools continue to be unsuccessful in furthering the **acculturation** of Mexicans. Of all minorities, only American Indians have a lower **median** income than Mexican Americans. Economically, Chicanos in California enjoy the most favorable position, while those in Texas are least well off. But in whatever state, they continue to earn less in all occupational **categories** than do Anglo-Americans, by between 20 to 40 percent; there has been considerable improvement since World War II, but much more progress needs to be made. 15 20

Of critical concern, however, is the rate of change in **ameliorating** the conditions of Chicanos. To **rectify** the tremendous **inequalities** experienced by Mexican Americans in our society and to satisfy **vociferous** demands being made today by Mexican Americans for a greater share in American political, economic, and social benefits, the process of change must be greatly accelerated. This can be accomplished only if Mexican American leaders successfully **articulate** the common **aspirations** of "la raza"[1] and if they and Anglo-American leaders organize and **mobilize** the resources, human and material, needed to achieve these aspirations. 25 30

[1] la raza: literally "the race," used especially in regard to New World Spanish-speaking people

Refining Your Understanding

For each of the following items consider how the target word is used in the passage. Write the letter of the word or phrase that best completes each sentence.

_____ 1. A synonym of *tactics* (line 8) is   a. strategies   b. objectives   c. hopes.

_____ 2. An example of "*acculturation* of Mexicans" (line 16) would be
a. learning the English language   b. getting better jobs   c. adhering to Mexican customs.

_____ 3. The rate at which the lives of Chicanos are being *ameliorated* (line 22) is, according to Meier and Rivera,   a. too fast   b. too slow   c. about right.

_____ 4. *Inequalities* (line 23) are incompatible with   a. democracy
b. minorities   c. favoritism.

_____ 5. The meaning of *articulate* (line 28) the authors use here is   a. speak clearly   b. express   c. fit together.

Number correct _____ (total 5)

Part C   *Ways to Make New Words Your Own*

By now you are familiar with the target words and their meanings. This section presents reinforcement activities that help you make these words part of your permanent vocabulary.

Using Language and Thinking Skills

Finding Examples Write the letter of the situation that best demonstrates each word's meaning.

_____ 1. **acculturation**
   a. Vietnamese immigrants living temporarily with relatives
   b. German immigrants holding an annual reunion
   c. Mexican immigrants celebrating July 4th

_____ 2. **ameliorate**
   a. using aerosol sprays that increase air pollution
   b. taking aspirin to reduce a fever
   c. arguing with your brother about who should do the dishes

_____ 3. **articulate**
   a. putting your feelings into words
   b. practicing your drawing technique
   c. meditating while listening to music

_____ 4. **aspiration**
   a. cleaning out your closet
   b. deciding to become the best pole-vaulter in your school
   c. wishing you had studied harder for the biology test

_____ 5. **economic**
   a. eating dinner in a restaurant because you're too tired to cook
   b. taking a job to earn money
   c. feeling you must give your classmate a birthday gift because she gave you one

_____ 6. **ethnicity**
   a. eating at a fast-food restaurant
   b. following the Golden Rule
   c. wearing green on St. Patrick's Day

_____ 7. **heritage**
   a. retelling stories about your ancestors
   b. filling out a college application
   c. driving a used car

_____ 8. **inequality**
   a. sitting in the back of the auditorium because you arrived late
   b. getting a bigger allowance than your twin sister
   c. sharing your lunch with a friend

_____ 9. **median**

  a. an area between two highways
  b. an excellent test score
  c. a person who tells jokes

_____ 10. **segment**

  a. potatoes in a stew
  b. a one-mile stretch of highway that is closed for repairs
  c. the hydrogen in water

Number correct _____ (total 10)

Words on a Continuum In each of the five sets of words below, **1** is placed beside a target word; find that word's antonym and place a **4** beside it. Then number the two remaining words. Put **2** beside the word that is closer in meaning to word **1**. Put **3** next to the word that is closer in meaning to word **4**.

Example:

3 fair
2 good
1 excellent
4 poor

1.

1 attainment
_____ attempt
_____ discouragement
_____ failure

2.

_____ insistent
_____ reserved
_____ silent
1 vociferous

3.

1 mobilize
_____ ignore
_____ train
_____ inhibit

4.

_____ unusual
1 mundane
_____ predictable
_____ interesting

5.

1 unify
_____ connect
_____ segment
_____ dissolve

Number correct _____ (total 15)

Practicing for Standardized Tests

Synonyms Write the letter of the word whose meaning is closest to that of the capitalized word.

_____ 1. MEDIAN: (A) minimal (B) optimal (C) irrelevant (D) indecisive (E) intermediate

_____ 2. ARTICULATE: (A) mislead (B) express (C) confuse (D) rectify (E) entertain

_____ 3. VOCIFEROUS: (A) soft-spoken (B) abusive (C) offensive (D) musical (E) outspoken

_____ 4. CATEGORY: (A) class (B) size (C) team (D) enclosure (E) meaning

_____ 5. UNIFY: (A) diversify (B) add (C) consolidate (D) modify (E) undo

_____ 6. MOBILIZE: (A) refuel (B) enlarge (C) stabilize (D) halt (E) prepare

_____ 7. TACTIC: (A) union (B) fight (C) strategy (D) task (E) analysis

_____ 8. CONSENSUS: (A) permission (B) interaction (C) dissension (D) consideration (E) agreement

_____ 9. RECTIFY: (A) coerce (B) relate (C) direct (D) electrify (E) correct

_____ 10. INTERPRETATION: (A) impression (B) letter (C) investigation (D) explanation (E) inquiry

Number correct _____ (total 10)

Spelling and Wordplay

Crossword Puzzle

ACROSS
1. Adjustment to a new culture
13. Past tense of *mean*
14. Parts
16. All or complete
17. Abbr. *Commanding Officer*
18. Noun suffix meaning "little"
19. To appear to be
21. Present participle suffix
22. Middle
26. Abbr. *On Account*
28. To unite
30. Abbr. *British*
31. Abbr. *Royal Naval Reserve*
32. Sharp cry of pain
34. That thing
35. Alpine singing
37. Islamic name
38. Chem. symbol for techvitium
40. Concerned with money matters
44. To consume
45. Negative word
47. Abbr. *Audio Visual*
48. ___ ___lu tribe, a Bantu people of South Africa
49. Birthright
51. Short for *Elevated Railway*
52. That man
53. Raw metal
55. Ambition
62. Door___ ___ ___
64. To explain
65. Abbr. *Tight End*

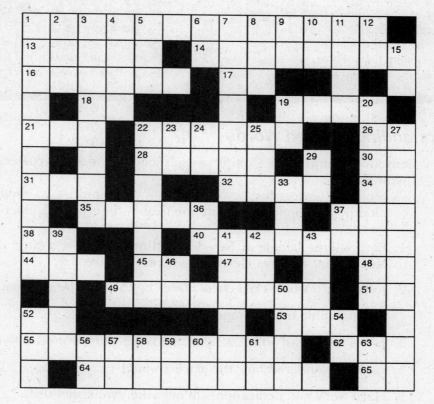

DOWN
1. To improve
2. Abbr. *Center*
3. Classification
4. Single, distinct part
5. Abbr. *Letter*
6. Objective case of *we*
7. To correct
8. Past
9. Abbr. *Trademark*
10. Abbr. *id est*
11. One time only
12. Abbr. *New Testament*
15. Spanish *yes*
19. Chem. symbol for tin

20. To organize
22. Commonplace
23. Spelling of the letter *n*
24. Prefix for "twice"
25. Vote of yes
27. To express clearly
29. Not down
33. Short for *Leonard*
36. Abbr. *Left End*
37. Abbr. *Morning*
39. Sleeveless garments
41. Plant liked by cats
42. Plural of *ovum*
43. Done

46. Word of choice
50. Departed
52. Head covering
54. Spelling of the letter *m*
56. 3.14159265
57. Not out
58. Abbr. *Route*
59. Abbr. *Associate of Education*
60. Abbr. *Treasurer*
61. Suffix for "person or thing that"
63. On, in, near, or by

Part D Related Words

A number of words are closely related to the target words you have studied. Use your knowledge of the target words and of word parts to determine the meanings of these words. (For information about word parts analysis, see pages 6–12.) If you are unsure of any definitions, use your dictionary. Learning these related words expands your vocabulary and helps you learn the target words more thoroughly.

1. articulation (är tik′yə lā′shən) n.
2. aspire (ə spīr′) v.
3. attain (ə tān′) v.
4. categorical (kat′ə gör′i k′l, -gär′-) adj.
5. categorize (kat′ə gə rīz′) v.
6. economist (i kän′ə mist) n.
7. equality (i kwäl′ə tē, -kwôl′-) n.
8. ethnic (eth′nik) adj.
9. immobilize (i mō′bə līz′) v.
10. inheritance (in her′it əns) n.
11. inspire (in spīr′) v.
12. interpret (in tʉr′prit) v.
13. mediate (mē′dē it) adj. (-āt′) v.
14. mobility (mō bil′ə tē) n.
15. tactician (tak tish′ən) n.
16. unification (yoo′nə fi kā′shən) n.

Understanding Related Words

Sentence Completion Complete each sentence with the correct word from the following list.

aspire   categorize   ethnic   inspire   mediate
attain   economist   immobilize   interpret   tactician

1. Each fall the people of New Ulm, Minnesota, have a (an) _____ festival that features German food and culture.

2. Johannes, a world-class chess player by the time he was nine years old, has a photographic memory and is a brilliant _____ .

3. Jake's heavy cast will _____ him from the waist down.

4. Lindsay wondered how the actress would _____ the role.

5. Hard work and dedication will help the gymnastics team _____ its goal—to win the state championship.

6. Because Ellen had always been interested in the production, distribution, and consumption of goods, she pursued a career as an _____ .

7. Will you help me _____ these books so that I can shelve them?

8. A third party was called in to _____ the disagreement between the union and the company managers.

9. Reading good books can _____ a person to become a writer.

10. The career of Chris Evert has made me _____ to be a professional tennis player.

Number correct _____ (total 10)

Turn to **Words Ending in y** on pages 207–209 of the **Spelling Handbook.**
Read the rule and complete the exercises provided.

Matching Definitions Match each word with its definition. Write the letter of the matching word in the blank.

_____ 1. a way of talking or pronouncing

_____ 2. a financial expert

_____ 3. to explain the meaning of

_____ 4. something acquired from a past generation; a bequest

_____ 5. the act of joining into a single whole

_____ 6. to be ambitious

_____ 7. the ability to move

_____ 8. unconditional or absolute

_____ 9. a strategist

_____ 10. balance

a. articulation

b. aspire

c. categorical

d. economist

e. equality

f. inheritance

g. interpret

h. mobility

i. tactician

j. unification

Number correct _____ (total 10)

Analyzing Word Parts

The Latin Root _med_ The target word _median_ derives from the Latin word _medius,_ which means "middle." English words derived from the root _med_ include the related word _mediate_ and others, such as _media, medial, medieval,_ and _mediocre._ These words all are associated with a position between two extremes. Interestingly, some words emphasize this "middleness" by adding the prefix _inter,_ meaning "between," to words that already have the _med_ root; _intermediary_ and _intermediate_ are examples. Write the word from the list below that best completes each of the following sentences. Use your dictionary as needed.

media   medieval
medial   mediocre
mediate

1. Our debate topic during the last presidential election was "The

   _____ no longer just report the news; they help create it."

2. The drama club gave a _____ performance; Allison wasn't sorry she saw it, but certainly she wouldn't go to see it again.

3. "If you two don't settle your disagreement in fifteen minutes," my mother

   threatened, "I'll have to step in and _____ it myself."

43

4. Martin chose a _____ position in the tug-of-war line, hoping that he would have to exert himself less than would those at the beginning and end of the line.

5. The millenium from A.D. 476 to about A.D. 1450 that separates ancient from modern times in Western civilization is called the _____ period, or Middle Ages.

Number correct _____ (total 5)

The Latin Root *spir* The target word *aspiration*, the related words *aspire* and *inspire*, and many other English words, such as *expire*, *respiration*, and *spirit*, contain the Latin root *spir* from the word *spirare*, meaning "to breathe." All of these words, and others based on the same root, have meanings related to breathing or breath. In the blank, write the word that best describes each situation.

aspire   expire   inspire   respiration   spirit

_____ 1. The pollution on hot, humid summer days makes it difficult for people with heart and lung diseases to breathe.

_____ 2. Aldo did not survive the plane crash that killed more than half the passengers and crew on the flight to Seattle.

_____ 3. Although the college football team had not won a game in three years, they practiced hard and tried to learn from the teams who defeated them.

_____ 4. When she was three years old, Greta decided that she wanted to be a dancer and never wavered from that decision.

_____ 5. Percy said he was too tired to mow the lawn but changed his mind when he saw the neighbor's teen-age daughter sunbathing in her yard.

Number correct _____ (total 5)

Number correct in Unit _____ (total 90)

Word's Worth: mundane

If you describe your life as *mundane*, you're telling people that you're bored with everything and that nothing exciting ever happens to you. Originally, however, this word had a very different, and much broader, meaning. It is derived from the Latin word *mundus*, meaning "universe." From *mundus* came the Latin word *mondain*, meaning "of this world," as opposed to "of the other world" or "sacred" or "eternal." In English, *mundane* has retained that worldly meaning but more often is used to mean "common" or "ordinary"— coming a long way from its original reference to the whole universe.

The Last Word

Writing

Write a short essay describing three aspects of your cultural *heritage* you want to pass on to your children and three that you would prefer not to pass on. Explain why each positive aspect is valuable and each negative aspect is useless or harmful.

Speaking

Describe a problem you have faced and the *tactics* you used to solve it. Indicate other approaches that might have worked as well or better.

Group Discussion

Have you ever wondered how witnesses to an accident or crime can give such different accounts of the event? As a class, discuss the problems that arise because everyone has a slightly different *interpretation* of an experience. You might want to consider the following questions:

1. If there is an objective answer to the question "What happened?" how can you find it?
2. What factors make one interpretation of events more valuable than another, or are all interpretations equally valid?

UNIT 4: Review of Units 1–3

Part A   Review Word List

Unit 1 Target Words

1. absurdly
2. acquiesce
3. ascend
4. beneficent
5. coerce
6. conference
7. contemplate
8. correspondent
9. distinction
10. dominate
11. enable
12. fundamentally
13. impress
14. indifferent
15. oblige
16. plausible
17. plight
18. serenity
19. shroud
20. singular

Unit 1 Related Words

1. absurdity
2. ascent
3. benefactor
4. beneficiary
5. benefit
6. benevolent
7. coercion
8. confer
9. contemplation
10. correspond
11. descend
12. descendant
13. distinctive
14. dominant
15. implausible
16. impression
17. indifference
18. serenade
19. singularity
20. transcend

Unit 2 Target Words

1. abode
2. alter
3. contamination
4. counterpart
5. diversify
6. impetuous
7. initiate
8. interaction
9. irrecoverable
10. irreversible
11. lethal
12. magnitude
13. millennium
14. modify
15. radiation
16. relatively
17. sinister
18. species
19. universal
20. vegetation

Unit 2 Related Words

1. alteration
2. altercation
3. contaminate
4. diverse
5. diversification
6. diversion
7. divert
8. initial
9. initiation
10. interact
11. magnanimous
12. modification
13. radiate
14. reversible
15. universe
16. vegetate

Unit 3 Target Words

1. acculturation
2. ameliorate
3. articulate
4. aspiration
5. attainment
6. category
7. consensus
8. economic
9. ethnicity
10. heritage
11. inequality
12. interpretation
13. median
14. mobilize
15. mundane
16. rectify
17. segment
18. tactic
19. unify
20. vociferous

Unit 3 Related Words

1. articulation
2. aspire
3. attain
4. categorical
5. categorize
6. economist
7. equality
8. ethnic
9. immobilize
10. inheritance
11. inspire
12. interpret
13. mediate
14. mobility
15. tactician
16. unification

Inferring Meaning from Context

For each sentence write the letter of the word or phrase that is closest to the meaning of the word or words in italics.

_____ 1. Because Raman already spoke Japanese, he had few problems with _acculturation_ during his stay in Japan.
a. changed diet   b. cultural adjustment   c. leisure activities
d. foreign currency

_____ 2. The Dewey Decimal System divides library sources into ten basic subject matter _categories_.
a. classifications   b. benefits   c. locations   d. catalogs

_____ 3. Jane's brother _coerced_ her into doing his chores.
a. forced   b. modified   c. diverted   d. inspired

_____ 4. Because of the power blackout, the _correspondent_ had difficulty submitting stories to her paper on time.
a. news reporter   b. librarian   c. teacher   d. public speaker

_____ 5. The design of the solar-powered car is _fundamentally_ sound, but the solar cell must be modified because it doesn't produce enough energy.
a. categorically   b. implausibly   c. basically   d. tactically

_____ 6. Studying the origins of American democracy helps acquaint us with our country's _heritage_.
a. culture   b. tradition   c. equality   d. political future

_____ 7. The club's secret meeting place is _shrouded with_ vegetation.
a. dominated by   b. contaminated with   c. covered with   d. rectified by

_____ 8. "What is your _interpretation_ of the events that occurred during the holdup?" the witness was asked.
a. explanation   b. justification   c. initiation   d. attainment

_____ 9. Everyone realized the _magnitude_ of the problem, but no one could think of a solution.
a. importance   b. origin   c. future implications   d. unfortunate consequences

_____ 10. If I hadn't been so _impetuous_ in buying the purple shoes, I would have realized that I'd probably never wear them.
a. beneficent   b. indifferent   c. hasty   d. mundane

_____ 11. Henry Ford tried to _ameliorate_ America's transportation problems by using assembly-line techniques to mass-produce the Model-T Ford.
a. improve   b. articulate   c. modify   d. dominate

_____ 12. The Zen master had worked very hard for many years to achieve _serenity_ and contentment.
a. ethnicity   b. consensus   c. peace   d. acculturation

_____ 13. Almost all of the seniors decided to take a bus up the mountain and hike down, but George, in his *singular* way, wanted to hike up and ride down.

a. traditional   b. indifferent   c. unique   d. irreversible

_____ 14. Many people think that the koala bear is *a species of* bear, but actually it is related to the kangaroo.

a. an enemy of the   b. a kind of   c. afraid of the   d. an ancestor of the

_____ 15. Although the Rodriguez family had been asleep when the fire started, they *mobilized* themselves within minutes after the fire started, and all escaped safely.

a. readied   b. confused   c. congratulated   d. rectified

Number correct _____ (total 15)

Using Review Words in Context

Use context clues to determine which word from the list below fits logically in each blank. Write the word in the blank. Each word in the word list is used once.

absurdly	impress	mundane
attain	initiate	rectify
conference	interactions	reversible
consensus	lethal	segments
enable	mobilize	vociferously

TV or Not TV

Late Friday afternoon Sasha James, production manager of QRX-TV, called an emergency _____ with her staff. Although low ratings had left the station in desperate straits, Sasha firmly believed that the situation was

_____ and she decided to _____ all of the station's talent to turn things around.

"We have to _____ some changes immediately, if not sooner," she told her harried staff. "It would be _____ unrealistic to think that we could _____ number-one ratings overnight, but we have to try. If anyone can do it, you people can."

One of the writers spoke up. "I think everyone agrees that the last several _____ of *Crime Patrol* have been _____ to our ratings, and nothing is more deadly to ratings than a bored audience. Even our own production crew fell asleep. The _____ of the crew was that we would have gotten better ratings if we had run an hour of old cartoons. We absolutely have to _____ this situation. Our jobs are on the line."

Another writer added, "The real problem is that our shows have no artistic value. The stories are very _____ and people are sick of everyday situations. They get enough of those in life. The _____ among the characters are forced and not really believable. We need to take some risks and write scripts that will set our programs apart from others, scripts that will _____ us to captivate the viewers and _____ our bosses."

"Hear, hear!" everyone yelled loudly and _____ .

"Now we just have to figure out how to do it," Sasha said. "Let's get this show on the road."

Number correct _____ (total 15)

Part B   Review Word Reinforcement

Using Language and Thinking Skills

Finding the Unrelated Word Write the letter of the word that is not related in meaning to the other words in the set.

_____ 1. a. authorize   b. enable   c. acquiesce   d. empower

_____ 2. a. change   b. modify   c. alter   d. divert

_____ 3. a. abide   b. stay   c. remain   d. abode

_____ 4. a. articulate   b. ameliorate   c. express   d. interpret

_____ 5. a. destroy   b. correct   c. rectify   d. amend

_____ 6. a. abrupt   b. impetuous   c. hurried   d. dominating

_____ 7. a. correspond   b. conform   c. confer   d. agree

_____ 8. a. shroud   b. cover   c. wrap   d. contaminate

_____ 9. a. duplicate   b. counterpart   c. enemy   d. match

_____ 10. a. distinctive   b. singular   c. rare   d. mundane

Number correct _____ (total 10)

Practicing for Standardized Tests

Antonyms Write the letter of the word that is most nearly *opposite* in meaning to the capitalized word.

_____ 1. ABSURDLY: (A) logically   (B) initially   (C) universally   (D) understandably   (E) senselessly

_____ 2. ACQUIESCE: (A) aspire   (B) consent   (C) ascend   (D) coerce   (E) resist

_____ 3. ATTAINMENT: (A) amelioration (B) success (C) aspiration (D) altercation (E) failure

_____ 4. CONSENSUS: (A) conference (B) unification (C) accord (D) disagreement (E) plausibility

_____ 5. CONTAMINATION: (A) coercion (B) pollution (C) condemnation (D) purification (E) modification

_____ 6. DISTINCTION: (A) indifference (B) similarity (C) plight (D) rectification (E) singularity

_____ 7. ENABLE: (A) authorize (B) coerce (C) ascend (D) lead (E) hinder

_____ 8. IMPETUOUS: (A) hasty (B) distinctive (C) deliberate (D) impressive (E) impertinent

_____ 9. LETHAL: (A) safe (B) tactical (C) vociferous (D) fatal (E) obliging

_____ 10. MUNDANE: (A) plausible (B) commonplace (C) universal (D) spectacular (E) mobilized

_____ 11. PLAUSIBLE: (A) singular (B) incredible (C) beneficial (D) categorical (E) believable

_____ 12. REVERSIBLE: (A) unchangeable (B) transposable (C) irrelevant (D) unable (E) mobile

_____ 13. SERENITY: (A) chaos (B) absurdity (C) indifference (D) consensus (E) median

_____ 14. SINGULAR: (A) distinctive (B) impressive (C) conventional (D) radiating (E) coercive

_____ 15. VOCIFEROUS: (A) boisterous (B) subdued (C) dominant (D) indifferent (E) articulate

Number correct _____ (total 15)

Synonyms Write the letter of the word whose meaning is closest to that of the capitalized word.

_____ 1. ALTER: (A) acquiesce (B) diversify (C) modify (D) initiate (E) mobilize

_____ 2. AMELIORATE: (A) abide (B) improve (C) deteriorate (D) mediate (E) radiate

_____ 3. ARTICULATE: (A) paint (B) express (C) unite (D) stutter (E) defend

_____ 4. BENEFICENT: (A) radiant (B) distinctive (C) categorical (D) charitable (E) acquiescent

_____ 5. CATEGORY: (A) grouping (B) catalog (C) consensus (D) millennium (E) chaos

_____ 6. COERCE: (A) forbid (B) coax (C) force (D) refuse (E) consent

7. CONTEMPLATE: (A) initiate (B) consider (C) mediate (D) refuse
(E) consent

8. COUNTERPART: (A) category (B) distinction (C) alteration
(D) match (E) difference

9. IMPRESS: (A) oblige (B) squeeze (C) bore (D) influence (E) mobilize

10. INITIATE: (A) halt (B) dominate (C) stop (D) interact (E) begin

Number correct _____ (total 10)

Spelling and Wordplay

Word Pyramid The root *ver* comes from the Latin word *vertere*, "to turn."
Build a word pyramid of *ver* words by following the code at the base of this pyramid.

VER

__ , __ VER __
4 7   13

__ __ VER __ __ __ __
4 7   12 7 10 9

__ __ __ VER __ __ __
14 9 7   12 1 8

__ __ __ __ VER __ __ __ __ __
7 11 11 5   12 7 2 8 5

__ __ VER __ __ __ __ __ __ __ __ __
4 7   12 7 6 7 3 1 13 7 10 9

A B C D E F I L N O R S T U Y
1 2 3 4 5 6 7 8 9 10 11 12 13 14 15

Match your pyramid words to the definitions below. Write the word in the
appropriate blank.

_____ 1. to deflect

_____ 2. occurring everywhere

_____ 3. the act of adding variety to something

_____ 4. unable to be changed back into an earlier form

_____ 5. a distraction of attention

Number correct _____ (total 10)

Part C *Related Word Reinforcement*

Using Related Words

Sentence Completion Write the related word from the list below that best completes each sentence.

altercation	inheritance
attain	interpret
contaminate	mobility
distinctive	universe
implausible	vegetate

1. The average American uses 110 gallons of water each day, so it is essential

   that we not _____ our water sources with pollutants.

2. Americans have tremendous _____ : they drove a total of 1.9 trillion miles in 1987.

3. A _____ feature of the U.S. twenty-five-cent piece is George Washington's face on one side.

4. The Eskimos have more than twenty words to describe snow, a fact that is not

   difficult to _____ considering where they live.

5. Although it seems _____ Napoleon in fact conquered Italy by the time he was twenty-six years old.

6. Because President John Tyler had fifteen children, the _____ that he passed on to his family was split many ways.

7. Astronomers have estimated the size of the _____ to be 35 billion light-years, or 210,000,000,000,000,000,000,000,000 miles.

8. The fierce _____ between the neighbors finally ended in court when the Jergans were given permission to build the fence they had planned.

9. Tidal waves have been known to _____ speeds of more than five hundred nautical miles per hour.

10. After the hectic week, all we wanted to do was watch TV

    and _____ for a couple of days.

Number correct _____ (total 10)

Reviewing Word Structures

Word Parts Write the word part from the list below that completes each of the following words. Each word part may be used more than once. Then use the word in a sentence.

ab   bene   con   inter   med   uni   vert

1. _____ i a n

   _____

2. _____ f a c t o r

   _____

3. _____ s u r d i t y

   _____

4. _____ t e m p l a t i o n

   _____

5. _____ a c t

   _____

6. _____ v e r t

   _____

7. _____ f i c a t i o n

   _____

8. _____ i a t e

   _____

9. _____ f i c e n t

   _____

10. _____ t a m i n a t e

   _____

Number correct _____ (total 10)

Number correct in Unit _____ (total 95)

Vocab Lab 1

FOCUS ON: **The Environment**

To increase your awareness of environmental issues, study the following terms.

acid rain (as′id rān) n. a corrosive precipitation that results when sulfur dioxide and nitrogen oxide mix with water vapor in the air to form sulfuric acid. • The United States and Canada are cooperating to regulate the emission of gases that contribute to the production of *acid rain*.

carcinogen (kär sin′ə jən, -jen′) n. any substance that produces cancer. • When nicotine was discovered to be a *carcinogen*, the Surgeon General advised people not to smoke or chew tobacco.

desalination (dē sal′ə nā′shən, -sā′ lə-) n. a process for removing salt from water to make it drinkable. • Scientists have not yet devised a method of *desalination* that is inexpensive enough to be used on a large scale.

ecosystem (ē′kō sis′təm, ek′ō-) n. the animals, plants, and other living things that live together in a particular environment. • That pond is a perfect *ecosystem* in which both plants and animals thrive.

emissions standards (i mish′əns stan′dərdz) n. the maximum amount of a pollutant that legally can be discharged from a single source. • The Environmental Protection Agency sets *emissions standards* for exhaust systems.

environmental impact (in vī′rən men′t′l im′pakt) n. the effect of a change in one component of the environment, such as an increase in population, on the rest of the environment. • The urban planners did not take into account the possible *environmental impact* of the new factory.

epicenter (ep′ə sen′tər) n. the part of the earth's surface that is directly above the origin of an earthquake. • The greatest damage from an earthquake usually occurs close to its *epicenter*.

hydrologic cycle (hī′ drə läj′ik sī′k′l) n. the continual movement of the earth's water supply in which water evaporates, falls back to earth as rain or snow, sinks into the ground, runs back into rivers, lakes, and seas, and again evaporates. • An extended drought can seriously interfere with the *hydrologic cycle* in a particular area.

mutagen (myo͞ot′ə jən) n. a substance that can cause genetic changes and abnormalities. • Because radioactivity is a powerful *mutagen*, many people are concerned about the use of nuclear products.

particulates (pär tik′yə lits, -lāts′) n. solid particles, such as soot, dust, and asbestos, that are suspended in the air. • Many industrial processes give off *particulates* that are a major component of air pollution.

photochemical smog (fot′ō kem′i k′l smôg, -smäg) n. an eye-irritating atmospheric condition resulting from the mixture of certain air pollutants and sunshine. • *Photochemical smog* frequently develops when great quantities of pollutants enter the atmosphere during a prolonged period of sunny weather.

population crash (päp′ yə lā′shən krash) n. a massive dying off of a species, occurring when the environment can no longer support its population. • Because resources in the forests are limited, a certain percentage of deer and moose are permitted to be shot each year during the hunting season to prevent a *population crash*.

synergy (sin′ər jē) n. the combined action of several agents that produces an effect greater than the sum of the individual effects. ● Environmental pollutants are such a serious problem because *synergy* makes these substances more dangerous in combination than they would be alone.

temperature inversion (tem′prə chər in vur′zhən, -pər ə-, -shə n) n. a condition in which a warm layer of air traps a cool layer underneath it, allowing dangerous pollutants to collect. ● Because Los Angeles is surrounded by mountains and water, polluted air cannot escape and *temperature inversions* often occur.

threshold effect (thresh′ōld ə fekt′, -hōld, i-) n. a response to an agent that occurs only when a particular level, or threshold, has been reached. ● Rachel Carson noted that DDT had a *threshold effect*, damaging the reproductive systems of birds only after many years.

Sentence Completion In the blank write the word from the list that completes each sentence.

1. The oceans will provide a virtually endless source of fresh water once the process of _____ becomes practical.

2. The recent earthquake in California was so strong that it killed more than two hundred people, more than forty miles from its _____ .

3. To decrease their chances of having children with genetic defects, people of child-bearing age should avoid contact with any substance that is known to be a _____ .

4. Cleopatra's Needle, a famous Egyptian carved stone pillar, had shown no signs of deterioration for centuries in the desert, but it began to corrode rapidly due to the effects of _____ when it was moved to Central Park in New York City.

5. A (an) _____ could occur if drought caused a severe food shortage in a heavily populated area.

6. The _____ ensures that the earth will have a perpetual supply of water.

7. Filters on industrial smokestacks can prevent _____ from escaping into the air.

8. Phosphates from laundry detergents that enter a body of water remain harmless until they accumulate and the _____ upsets the natural balance.

9. There probably is not a (an) _____ on earth that has not been affected by the byproducts of industrialization.

10. Until strict _____ are enforced, the smoke and ash from industrial smokestacks will continue to pollute the earth's atmosphere.

Number correct _____ (total 10)

FOCUS ON: *Analogies*

In the first four units of this book, you completed various activities that help build vocabulary skills, such as synonym, antonym, and sentence completion exercises. An analogy exercise is another way to enrich your understanding of words. An **analogy** shows a relationship between words. A typical analogy problem looks like this:

> Choose the lettered pair of words that best expresses a relationship similar to that expressed in the original pair.

> _____ 1. SILVER : MINE :: (A) wood : carving (B) marble : quarry (C) garden : crop (D) excavation : cave (E) corn : grain

The analogy can be expressed this way: "*Silver* is to *mine* as __?__ is to __?__ ."

To answer an analogy problem, first determine the relationship between the original pair of words. State this relationship in a sentence:

"*Silver* comes from a *mine*."

Then decide which of the other word pairs expresses a similar relationship. You can test your choice by substituting the pair of words for the original pair in the sentence. It becomes apparent that *(B)* is the best answer to this problem when you use the test:

"*Marble* comes from a *quarry*."

Here are the most common types of relationships used in analogies:

Type of Analogy	Example
cause to effect	virus : cold :: carelessness : errors
part to whole	finger : hand :: spoke : wheel
object to purpose	car : transportation :: lamp : illumination
action to object	dribble : basketball :: fly : kite
item to category	salamander : amphibian :: corn : vegetable
age	kitten : cat :: cygnet : swan
type to characteristic	owl : nocturnal :: lion : carnivorous
word to synonym	nice : pleasant :: gratitude : thankfulness
synonym variants	pliant : flexibility :: unruly : disobedience
word to antonym	nice : unpleasant :: lazy : industrious
antonym variants	spotless : filth :: faultless : accuracy
object to its material	shoe : leather :: necklace : gold
product to source	apple : tree :: milk : cow
worker and creation	composer : symphony :: author : novel
worker and tool	carpenter : hammer :: surgeon : scalpel
worker and work place	mechanic : garage :: judge : courtroom
time sequence	sunrise : sunset :: spring : winter
spatial sequence	mountain top : valley :: engine : caboose
word and derived form	act : action :: image : imagine
degree of intensity	pleased : ecstatic :: drizzle : downpour
manner	shout : speak :: swagger : walk

Analogies Solve the following analogy problems, which use words from previous units. Write the letter of the word pair that best completes the analogy.

_____ 1. SERENITY : TRANQUILITY :: (A) millennium : decade
(B) interaction : repulsion (C) magnitude : size
(D) contamination : purification (E) segment : whole

_____ 2. ASCEND : DESCEND :: (A) radiate : absorb (B) dominate : control
(C) impress : affect (D) transcend : overcome (E) rectify : correct

_____ 3. ATTAIN : GOAL :: (A) unify : wedding (B) alter : dress (C) mediate
: consensus (D) initiate : conclusion (E) contemplate : contemplation

_____ 4. TREE : VEGETATION :: (A) rose : rosebush (B) vegetable :
asparagus (C) bear : animal (D) computer : computation
(E) beaver : dam

_____ 5. LETHAL : SAFE :: (A) mundane : common (B) fatal : deadly
(C) impetuous : impulsive (D) beneficent : kindly (E) singular :
multiple

_____ 6. ORATOR : ARTICULATE :: (A) gardener : vegetate (B) musician :
harmonize (C) automobile : mobilize (D) economist : spend
(E) shroud : reveal

_____ 7. TAILOR : ALTER :: (A) adjective : modify (B) graduation :
graduate (C) student : educate (D) radio : radiate
(E) mechanic : mechanize

_____ 8. FUNDAMENTALLY : BASICALLY :: (A) relatively : absolutely
(B) absurdly : senselessly (C) distinctly : vaguely (D) articulately :
unintelligibly (E) universally : individually

_____ 9. IRREVERSIBLE : REVERSIBLE :: (A) median : middle
(B) benevolent : compassionate (C) immobile : mobile (D) sinister :
ominous (E) indifferent : different

_____ 10. AMELIORATE : RECTIFY :: (A) ascend : descend (B) shroud :
uncover (C) attain : fail (D) inspire : motivate (E) harm : benefit

Number correct _____ (total 10)

Number correct in Vocab Lab _____ (total 20)

UNIT 5

Part A Target Words and Their Meanings

1. aggregation (ag′rə gā′shən) n.
2. assimilate (ə sim′ə lāt′) v.
3. augment (ôg ment′) v.
4. collision (kə lizh′ən) n.
5. comparatively (kəm par′ə tiv lē) adv.
6. component (kəm pō′nənt) adj., n.
7. condensation (kän′dən sā′shən) n.
8. conjecture (kən jek′chər) n., v.
9. deduction (di duk′shən) n.
10. eject (i jekt′, ē-) v.
11. extrapolate (ik strap′ə lāt′) v.
12. immerse (i murs′) v.
13. incipient (in sip′ē ənt) adj.
14. obscure (əb skyoor′, äb-) v., adj.
15. postulate (päs′chə lit, -lāt′) n.
    (päs′chə lāt′) v.
16. reconcile (rek′ən sīl′) v.
17. simulate (sim′yoo lāt′) v.
18. solar (sō′lər) adj.
19. subsequently (sub′si kwənt lē, -kwent′-) adv.
20. volatile (väl′ə t′l) adj.

Inferring Meaning from Context

For each sentence write the letter of the word or phrase that is closest to the meaning of the word or words in italics. Use context clues to help you.

_____ 1. The new exhibit at the museum featured *an aggregation* of relics from pioneer days, including farm implements, milk cans, and pottery.

   a. a collection   b. a horde   c. a confusion   d. a jumble

_____ 2. Immigrants often question the value of becoming *assimilated into* American culture. Many try to retain their heritage.

   a. hostile toward   b. corrupted by   c. absorbed into d. beneficial to

_____ 3. Our troops were *augmented* in order to handle the growing number of rebel attacks.

   a. on leave   b. increased   c. isolated   d. reduced

_____ 4. The *collision* only dented my fender; however, the other vehicle was nearly destroyed.

   a. decision   b. treachery   c. crash   d. tactic

_____ 5. After spending time in a crowded refugee camp, the Vietnamese family thought their two-room apartment was *comparatively* large.

   a. unbelievably   b. less   c. relatively   d. obviously

_____ 6. Yeast is a crucial *component* of baked bread; without it, the bread will not rise.

   a. compliment   b. modification   c. ingredient   d. idea

58

_____ 7. As the room became humid, *condensation* collected on the cold windows.
   a. droplets of water   b. moths   c. streaks of dirt   d. evaporation

_____ 8. The defense lawyer insisted that the prosecution's case lacked factual information and contained nothing but *conjecture*.
   a. consensus   b. confusion   c. guesswork   d. truth

_____ 9. "Watson, when I saw the unusual footprints along the trail leading to the house, my *deduction* was that Peg-Leg Jones was the murderer."
   a. hope   b. inspiration   c. fear   d. conclusion

_____ 10. The boys caused a disturbance and were *ejected from* the theater.
   a. overwhelmed by   b. thrown out of   c. praised by   d. imprisoned by

_____ 11. By studying sales for the first three months, Ms. Lorca was able to *extrapolate* sales for the entire year.
   a. ignore   b. estimate   c. contemplate   d. demand

_____ 12. Lorna *immersed* the greasy pan in soapy water and left it to soak.
   a. spun   b. sprayed   c. floated   d. submerged

_____ 13. Cancer is most treatable if caught in its *incipient* stage, before it has a chance to spread.
   a. middle   b. treacherous   c. beginning   d. contagious

_____ 14. That new house partially *obscures* our view of the lake.
   a. blocks   b. improves   c. unifies   d. reflects

_____ 15. Early American colonists *postulated* that England had no right to collect taxes from them as long as they had no right to vote.
   a. claimed   b. suggested   c. pretended   d. obscured the fact

_____ 16. The tribes *reconciled* their differences and stopped fighting.
   a. settled   b. revealed   c. confessed   d. decided on

_____ 17. The new Coast Guard recruits *simulated* the rescue of a fishing boat in order to learn each step in the rescue procedure.
   a. blocked   b. staged   c. endangered   d. accelerated

_____ 18. Because Denver has three hundred days of sunshine per year, many residents build homes powered by *solar* energy.
   a. electric   b. sun   c. wind   d. lunar

_____ 19. Ronald Reagan and Mikhail Gorbachev agreed on several key issues during their meetings in 1987 and 1988; *subsequently*, the relationship between the United States and the Soviet Union improved.
   a. previously   b. unrelatedly   c. since then   d. on the other hand

_____ 20. Fred worried about the possibility of an explosion as he drove a truck load of *volatile* nitroglycerin over the bumpy mountain road.
   a. excess   b. valuable   c. poisonous   d. unstable

Number correct _____ (total 20)

You should now have a general idea of the meaning of each target word. Refine your understanding by examining the shades of meaning these words have in the following excerpt.

The Earth's Origin

T.F. Gaskell

In this excerpt from his book Physics of the Earth, *T.F. Gaskell reveals some of the theories about how our planet Earth originally formed.*

The beginning of the earth will always be shrouded[1] in mystery. No one was present to report how it all happened nearly 5,000-million years ago, and it is unlikely that a similar occurrence will ever be witnessed. Moreover, the operation is far too vast to be **simulated** in a modern experiment, even on a model scale. In order to make a reasonable **conjecture** about the origin of the   5
earth, we must rely on **deductions** from the world that we can see today, and must **extrapolate** backwards using known laws governing the behavior of matter.

The eighteenth-century philosopher Kant proposed that a swirling nebula[2] of hot gas originally gave rise to the sun and the planets by a series of local   10
condensations of matter. In 1796, the astronomer and mathematician Laplace modified this concept by proposing condensation to form the sun, which then, owing to the centrifugal[3] effect of its rotation, **ejected** the planets, the outer planets being thrown off first. These theories are difficult to **reconcile** with the
comparatively slow rotation of the sun. This is because most of the rotational   15
energy of the **solar** system resides with the planets, although the sun is nearly a thousand times as massive as all the planets put together. Perhaps this rotational problem can be overcome by **postulating** the action of a second body. Another star could pass close by the sun and wrench away a string of droplets which would then condense to form the planets. However, it is probable that   20
any such droplets which remained within the sun's gravitational field would eventually fall back into the parent body. Only if the sun originally had a companion star that was removed by the near miss of a third star would it be possible to account for the orbital paths of these droplets.

Present-day ideas favor an initially cold planet rather than condensation from   25
a hot gas to a molten liquid which **subsequently** solidified. Dense "dust clouds" or "globules" can be seen in the night sky partially **obscuring** the stars. Some of these clouds are comparatively nearby, between 10,000 and 100,000 times as distant as the sun, and may possibly have resulted from the break-up of a companion star to the sun; from a **collision** of this companion star with a third,   30
resulting in a finely vaporized material; or merely from the capture of a stray cloud by the sun. Such gaseous material would have cooled and its less **volatile components** would have condensed to give a mixture of liquid droplets and solid particles **immersed** in gas.

This mixture probably rotated in the form of a vast disc with the sun at its   35
center, and stretched out as far as the present path of Neptune and Pluto. At
first, particles would stick together only when they collided, but later, where
sufficiently large **aggregations** had formed, gravitational attraction would cause
more material to **augment** the growing body. As its mass increased, a planet
would eventually attract a wide swathe[4] of particles, and would starve its smaller   40
competitors. Some of the asteroids, which are bodies up to a few hundred miles
in diameter, may represent **incipient** planets, stunted in their youth because
their larger neighbors snatched the raw material of growth before they could
assimilate it.

_____

[1] shrouded: hidden
[2] nebula: a vast cloudlike patch seen in the night sky, consisting of a very distant group of stars, of
   gaseous masses, or of galaxies
[3] centrifugal: moving or tending to move away from a center
[4] swathe: a strip or band

Refining Your Understanding

For each of the following items consider how the target word is used in the
passage. Write the letter of the word or phrase that best completes each sentence.

_____   1. "These theories are difficult to *reconcile* with the . . . slow rotation of the
         sun." This statement (lines 14-15) suggests that the sun's slow rotation
         a. undercuts these theories   b. validates these theories   c. slows the
         scientific method.

_____   2. "Perhaps this rotational problem can be overcome by *postulating* the
         action of a second body (lines 17-18)." The word *postulating* is used
         here to mean   a. proving   b. positioning   c. theorizing.

_____   3. If dust clouds or globules *obscure* the stars (line 27), then astronomers
         a. can easily observe the stars   b. are in a dangerous situation   c. have
         difficulty seeing the stars.

_____   4. If more material *augments* the planet (line 39), this would mean that the
         planet would   a. expand   b. contract   c. drift away from the sun.

_____   5. "Some of the asteroids . . . may represent *incipient* planets" (lines 41-42)
         means that asteroids may be   a. planets in an early stage   b. planets
         about to explode   c. false planets.

Number correct _____ (total 5)

Part C Ways to Make New Words Your Own

By now you are familiar with the target words and their meanings. This section presents reinforcement activities that will help you make these words part of your permanent vocabulary.

Using Language and Thinking Skills

True-False Decide whether each statement is true or false. Write **T** for True and **F** for False.

_____ 1. Eggs are *components* of omelets.

_____ 2. Unstable substances can be *volatile*.

_____ 3. To *simulate* means "to pretend."

_____ 4. You will *augment* your weight if you carefully follow a reducing diet.

_____ 5. When you push the *eject* button on a tape player, the music begins to play.

_____ 6. Darkness *obscures* a landscape.

_____ 7. *Collisions* between subway trains are rarer than car crashes.

_____ 8. The computer is a *comparatively* recent invention.

_____ 9. Most students can *assimilate* all the concepts in algebra within a day.

_____ 10. Your car's breaking down on the highway could be considered an *aggregation*.

Number correct _____ (total 10)

Finding Examples Write the letter of the situation that best demonstrates the meaning of each word.

_____ 1. **volatile**
   a. A monk prays in a monastery.
   b. Someone dives into a swimming pool.
   c. A match drops onto a crate of explosives.

_____ 2. **ejected**
   a. Someone is discouraged after finishing last in a race.
   b. A pilot whose jet fighter is about to crash is propelled out of the pilot's seat.
   c. The astronaut reenters the spacecraft.

_____ 3. **reconcile**
   a. You detest your loud-mouthed neighbor.
   b. You become friendly again with a cousin after feuding for years.
   c. Your company transfers you to a branch office in another city.

_____ 4. **extrapolate**
   a. Based on the week's workouts, the coach could predict fairly accurately how his runner would do in the race.
   b. The artist was nearly finished painting the ceiling of the chapel.
   c. That boy told the biggest lies you ever heard.

_____ 5. **condensation**
   a. The writer created a 1,000-page version of a 200-page novel.
   b. The editor turned a 1,000-page manuscript into a 100-page summary.
   c. The piano tuner was paid well for her work.

_____ 6. **conjecture**
   a. Dr. Lee discussed the possibility of life existing outside our planet.
   b. Dr. Santo described the procedure used in a heart transplant.
   c. Dr. Horowitz crossed the river at Antietam Bridge.

_____ 7. **solar**
   a. The planets in our system orbit around the same point.
   b. A strong wind blew in from the north last night.
   c. At that time of year at the North Pole, it is dark all day.

_____ 8. **subsequently**
   a. The tidal wave came after the earthquake.
   b. I used to ride the bus to school.
   c. Before I give that speech, I will rehearse.

_____ 9. **deduction**
   a. A spider lures an ant into its web.
   b. You call the restaurant, get no answer, and conclude that it is closed.
   c. You lose fifty pounds on a diet.

_____ 10. **augment**
   a. The police arrived at the scene of the crime too late.
   b. Mike used the last of the cereal for breakfast.
   c. The government increased surpluses of corn and wheat.

Number correct _____ (total 10)

Practicing for Standardized Tests

Synonyms Write the letter of the word whose meaning is closest to that of the capitalized word.

_____ 1. AGGREGATION: (A) fear (B) nervousness (C) mixture (D) goal (E) unit

_____ 2. AUGMENT: (A) lessen (B) unify (C) increase (D) initiate (E) acquire

_____ 3. COMPONENT: (A) part (B) electron (C) collection (D) problem (E) improvement

_____ 4. CONJECTURE: (A) guess (B) perjure (C) report (D) rectify (E) agree

_____ 5. DEDUCTION: (A) cause (B) background (C) refinement
(D) subtraction (E) gain

_____ 6. IMMERSE: (A) teach (B) clean (C) touch (D) discuss (E) dip

_____ 7. INCIPIENT: (A) odd (B) final (C) beginning (D) unknown (E) fierce

_____ 8. OBSCURE: (A) unify (B) conceal (C) quiet (D) enable (E) expose

_____ 9. POSTULATE: (A) mobilize (B) blend (C) rectify (D) claim (E) deny

_____ 10. SUBSEQUENTLY: (A) truly (B) causally (C) only (D) before
(E) afterward

Number correct _____ (total 10)

Spelling and Wordplay

Crossword Puzzle

ACROSS

1. To look or act like; to pretend
6. On, by, or near
9. Singles
10. A baby's utterances
12. Abbr. *Library of Congress*
13. Help
16. *Ex* often changes to this prefix when coming before *c* or *s*
18. Possible title for a married woman
19. A goal
21. Abbr. *Regarding*
22. Slang for *swindle*
23. Prefix for "two"
24. Abbr. *Revolutions Per Minute*
25. Letters used to form the past tense
26. Abbr. *Ton*
27. Not bright
29. Abbr. *United Artists*
31. Abbr. *Justice of the Peace*
32. Abbr. *Titanium*
33. To make friends again
36. Slang for *friend*
37. Prefix indicating "Indian"
38. A prank
39. Sixth tone of the music scale
40. Abbr. *New Testament*
44. To assume to be true without proof
47. To increase
50. See 21 Across
51. Abbr. *Royal Society*
52. To arrange according to class
53. An idea or plan

DOWN

1. Of the sun
2. Just beginning to appear
3. Myself
4. Letters for America
5. To throw out of; to discharge
6. Abbr. *Alternating Current*
7. A male cat
8. Absorbs and incorporates
11. Referring to the path of a satellite around a planet
14. Anger
15. A subtraction
17. To guess
20. Abbr. *Millimeter*
28. Tragic fate
30. What we breathe
33. Abbr. *Rhode Island*
34. Abbr. *Certificate of Deposit*
35. Fluff from cloth or yarn
41. Slang for *father*
42. Mate to 41 Down
43. The self
44. An animal kept as a companion
45. _ _ _ _ the Lion
46. To attempt
48. You and me
49. Mate to 18 Across

Part D Related Words

A number of words are closely related to the target words you have studied. Use your knowledge of the target words and of word parts to determine the meanings of these words. (For information about word parts analysis, see pages 6-12.) If you are unsure of any definitions, use your dictionary.

1. abject (ab′jekt, ab jekt′) adj.
2. aggregate (ag′rə gət) adj. (-gāt′) n.
3. assimilation (ə sim′ə lā′shən) n.
4. collide (kə līd′) v.
5. comparable (käm′pər ə b'l) adj.
6. condense (kən dens′) v.
7. deduce (di do͞os′, -dyo͞os′) v.
8. dejection (di jek′shən) n.
9. ejection (i jek′shən, ē-) n.
10. exponent (ik spō′nənt) adj.
    (ik spō′nənt, ek′spō′-) n.
11. extrapolation (ik strap′ə lā′shən) n.
12. immersion (i mʉr′shən, -zhən) n.
13. impose (im pōz′) v.
14. interject (in′tər jekt′) v.
15. obscurity (əb skyo͞or′ə tē, äb-) n.
16. opponent (ə pō′nənt) n., adj.
17. projectile (prə jek′t'l, -tīl) adj., n.
18. reconciliation (rek′ən sil′ē ā′shən) n.
19. repose (ri pōz′) v., n.
20. simulation (sim′yo͞o lā′shən) n.

Understanding Related Words

Sentence Completion Complete each sentence with the correct word from the following list.

assimilation	extrapolation
collide	immersion
condense	reconciliation
deduce	repose
dejection	simulation

1. When awake, the child wore a mischievous grin; but in _____ the boy had the face of an angel.

2. Using a (an) _____ from the first three quarters of the year, the Center for Crime Statistics predicted a decrease in crime.

3. Several factors prevented the _____ of that tribe into our culture, including their fierce independence.

4. Ladies and gentlemen of the jury, what can we _____ from these facts: the defendant had the motive, the means, and the opportunity to commit this robbery.

5. The objective of current U.S.-Russian policy is _____ through overcoming old differences.

6. An early popular analogy explained atomic chain reactions by showing *how* billiard balls _____ .

7. In some religions, baptism requires full-body _____ in water.

8. The _____ felt by the losing team was particularly intense because they had lost by one point in the final second of the game.

9. It is impossible to _____ a twelve-part television series into a half-hour program

10. A fire drill is the _____ of a real emergency.

Number correct _____ (total 10)

Turn to **The Prefix *com-*** on page 204 of the **Spelling Handbook.** Read the rule and complete the exercise provided.

Analyzing Word Parts

The Latin Root *ject* The target words *conjecture* and *eject* come from the Latin word *jacere*, "to throw." The following related words also come from *jacere*:

abject   dejection   ejection   interject   projectile

Keeping in mind the meaning of *jacere*, match each word with its correct definition.

_____ 1. (n.) the state of being depressed, downcast, or disheartened

_____ 2. (v.) to put in between other things; to insert

_____ 3. (n.) an object thrown, fired, or otherwise thrust forward

_____ 4. (n.) the act of being thrown out forcefully or expelled

_____ 5. (adj.) miserable; wretched; contemptible

Number correct _____ (total 5)

The Latin Root *pon/pos* The target word *component* comes from the Latin *ponere*, meaning "to put" or "to set." The following words also come from this Latin source (Notice that in some words *pon* has become *pos*.):

exponent   impose   opponent   proposition   repose

In your dictionary look up the definition of each word you do not know. Then use each word in one of the following sentences.

1. The wrestler Killer Typhoon glared across the ring at his _____ .

2. Ever since she stopped eating meat, Isabel has become a (an) _____ of vegetarianism.

3. Citizens gathered at the town meeting to debate the _____ that home construction be permitted on the hills above town.

4. In the intense heat of desert afternoons, many creatures simply

_____ in the shade until nightfall.

5. The British planned to _____ a tax on tea in the American colonies; the colonists responded with the Boston Tea Party.

Number correct _____ (total 5)

Number correct in Unit _____ (total 75)

Word's Worth: augment

Learning about one word often helps to shed light on relatives of that word. Consider the word *augment*. This word came into English from the Old French *augmenter*, and before that from the Latin *augere*, "to increase"—the same meaning that *augment* has today. In **Unit 2** (in relation to the word *sinister*), you read about *augury*, the practice of trying to foretell the future from omens. *Augury* shares the same root as *augment*. Apparently, augury was intended to increase one's knowledge. Another relative is the word *auction*. At an auction, the price of an item starts at one amount and then increases as people bid for the item.

The Last Word

Writing

Given the prevalence of conflict in our age, *reconciliation*, or peacemaking, is an important goal. Write a brief essay that explains what you think the necessary ground rules are for initiating *reconciliation* between hostile parties, whether they be individuals, gangs, or nations. Your paper should also offer some specific suggestions for resolving conflict.

Speaking

Extrapolation is a way of using the past or the present to make an educated guess about the future. Prepare a brief talk in which you predict a future occurrence by extrapolating from past or present facts and conditions.

Group Discussion

Working in a group, use encyclopedias and other references to gather information about the wide variety of ways *solar* energy is put to use. Discuss your findings among your group members.

UNIT 6

Part A Target Words and Their Meanings

1. aristocratic (ə ris′tə krat′ik, ar′is-) adj.
2. assertion (ə sur′shən) n.
3. barbarian (bär ber′ē ən) n., adj.
4. civilized (siv′ə līzd) adj.
5. contempt (kən tempt′) n.
6. cynical (sin′i k'l) adj.
7. deportment (di pôrt′mənt) n.
8. extortion (ik stôr′shən) n.
9. extract (ik strakt′) v. (eks′trakt) n.
10. lethargy (leth′ər jē) n.
11. lyric (lir′ik) adj., n.
12. methodical (mə thäd′i k'l) adj.
13. obstinately (äb′stə nit lē) adv.
14. polyglot (päl′i glät′) adj., n.
15. prose (prōz) n.
16. provincial (prə vin′shəl) adj.
17. pugnacious (pug nā′shəs) adj.
18. seamy (sē′mē) adj.
19. synonymous (si nän′ə məs) adj.
20. temperament (tem′prə mənt, -pər ə mənt, -pər mənt) n.

Inferring Meaning from Context

For each sentence write the letter of the word or phrase that is closest to the meaning of the word or words in italics. Use context clues to help you determine the correct answer. (For information about context clues, see pages 1–5.)

_____ 1. Francis was proud of his *aristocratic* heritage; his ancestors had been German barons with giant estates.

a. upper-class   b. lower-class   c. political   d. urban

_____ 2. The scientist made the *assertion* that a defensive shield could protect a country from nuclear attack; however, she did not offer any proof.

a. pledge   b. claim   c. mistake   d. invention

_____ 3. Orson wanted to be thought of as a cultivated person, not as *a barbarian,* so he tried to learn better manners.

a. an intelligent person   b. a mundane person   c. a crude person
d. a foolish person

_____ 4. With its fine local government and its love of the arts, the town was certainly one of the most *civilized* places on the frontier.

a. cultured   b. dominated   c. vociferous   d. inhospitable

_____ 5. Marie felt *contempt* for the person who had stolen her bicycle, and she searched the streets with anger in her eyes.

a. respect   b. reverence   c. pity   d. scorn

_____ 6. Parents who repeatedly break promises may raise children who *are cynical*.

   a. have good relationships with others   b. doubt others' sincerity
   c. are normal adults   d. are law-abiding

_____ 7. The parents were proud of their young child's *deportment* at the party.

   a. chores   b. conjecture   c. mischievousness   d. behavior

_____ 8. Taking money from people by threatening to ruin their reputations is a form of *extortion*.

   a. business   b. receiving compensation for losses   c. civilization
   d. getting something by force

_____ 9. It is illegal to *extract* a confession from a criminal by using force.

   a. request   b. record   c. simulate   d. obtain

_____ 10. I feel energetic in the morning; but after lunch, *lethargy* sets in.

   a. indecision   b. aspiration   c. assimilation   d. drowsiness

_____ 11. Lester's poetry, with its lilting rhythms, has a *lyric* quality; several of his poems have been set to music.

   a. convincing   b. melodious   c. boring   d. metallic

_____ 12. The expression "There is a method to his madness" describes a person who seems disorganized but is actually quite *methodical*.

   a. scatterbrained   b. vindictive   c. systematic   d. dishonest

_____ 13. We should have put Aunt Martha in a nursing home two years ago, but she *obstinately* refuses to listen to reason.

   a. stubbornly   b. sweetly   c. honorably   d. sensitively

_____ 14. The Swiss are *a polyglot* people; it is not unusual for a Swiss to speak German, French, English, and Italian.

   a. a commonplace   b. a memorable   c. a multilingual   d. an absurd

_____ 15. That author writes some poetry, but she is best known for her *prose*, particularly her fine essays on nature.

   a. songs   b. writing without rhyme or meter   c. profession   d. writing

_____ 16. Wayne spoke critically of the *provincial* townspeople, who showed little interest in the outside world.

   a. incipient   b. progressive   c. unified   d. narrow-minded

_____ 17. In the early years of college football, some officials permitted slugging and kicking on the field. This *pugnacious* playing caused eighteen deaths and more than 150 permanent injuries in the 1905 season.

   a. combative   b. illegal   c. enthusiastic   d. one-sided

_____ 18. Stephen Crane's novel *Maggie: A Girl of the Streets* shows the *seamy* side of life—the world of the trapped and the unfortunate.

   a. adventurous   b. wretched   c. absurd   d. untrue

_____ 19. "Righteous" is *synonymous with* the word "good."

a. of the same origin as   b. of the same rhythm as   c. of the same meaning as   d. of the same difficulty as

_____ 20. Angela was known for her pleasant *temperament*, a quality that allowed her to get along well with others.

a. appearance   b. intelligence   c. disposition   d. demonstration

Number correct _____ (total 20)

Part B   Target Words in Reading and Literature

You should now have a general idea of the meaning of each target word. Refine your understanding by examining the shades of meaning these words have in the following excerpt.

Ship of Fools

Katherine Anne Porter

At the beginning of her novel Ship of Fools, *Katherine Ann Porter describes a Mexican port city and its unusual inhabitants.*

August, 1931—The port town of Veracruz is a little purgatory[1] between land and sea for the traveler, but the people who live there are very fond of themselves and the town they have helped to make. They live as initiates in a local custom reflecting their own history and **temperament**, and they carry on their lives of alternate violence and **lethargy** with a pleasurable **contempt** for outside opinion, founded on the charmed notion that their ways and feelings are above and beyond criticism.

When they entertain themselves at their numerous private and public feasts, the newspapers publish **lyric prose** saying what an occasion it was; in what lavish and **aristocratic**—the terms are **synonymous**, they believe—taste the decorations and refreshments [were]; and they cannot praise too much the skill

5

10

with which the members of good society maintain in their **deportment** the delicate balance between high courtesy and easy merriment, a secret of the Veracruz world bitterly envied and unsuccessfully imitated by the **provincial** inland society of the capital. "Only our people know how to enjoy themselves with **civilized** freedom," they write. "We are generous, warmhearted, hospitable, sensitive," they go on, and they mean it to be read not only by themselves but by the **polyglot barbarians** of the upper plateau[2] who **obstinately** go on regarding Veracruz as merely a pestilential[3] jumping-off place into the sea. 15

There may be a small sign of uneasiness in this **pugnacious assertion** of high breeding; in this and in the **methodical** brutality of their common behavior towards the travelers who must pass through their hands to reach the temporary haven of some ship in harbor. The travelers wish only to be carried away from the place, and the Veracruzanos wish only to see the last of them; but not until every possible toll, fee, **extortion**, and bribe due to the town and its citizens has been **extracted**. It is to the passing eye a typical port town, **cynical** by nature, shameless by experience, hardened to showing its **seamiest** side to strangers; ten to one this stranger passing through is a sheep bleating for their shears, and one in ten is a scoundrel it would be a pity not to outwit. In any case, there is only so much money to be got out of each one, and the time is always short. 20 25 30

[1] purgatory: in Roman Catholic and other Christian doctrine, a state or place in which those who died in the grace of God suffer for a certain time for their sins.
[2] plateau: an elevated area of more or less level land
[3] pestilential: annoying, troublesome

Refining Your Understanding

For each of the following items, consider how the target word is used in the passage. Write the letter of the word or phrase that best completes each sentence.

_____ 1. "Lives of alternate violence and *lethargy*" (line 5) suggests that the people's lives are characterized by   a. happiness   b. purposefulness   c. contradiction.

_____ 2. *Lyric prose* (line 9) suggests writing that is   a. factual   b. concise   c. songlike.

_____ 3. The people of Veracruz regard *lavish* and *aristocratic* as synonyms (line 10); the suggestion is that the author does not regard these words as synonyms—probably because *aristocratic*, unlike *lavish*, is associated with   a. greed   b. nobility   c. money.

_____ 4. If the people of the inland capital are *provincial* (line 14), the Veracruzanos are, by contrast,   a. sophisticated   b. crowded   c. money-hungry.

_____ 5. Through *extortion* and other means (line 25), the Veracruzanos   a. get money from the travelers   b. murder some travelers   c. believe they are better than the travelers.

Number correct _____ (total 5)

Part C Ways to Make New Words Your Own

By now you are familiar with the target words and their meanings. This section presents a variety of reinforcement activities that will help you make these words part of your permanent vocabulary.

Using Language and Thinking Skills

Understanding Multiple Meanings Each boldfaced word in this exercise has several definitions. Read the definitions and then read the sentences that use the word. Write the letter of the definition that applies to each sentence.

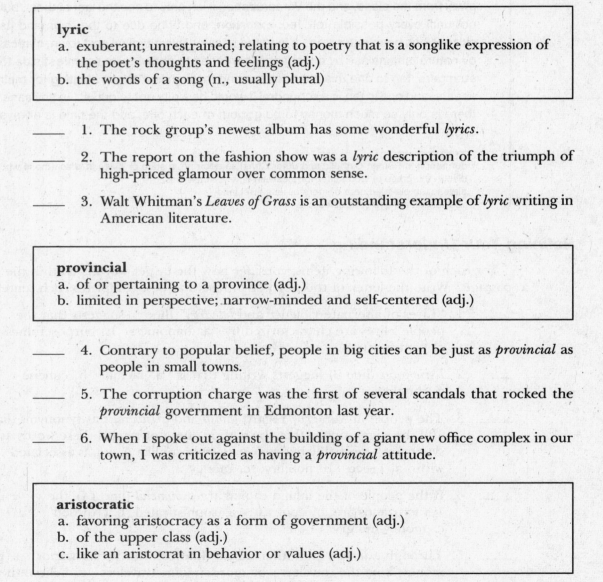

> **lyric**
> a. exuberant; unrestrained; relating to poetry that is a songlike expression of the poet's thoughts and feelings (adj.)
> b. the words of a song (n., usually plural)

_____ 1. The rock group's newest album has some wonderful *lyrics*.

_____ 2. The report on the fashion show was a *lyric* description of the triumph of high-priced glamour over common sense.

_____ 3. Walt Whitman's *Leaves of Grass* is an outstanding example of *lyric* writing in American literature.

> **provincial**
> a. of or pertaining to a province (adj.)
> b. limited in perspective; narrow-minded and self-centered (adj.)

_____ 4. Contrary to popular belief, people in big cities can be just as *provincial* as people in small towns.

_____ 5. The corruption charge was the first of several scandals that rocked the *provincial* government in Edmonton last year.

_____ 6. When I spoke out against the building of a giant new office complex in our town, I was criticized as having a *provincial* attitude.

> **aristocratic**
> a. favoring aristocracy as a form of government (adj.)
> b. of the upper class (adj.)
> c. like an aristocrat in behavior or values (adj.)

_____ 7. Robert E. Lee, head of the Confederate forces in the Civil War, fought for _aristocratic_ rule; he believed that the upper class was obligated to lead the rest of society.

_____ 8. Ellen's _aristocratic_ manner is probably a cover-up for her insecurities.

_____ 9. Franklin D. Roosevelt is a prime example of a person of _aristocratic_ background who was concerned about the needy and the downtrodden.

_____ 10. Mr. Floyd had an _aristocratic_ way about him—he seemed somewhat arrogant, but he also commanded respect from people.

Number correct _____ (total 10)

Practicing for Standardized Tests

Synonyms Write the letter of the word whose meaning is closest to that of the capitalized word.

_____ 1. METHODICAL: (A) pious   (B) organized   (C) unmerciful
(D) disorganized   (E) similar

_____ 2. CIVILIZED: (A) impolite   (B) cultivated   (C) unnatural   (D) initial
(E) crowded

_____ 3. CONTEMPT: (A) pessimism   (B) disdain   (C) contentment
(D) self-pity   (E) awkwardness

_____ 4. DEPORTMENT: (A) collection   (B) rejection   (C) section
(D) behavior   (E) culture

_____ 5. EXTRACT: (A) remove   (B) strengthen   (C) shorten   (D) begin
(E) summarize

_____ 6. PUGNACIOUS: (A) belligerent   (B) useful   (C) intelligent
(D) vociferous   (E) indifferent

_____ 7. LYRIC: (A) ameliorating   (B) obscure   (C) songlike   (D) dishonest
(E) flat

_____ 8. OBSTINATELY: (A) unfortunately   (B) reluctantly   (C) unyieldingly
(D) illegally   (E) sluggishly

_____ 9. POLYGLOT: (A) polyester   (B) aristocratic   (C) mute
(D) multilingual   (E) unsympathetic

_____ 10. TEMPERAMENT: (A) consensus   (B) ill will   (C) anger
(D) development   (E) disposition

Number correct _____ (total 10)

Analogies Each item below consists of a related pair of words followed by five other pairs of words. Write the letter of the word pair that best expresses a relationship similar to that expressed in the original pair.

_____ 1. EXTRACT : TOOTH ::   (A) celebrate : defeat   (B) extort : extortion   (C) reconcile : peace   (D) inject : vaccine   (E) sleep : repose

_____ 2. EXTORTION : BLACKMAIL ::   (A) cynic : skeptic   (B) pilot : aviation   (C) reconciliation : war   (D) flag : eagle   (E) explosion : dynamite

_____ 3. POETRY : PROSE ::   (A) fiction : book   (B) organizer : method   (C) astronomer : astronomy   (D) stanza : poetry   (E) walking : running

_____ 4. OPPOSITE : SYNONYMOUS ::   (A) victorious : successful   (B) tactical : strategic   (C) impartial : objective   (D) polluted : contaminated   (E) mundane : aristocratic

_____ 5. BARBARIAN : UNCIVILIZED ::   (A) poison : dangerous   (B) universe : local   (C) cheerleader : lethargic   (D) artist : uncreative   (E) shortage : augmented

_____ 6. CYNICAL : SCORNFUL ::   (A) incipient : final   (B) subsequent : previous   (C) plausible : unbelievable   (D) pugnacious : quarrelsome   (E) obscure : obvious

_____ 7. ASSERTION : DECLARE ::   (A) water : immerse   (B) fog : clear   (C) equality : equalize   (D) deterioration : ameliorate   (E) question : ask

_____ 8. SEAMY : SLUM ::   (A) aristocratic : estate   (B) treeless : arboretum   (C) French : province   (D) hostile : temperament   (E) dirty : hospital

_____ 9. CIVILIZED : CULTURED ::   (A) synonymous : antonymous   (B) orbiting : solar   (C) unsophisticated : naive   (D) last : incipient   (E) impetuous : controlled

_____ 10. ILLNESS : LETHARGY ::   (A) deduction : subtraction   (B) map : directions   (C) deportment : behavior   (D) collision : damage   (E) simulation : fire drill

Number correct _____ (total 10)

Spelling and Wordplay

Word Maze Find and circle each target word in this maze.

```
M  E  T  H  O  D  I  C  A  L  X  A  P  P  R
A  L  R  Q  O  B  I  B  A  K  P  N  R  D  A
C  R  E  L  A  C  I  N  Y  C  U  O  O  N  H
I  M  I  T  Y  I  C  M  P  O  G  I  B  G  S
P  E  A  S  H  R  Q  L  C  N  N  T  S  D  N
O  X  S  E  T  A  I  T  P  T  A  R  T  E  A
L  T  S  Y  K  O  R  C  J  E  C  O  I  P  I
Y  R  E  E  T  E  C  G  I  M  I  T  N  O  R
G  A  R  S  A  A  I  R  Y  P  O  X  A  R  A
L  C  T  O  J  M  Y  I  A  T  U  E  T  T  B
O  T  I  R  X  L  Y  R  W  T  S  Z  E  M  R
T  D  O  P  R  O  V  I  N  C  I  A  L  E  A
S  Y  N  O  N  Y  M  O  U  S  D  C  Y  N  B
P  F  J  T  N  E  M  A  R  E  P  M  E  T  E
G  C  I  V  I  L  I  Z  E  D  E  T  H  F  B
```

aristocratic
assertion
barbarian
civilized
contempt
cynical
deportment
extortion
extract
lethargy
lyric
methodical
obstinately
polyglot
prose
provincial
pugnacious
seamy
synonymous
temperament

Part D Related Words

A number of words are closely related to the target words you have studied. Use your knowledge of the target words and of word parts to determine the meanings of these words. (For information about word parts analysis, see pages 6–12.) If you are unsure of any definitions, use your dictionary. Learning these related words expands your vocabulary and helps you learn the target words more thoroughly.

1. aristocracy (ar′ə stäk′rə sē) n.
2. aristocrat (ə ris′tə krat′, ar′is-) n.
3. assert (ə sʉrt′) v.
4. assertive (ə sʉr′ tiv) adj.
5. barbaric (bar ber′ik) adj.
6. civil (siv′′l) adj.
7. civilian (sə vil′yən) n., adj.
8. civilization (siv′ə lə zā′shən) n.
9. contemptuous (kən temp′choo wəs) adj.
10. cynic (sin′ik) n.
11. deportation (dē′ pôr tā′shən) n.
12. extort (ik stôrt′) v.
13. lethargic (li thär′jik) adj.
14. lyricism (lir′ə siz′m) n.
15. prosaic (prō zā′ik) adj.
16. province (präv′ins) n.
17. provincialism (prə vin′shəl iz′m) n.
18. pugilist (pyoo′jə list) n.
19. temper (tem′pər) n., v.
20. temperamental (tem′prə men′t′l, -pər ə men′t′l, -pər men′t′l) adj.
21. uncivilized (un siv′ə līzd′) adj.

Understanding Related Words

Finding Examples Write the word from the list below that most closely describes the idea in the sentence.

aristocrat   extort
assert   lethargic
barbaric   prosaic
contemptuous   pugilist
cynic   temperamental

_____ 1. On the set of *Murder on Wall Street*, Lance Richards was impossible. He never appeared before 11:00 A.M., demanded a valet and catered meals in his dressing room, and stomped out of a scene if the director criticized him.

_____ 2. In the final round, the boxer forced his opponent into the corner.

_____ 3. Chatworth Whittington Osbourne ("Ozzy") IV was born with a silver spoon in his mouth, a trust fund in the bank, and a family fondness for African safaris.

_____ 4. I was not impressed by the lecturer's stale, unimaginative remarks.

_____ 5. Dale declared that foreign cars are undependable and overpriced.

_____ 6. Osric the Mighty never learned to read or write, but for forty years he held the world's record for pillaging towns and terrorizing the population.

_____ 7. Robert spent every weekend lounging on the couch, watching television for hours without stirring. His biggest decision of the day was whether or not to sit up.

_____ 8. Candace claims that she does not trust anyone over age thirty.

_____ 9. When the informant walked by the jail cell a free man, the other convicts spat and cursed at him.

_____ 10. Harry's scheme to blackmail his brother-in-law backfired.

Number correct _____ (total 10)

Turn to **The Prefix *ex-*** and **The Letter *g*** on pages 206 and 217 of the **Spelling Handbook**. Read the rules and complete the exercises provided.

Analyzing Word Parts

The Latin Root *civ* *Civilized* comes from the Latin root *civis*, meaning "citizen." English words derived from *civis* are related to the idea of citizenship. *City*, a collection of citizens, comes from this root, and a city will function best if most of its citizens are *civic-minded*. Keeping these meanings in mind, write the word from the following list that best completes each sentence. Use your dictionary as needed.

civics   civil   civilian   civilization   uncivilized

1. Many states require high school students to take a course in _____ , the study of government and politics.

2. Long before Columbus came to North America, Japan had a highly developed _____ .

3. Occasionally one hears of a child who has been raised by wolves or other wild animals; usually such a child is completely _____ .

4. The military people in that town get along well with the _____ population.

5. To be _____ even toward your enemies is a mark of maturity.

Number correct _____ (total 5)

Word's Worth: seamy

If you thought *seamy* was a word about sewing—you are right. *Seamy* is an adjective formed from the word *seam*. *Seamy* was originally used to describe a poor job of sewing in which the rough edges, or seams, were visible on the underside of a garment. Scholars believe that the playwright William Shakespeare was the first to use *seamy* in a figurative sense—to describe the rough side of a person or of life.

The Prefix *poly-* *Poly-* is a common prefix derived from the Greek word *polus*, meaning "many." It combines with various roots to form many English words. For example, *poly-* combined with *gamy* ("marriage") forms *polygamy*, the practice of being married to several spouses at the same time. Look up the following *poly-* words in your dictionary. Then write a sentence for each word.

1. polygraph:

   _____

2. polymorphous:

   _____

   _____

3. Polynesian:

_____

4. polynomial:

_____

_____

5. polyunsaturated:

_____

_____

Number correct _____ (total 5)

Number correct in Unit _____ (total 75)

The Last Word

Writing

What constitutes a *civilization*? In a brief paper, describe the accomplishments and attributes that make a country or a people civilized.

Speaking

Prepare to give an oral reading to the class of a favorite poem or a *lyric* piece of *prose*. Give special attention to the vocal expression that is necessary for an effective, lyrical presentation.

Group Discussion

Although our country is officially a democracy, some people believe that a powerful *aristocracy* still exists. Do you agree? If so, who belongs to that class, and what are their characteristics and accomplishments? Divide into groups and discuss these questions. Then report your thoughts to the class.

UNIT 7

Part A Target Words and Their Meanings

1. agitate (aj'ə tāt') v.
2. ardor (är'dər) n.
3. aspect (as'pekt) n.
4. catastrophic (kat'ə sträf'ik) adj.
5. compose (kəm pōz') v.
6. convulsive (kən vul'siv) adj.
7. delineate (di lin'ē āt') v.
8. dreary (drir'ē) adj.
9. endeavor (in dev'ər) v., n.
10. endure (in door', -dyoor') v.
11. exceed (ik sēd') v.
12. inanimate (in an'ə mit) adj.
13. infuse (in fyooz') v.
14. lassitude (las'ə tood', -tyood') n.
15. lustrous (lus'trəs) adj.
16. luxuriance (lug zhoor' ē əns) n.
17. moderation (mäd'ə rā'shən) n.
18. shrivel (shriv''l) v.
19. toil (toil) n., v.
20. traverse (tra vɥrs', trav'ərs) v.

Inferring Meaning from Context

For each sentence write the letter of the word or phrase that is closest to the meaning of the word or words in italics. Use context clues to help you determine the correct answer. (For information about context clues, see pages 1–5.)

_____ 1. The boy took every opportunity to *agitate* his little sister, pulling her hair, taking her toys, and scaring her.
   a. ignore b. injure c. befriend d. upset

_____ 2. The *ardor* with which Winston Churchill spoke to the British people during World War II helped to inspire and sustain them.
   a. aristocratic manner b. passion c. tranquility d. lethargy

_____ 3. With spikes sticking out in all directions, the straight-spined barrel cactus certainly has a threatening *aspect*.
   a. appearance b. life cycle c. color d. deportment

_____ 4. Marcus's reign as emperor came to a *catastrophic* end when his country was invaded by barbarians and he was imprisoned.
   a. lethargic b. celebrated c. disastrous d. well-deserved

_____ 5. During Michelle's farewell speech, tears streamed down her face, and she had to stop several times to *compose* herself.
   a. clarify b. calm c. civilize d. talk to

_____ 6. When Rocky the parrot began to sing "Three Coins in a Fountain," Ramon fell to the floor in a *convulsive* fit of laughter.
   a. shaking b. confused c. contemptuous d. temperamental

79

_____ 7. In her lecture, Professor Ernst *delineated* the factors that led to World War I, beginning with the European arms race.

    a. obscured b. de-emphasized c. outlined d. condensed

_____ 8. The North Pole can be a very *dreary* place; for 186 days there is little or no sunlight.

    a. pleasant b. crime-ridden c. barbaric d. gloomy

_____ 9. Rosa Bonheur, a nineteenth-century French painter, *endeavored* to paint animals realistically. To this end, she kept lions, gazelles, chamois, and deer in her yard.

    a. strived b. failed c. gave up everything d. disliked having

_____ 10. People living in Death Valley, California, have *endured* hot days of over 120 degrees.

    a. withstood b. prayed for c. enjoyed d. taken advantage of

_____ 11. In laughter, men *exceed* women: men laugh longer, louder, and more often, according to recent research.

    a. show higher ability than b. simulate c. surpass d. are inferior to

_____ 12. Some people think that the desert is merely a vast stretch of sand, *an inanimate* landscape. Actually, the desert is teeming with life; it is home to hundreds of plants, birds, mammals, and reptiles.

    a. an alien b. a lifeless c. a diverse d. a provincial

_____ 13. Their winning streak *infused* the players with a new confidence, and now the team felt that they could beat the world.

    a. filled b. confused c. dissatisfied d. promoted

_____ 14. Her feeling of *lassitude* came from working fourteen-hour days for weeks.

    a. cynicism b. competition c. lethargy d. zest

_____ 15. The new wax and hours of polishing gave the car its *lustrous* appearance.

    a. expensive b. unused c. glowing d. new

_____ 16. Ferns like shade; in a damp, wooded area they will grow in *luxuriance*.

    a. reluctance b. luxury c. a methodical way d. abundance

_____ 17. Most kings have not believed in *moderation*. For example, King Louis XIV had 413 beds in his palace.

    a. avoiding extremes b. living like a king c. sleep d. extortion

_____ 18. After a month in a cast, my leg muscles had *shriveled*.

    a. expanded b. disappeared c. deteriorated d. remained unchanged

_____ 19. After hours of *toil*, the firefighters had almost stopped the fire's progress.

    a. danger b. work c. fascination d. technology

_____ 20. In 1981, a three-person party *traversed* Antarctica, traveling 2,600 miles by snowmobile.

    a. arrived in b. studied c. crossed d. viewed

Number correct _____ (total 20)

Part B Target Words in Reading and Literature

You should now have a general idea of the meaning of each target word. Refine your understanding by examining the shades of meaning these words have in the following excerpt.

Frankenstein

Mary Shelley

The Frankenstein story is probably familiar to you. But you may be surprised to know that a twenty-one year old woman, Mary Shelley, wrote the original Frankenstein novel more than 150 years ago. In Shelley's novel, Dr. Frankenstein is a young medical student who creates a monster that ultimately destroys him. In the following excerpt, Dr. Frankenstein, the narrator, brings his creation to life—and feels awe and terror at what he has done.

It was on a **dreary** night of November that I beheld the accomplishment of my **toils**. With an anxiety that almost amounted to agony, I collected the instruments of life around me, that I might **infuse** a spark of being into the lifeless thing that lay at my feet. It was already one in the morning; the rain pattered dismally against the panes, and my candle was nearly burnt out, when by the glimmer of the half-extinguished light, I saw the dull yellow eye of the creature open; it breathed hard, and a **convulsive** motion **agitated** its limbs.

5

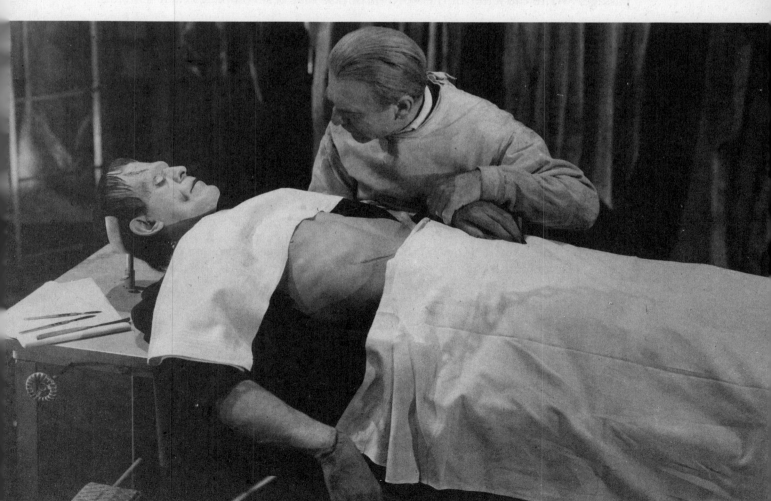

How can I describe my emotions at this **catastrophe**, or how **delineate** the wretch whom with such infinite pains and care I had **endeavored** to form? His limbs were in proportion, and I had selected his features as beautiful. 10 Beautiful! . . . His yellow skin scarcely covered the work of muscles and arteries beneath; his hair was of a **lustrous** black, and flowing; his teeth of a pearly whiteness; but these **luxuriances** only formed a more horrible contrast with his watery eyes, that seemed almost of the same color as the dun white sockets in which they were set, his **shriveled** complexion, and straight black lips. 15

I had worked hard for nearly two years, for the sole purpose of infusing life into an **inanimate** body. For this I had deprived myself of rest and health. I had desired it with an **ardor** that far **exceeded moderation**; but now that I had finished, the beauty of the dream vanished, and breathless horror and disgust filled my heart. Unable to **endure** the **aspect** of the being I had created, I rushed 20 out of the room, and continued a long time **traversing** my bedchamber, unable to **compose** my mind to sleep. At length **lassitude** succeeded to the tumult I had before endured; and I threw myself on the bed in my clothes, endeavoring to seek a few moments of forgetfulness. But it was in vain: I slept, indeed, but I was disturbed by the wildest dreams. 25

Refining Your Understanding

For each of the following items, consider how the target word is used in the passage. Write the letter of the word or phrase that best completes each sentence.

_____ 1. The creature's motion was *convulsive* (line 7), meaning that the creature came to life   a. in a confused state   b. slowly and peacefully   c. with a jerk.

_____ 2. *Delineate* (line 8) in this context is synonymous with   a. cure   b. describe   c. love.

_____ 3. The *luxuriances* (line 13) the narrator refers to are   a. flowing hair and beautiful teeth   b. watery eyes and shriveled complexion   c. the electric shocks given to the creature.

_____ 4. The narrator used the word *ardor* (line 18) to indicate that he had approached this scientific experiment with   a. fear b. enthusiasm c. a sense of duty.

_____ 5. The *lassitude* (line 22) the narrator experiences at the end of this evening is probably due to   a. emotional turmoil   b. hard physical labor   c. the convulsions.

Number correct _____ (total 5)

Part C Ways to Make New Words Your Own

By now you are familiar with the target words and their meanings. This section presents a variety of reinforcement activities that will help you make these words part of your permanent vocabulary.

Using Language and Thinking Skills

Matching Sayings and Target Words Each of the sayings below suggests one of the target words in this unit. Match the saying with the target word. Write the appropriate target word in the blank.

agitate	endeavor	exceed	lassitude	moderation
dreary	endure	inanimate	luxuriance	toil

_____ 1. to have one's nose to the grindstone

_____ 2. to get in someone's hair

_____ 3. to overshoot the mark

_____ 4. Try and try again.

_____ 5. If you've got it, flaunt it.

_____ 6. Overdone is poorly done.

_____ 7. dead as a doornail

_____ 8. Hang in there.

_____ 9. down in the dumps

_____ 10. He who snoozes loses.

Number correct _____ (total 10)

Practicing for Standardized Tests

Antonyms Write the letter of the word that is most nearly *opposite* in meaning to the capitalized word in each set.

_____ 1. INFUSE: (A) instill (B) reject (C) refuse (D) ameliorate (E) extract

_____ 2. CONVULSIVE: (A) calm (B) incipient (C) thoughtless (D) vociferous (E) necessary

_____ 3. CATASTROPHIC: (A) energetic (B) tropical (C) disastrous (D) uneventful (E) lethargic

_____ 4. DELINEATE: (A) educate (B) obscure (C) immerse (D) extrapolate (E) distinguish

_____ 5. LUSTROUS: (A) luminous (B) unimaginative (C) solar (D) dull (E) volatile

_____ 6. SHRIVEL: (A) reconcile (B) wither (C) grow (D) avoid (E) detract

_____ 7. ARDOR: (A) lassitude (B) temperament (C) tradition (D) intensity (E) consensus

_____ 8. COMPOSE: (A) perform (B) impose (C) agitate (D) soothe (E) observe

_____ 9. TOIL: (A) labor (B) pretend (C) rest (D) dominate (E) ignore

_____ 10. INANIMATE: (A) final (B) civilized (C) rocklike (D) lively (E) dull

Number correct _____ (total 10)

Spelling and Wordplay

Crossword Puzzle Read each clue to determine what word will fit in the corresponding squares. There are several target words in the puzzle.

ACROSS
2. Disastrous
10. Contraction of *I am*
12. Man's title
13. Word of laughter
14. Negative word
15. Attempts
20. _ _ _ _ chowder
21. Prone to violent disturbances
23. Chem. symbol for neptunium
25. A boy
26. Abbr. *Information Officer*
27. The absence of excess
31. Abbr. *Mornings*
32. Abbr. *Versus*
33. Abbr. *Area*
34. Scottish for *riverbank*
35. To go beyond requirements
38. Appearance or view
41. As regards
42. Santa's laugh
43. Abbr. *East Indies*
45. Gloomy
48. Passion
50. Historical period
51. Singular of *these*
52. Not on
53. A device for dicing food
55. Abbr. *Anno Domini*
56. Short for *elevated railway*
58. To depict or describe
60. Unhappy
61. To work hard
62. Biblical *you*

DOWN
1. To stop living
3. Word after prayer
4. To cross an area
5. Sailors
6. An exclamation of surprise or pain
7. Walked back and forth
8. Lifeless
9. To calm (oneself)
11. Abbr. *Multinational Corporation*
16. To perform an act
17. Abbr. *Valparaiso University*
18. Suffix used to indicate an alcohol
19. Missile storehouse
22. An enclosed truck
24. 1st person singular of *to be*
28. Adam and _ _ _
29. Scottish for *the*
30. Abbr. *Individual Retirement Account*
31. Joan of _ _ _
34. To exist
35. Puts up with
36. Statement of belief
37. Not wet
39. To wither
40. Groups of whales
44. To pour in or instill
46. Very dry
47. A speed contest
48. Open wide and say, "_ _"
49. Past tense of *ride*
51. A group of three
54. Abbr. *English Language Teaching*
55. Past tense of *eat*
57. Abbr. *Los Angeles*
59. Chem. symbol for nickel

Part D Related Words

A number of words are closely related to the target words you have studied. Use your knowledge of the target words and of word parts to determine the meanings of these words. (For information about word parts analysis, see pages 6–12.) If you are unsure of any definitions, use your dictionary. Learning these related words expands your vocabulary and helps you learn the target words more thoroughly.

1. agitation (aj′ə tā′shən) n.
2. animation (an′ə mā′shən) n.
3. ardent (är′d'nt) adj.
4. catastrophe (kə tas′trə fē) n.
5. convulsion (kən vul′shən) n.
6. convoluted (kän′və lōōt′id) adj.
7. delineation (di lin′ē ā′shən) n.
8. durable (door′ə b'l, dyoor′-) adj.
9. endurance (in door′əns, -dyoor′-) n.
10. immoderate (i mäd′ər it) adj.
11. infusion (in fyoo′zhən) n.
12. luster (lus′tər) n.
13. moderate (mäd′ər it) adj.
14. moderator (mäd′ə rāt′ər) n.

Understanding Related Words

Sentence Completion Write the word from the preceding list that best completes the meaning of the sentence.

1. The twenty-mile mountain hike became a (an) _____ test for the new recruits.

2. The Armenian earthquake of 1988 proved to be one of history's worst natural _____ .

3. Club members decided that a (an) _____ of money was needed to increase the organization's services.

4. _____ by the defenders of the homeless group has included criticism of government inaction and calls for free housing in public buildings.

5. Parked for months in the hot sun, Jeremy's new sports car lost its _____ .

6. Because of the high fever, the child suffered a _____ and was rushed to the hospital.

7. One of the most famous names in film _____ is Walt Disney.

8. The directions to his house were so _____ that we got lost.

9. A topographical map includes the _____ of land elevations.

10. Benjamin Franklin advised people to be _____ and to avoid extremes.

Number correct _____ (total 10)

Turn to **Words with the "Seed" Sound** on page 216 of the **Spelling Handbook.** Read the rule and complete the exercise provided.

Analyzing Word Parts

The Prefix cata- *Cata-*, a prefix from the Greek, means "down." In Greek, the word *catastrophe* literally meant a "down" *(cata)* "turn" *(strophe)* and was used to describe the overthrow of a government. Several other words have the *cata-* prefix, such as *cataclysm* and *catacomb*. Combine your knowledge of the *cata-* prefix and the following root word meanings to complete the exercise below.

clysm=to wash   *lyst*=to loosen, to break   *tonic*=tension
comb=tomb   *pult*=to hurl

Write the *cata-* word that best completes the meaning of the sentence.

cataclysm   catacomb   catalyst   catapult   catatonic

1. Millions perished in the _____ of World War II.

2. The psychiatric patient, suffering a _____ fit, remained in the same position for hours.

3. Medieval soldiers were able to break through the castle walls by flinging

    boulders from a _____ .

4. Martin Luther King, Jr., was a _____ in the civil rights movement of the 1960's. His speeches and nonviolent approach served to awaken the country's awareness.

5. To avoid persecution, some early Christians hid underground

    in _____ .

Number correct _____ (total 5)

Number correct in Unit _____ (total 60)

Word's Worth: ardor

The word *ardor* comes from the Old French word *ardour*, which is still the British spelling of the word. It first came to the English language in Geoffrey Chaucer's *Canterbury Tales*. Chaucer used the word figuratively to mean "warmth of emotion." The literal sense of the word, from the Latin *ardere*, means "to burn." Thus, if you feel *ardor* about something, you are burning with enthusiasm. Interestingly, the word *arid* comes from the same Latin root and suggests something that has been burned so much that it is parched and dry.

The Last Word

Writing

Using the excerpt from Mary Shelley's novel as a model, write a scene from a horror story.

Speaking

People have *endured* catastrophes and later told how they not only endured but grew stronger as a result. Prepare a short speech about a person who has shown great endurance. You might choose as your subject a person who has coped with a handicap, a failure, or the loss of a loved one. In addition to explaining the obstacles faced, try to account for that person's ability to prevail: What strength was it that brought him or her through the difficulties?

Group Discussion

Why do horror stories appeal to so many people? What are the elements all great horror stories must have? What are the five greatest horror stories of all time? (Explain why each is great.) Divide into groups, discuss these questions, then report your findings to the class.

UNIT 8: Review of Units 5-7

Part A Review Word List

Unit 5 Target Words

1. aggregation
2. assimilate
3. augment
4. collision
5. comparatively
6. component
7. condensation
8. conjecture
9. deduction
10. eject
11. extrapolate
12. immerse
13. incipient
14. obscure
15. postulate
16. reconcile
17. simulate
18. solar
19. subsequently
20. volatile

Unit 5 Related Words

1. abject
2. aggregate
3. assimilation
4. collide
5. comparable
6. condense
7. deduce
8. dejection
9. ejection
10. exponent
11. extrapolation
12. immersion
13. impose
14. interject
15. obscurity
16. opponent
17. projectile
18. reconciliation
19. repose
20. simulation

Unit 6 Target Words

1. aristocratic
2. assertion
3. barbarian
4. civilized
5. contempt
6. cynical
7. deportment
8. extortion
9. extract
10. lethargy
11. lyric
12. methodical
13. obstinately
14. polyglot
15. prose
16. provincial
17. pugnacious
18. seamy
19. synonymous
20. temperament

Unit 6 Related Words

1. aristocracy
2. aristocrat
3. assert
4. assertive
5. barbaric
6. civil
7. civilian
8. civilization
9. contemptuous
10. cynic
11. deportation
12. extort
13. lethargic
14. lyricism
15. prosaic
16. province
17. provincialism
18. pugilist
19. temper
20. temperamental
21. uncivilized

Unit 7 Target Words

1. agitate
2. ardor
3. aspect
4. catastrophic
5. compose
6. convulsive
7. delineate
8. dreary
9. endeavor
10. endure
11. exceed
12. inanimate
13. infuse
14. lassitude
15. lustrous
16. luxuriance
17. moderation
18. shrivel
19. toil
20. traverse

Unit 7 Related Words

1. agitation
2. animation
3. ardent
4. catastrophe
5. convulsion
6. convoluted
7. delineation
8. durable
9. endurance
10. immoderate
11. infusion
12. luster
13. moderate
14. moderator

Inferring Meaning from Context

For each sentence write the letter of the word or phrase that is closest in meaning to the word or words in italics.

_____ 1. The cultivated Roman citizens thought that any non-Roman was *a barbarian*.

a. a savage   b. an aristocrat   c. a cynic   d. a polyglot

_____ 2. Vernon was so *pugnacious* that he would even pick fights with his own mother.

a. argumentative   b. articulate   c. absurd   d. magnanimous

_____ 3. After he had fasted for two days, Jeff felt *comparatively* full after eating only two pieces of bread.

a. obstinately   b. relatively   c. exceedingly   d. moderately

_____ 4. Mario had such *a cynical* attitude that he wondered what people wanted of him when they said, "Good morning!"

a. a coercive   b. an impetuous   c. a skeptical   d. a beneficent

_____ 5. Completely waterproof gear is impractical because *condensation* trapped inside clothing will make a person feel cold and clammy.

a. evaporation   b. liquid formed from vapor   c. humidity
d. liquid formed from freezing

_____ 6. The dog lay on the sidewalk in such *an inanimate* posture that we thought it was dead.

a. a composing   b. a lifeless   c. a delineated   d. an agitated

_____ 7. The students' *deportment* during the performance was generally good.

a. behavior   b. luxuriance   c. ardor   d. applause

_____ 8. Our science teacher, Mr. Zapata, tries to *infuse* in his students an understanding of the scientific method.

a. forget   b. eject   c. attain   d. implant

_____ 9. Based on your grades for the first five papers, your teacher can *extrapolate* your grades on the remaining assignments.

a. eject   b. predict   c. extort   d. ameliorate

_____ 10. Alex's favorite pastime is to become deeply *immersed in* a suspenseful detective novel.

a. distracted by   b. agitated by   c. disturbed by   d. absorbed in

_____ 11. Although the other parishioners glared at her, Donna could not help breaking out in *convulsive* laughter.

a. agitated   b. serene   c. dejected   d. catastrophic

_____ 12. Despite a pulled hamstring muscle that caused her considerable pain, Nicole *obstinately* refused to quit the relay race.

a. impetuously   b. dejectedly   c. stubbornly   d. nearly

_____ 13. The fog *obscured* our vision.
   a. revealed   b. defined   c. blocked   d. distilled

_____ 14. Just because he lives in a large, cosmopolitan city, Terry thinks that
      people from small towns must be *provincial*.
   a. assimilated   b. shrewd   c. stupid   d. narrow-minded

_____ 15. Nothing seems to bother Natalia; she has an even *temperament*.
   a. presentation   b. disposition   c. technique   d. endeavor

Number correct _____ (total 15)

Using Review Words in Context

Using context clues, determine which word from the list below best completes
each sentence in the story. Write the word in the blank. Each word is used once.

ardor	cynical	infuse
barbaric	deportment	lyrics
civilized	dreary	polyglot
composing	immersed	prose
contempt	inanimate	solar

A Would-Be Hermit

Bernard, the celebrated _____ who spoke seven languages, was
tired of urban life. To him the pollution, the congestion, and the impersonal
nature of the city made it a _____ and depressing place to live.

His appearance, his conversation, and his overall _____ reflected
his growing hatred and _____ for the city. Even the renowned
skyscrapers and sculpture of the city Bernard viewed as nothing but
lifeless, _____ objects. He said that they had been erected by
spirited young artists who seemingly had _____ for their work but
lacked the experience to _____ into their work anything truly
worthwhile or meaningful. Consequently, Bernard felt that their work
was _____ and uncivilized.

Inspired by the _____ of writers such as Henry David Thoreau,
Bernard dreamed of leaving _____ society and living in the
wilderness. Because he could not afford a permanent move to the wilderness,
Bernard set up a tent in his back yard. The fact that it was a snowy day in
mid-February did not stop him. He thought that the
natural _____ heat from the sun would keep him
warm. _____ in his thoughts, he sat inside his tent, strumming his
guitar and _____ songs. His song _____ told of the
glories of the wilderness and the horrors of the city.

On March 1, a blizzard struck. Alerted by neighbors, paramedics rescued Bernard and took him to the hospital. When Bernard got out of the hospital, his neighbors had a surprise party to welcome him home. Finally, Bernard's _____ attitude toward the city melted as he realized how lucky he was to have neighbors who cared. In all seven of his languages, he said, "It isn't the place; it's the people that make life worthwhile."

Number correct _____ (total 15)

Part B *Review Word Reinforcement*

Using Language and Thinking Skills

Words and Personalities List the letters of the adjectives from the list that mean much the same as the italicized adjective in the given phrase.

_____ 1. an *agitated* person: a. quiet b. perturbed c. seamy d. volatile e. pacific f. violent g. upset h. shaken

_____ 2. a *lethargic* person: a. lazy b. prompt c. obscure d. sluggish e. passive f. assertive g. listless h. lackadaisical

_____ 3. a *dejected* person: a. discouraged b. gloomy c. exhilarated d. aristocratic e. depressed f. sad g. moderate h. crestfallen

_____ 4. a *barbaric* person: a. coarse b. cultural c. uncivilized d. vulgar e. assimilated f. wild g. uncouth h. lyrical

Number correct _____ (total 20)

Practicing for Standardized Tests

Analogies Write the letter of the word pair that best expresses a relationship similar to that expressed in the original pair.

_____ 1. ASSIMILATION : IMMIGRANT :: (A) indigestion : medicine (B) health : doctor (C) stomach : enzymes (D) digestion : food (E) ammunition : rifle

_____ 2. WATER : CONDENSATION :: (A) vapor : evaporation (B) correspondence : letter (C) current : tide (D) x-ray : radiation (E) fume : smoke

_____ 3. ARGUE : RECONCILE :: (A) criticize : corrupt (B) commend : complain (C) whine : whimper (D) coerce : convince (E) protest : march

_____ 4. SOLAR : SUN ::   (A) azure : sky   (B) prehistoric : civilization
(C) moderate : moderation   (D) extinct : dinosaur   (E) lunar : moon

_____ 5. CONTEMPT : ENEMY ::   (A) reunion : relative   (B) love : spouse
(C) endeavor : aspiration   (D) negligence : collision   (E) elation :
dejection

_____ 6. LANGUAGE : POLYGLOT ::   (A) prose : poetry   (B) pugilist :
fighter   (C) lassitude : weariness   (D) numbers : mathematician
(E) catastrophe : earthquake

_____ 7. STATUE : INANIMATE ::   (A) postulate : factual   (B) dynamite :
volatile   (C) military : nontactic   (D) license : expired   (E) serenade :
discordant

_____ 8. DETECTIVE : DEDUCTION ::   (A) magician : illusion   (B) civilian :
government   (C) worker : wage   (D) water : solution   (E) cynic : belief

_____ 9. LASSITUDE : WEARINESS ::   (A) overwork : fatigue   (B) luxuriance
: poverty   (C) inflation : balloon   (D) simulation : imitation
(E) extortion : gangster

_____ 10. SEAMY : WHOLESOME ::   (A) barbaric : civilized   (B) methodical :
orderly   (C) cultured : civilized   (D) incipient : beginning
(E) infected : contaminated

Number correct _____ (total 10)

Synonyms Write the letter of the word whose meaning is closest to that of the
capitalized word.

_____ 1. ARDOR: (A) passion   (B) indifference   (C) happiness (D) lassitude
(E) coldness

_____ 2. ARISTOCRACY: (A) nobility   (B) masses   (C) commoners
(D) civilians   (E) peasants

_____ 3. BARBARIC: (A) volatile   (B) obstinate   (C) savage   (D) gracious
(E) civilized

_____ 4. COMPONENT: (A) whole   (B) deportment   (C) ingredient
(D) compound   (E) counterpart

_____ 5. CONJECTURE: (A) consensus   (B) endeavor   (C) fact   (D) conjunction
(E) guess

_____ 6. DEDUCTION: (A) enigma   (B) conclusion   (C) addition   (D) distinction
(E) diversion

_____ 7. DELINEATE: (A) diversify   (B) extort   (C) rectify   (D) mediate
(E) describe

_____ 8. INANIMATE: (A) lifeless   (B) lustrous   (C) agitated   (D) imitative
(E) lively

_____ 9. PUGNACIOUS: (A) pacific (B) impetuous (C) quarrelsome
(D) friendly (E) negligent

_____ 10. SEAMY: (A) serene (B) absurd (C) unpleasant (D) wholesome
(E) wrinkled

Number correct _____ (total 10)

Antonyms Write the letter of the word that is most nearly *opposite* in meaning to
the capitalized word.

_____ 1. ASSIMILATE: (A) relieve (B) incorporate (C) segregate
(D) digest (E) assist

_____ 2. AUGMENT: (A) decrease (B) enable (C) modify (D) inflate
(E) convulse

_____ 3. CIVILIZED: (A) methodical (B) cultured (C) barbaric
(D) aristocratic (E) refined

_____ 4. ENDURE: (A) infringe (B) sustain (C) give up (D) ratify
(E) withstand

_____ 5. CONTEMPT: (A) love (B) lethargy (C) scorn (D) indifference
(E) ridicule

_____ 6. DREARY: (A) gloomy (B) distinctive (C) oppressive (D) cheerful
(E) tragic

_____ 7. EJECT: (A) banish (B) reject (C) deduce (D) coerce (E) receive

_____ 8. LUSTROUS: (A) radiant (B) faithless (C) drab (D) gleaming
(E) deceitful

_____ 9. LASSITUDE: (A) travail (B) weariness (C) curiosity (D) apathy
(E) vitality

_____ 10. MODERATE: (A) reasonable (B) obscure (C) bland (D) excessive
(E) provincial

Number correct _____ (total 10)

Spelling and Wordplay

Proofreading Choose the correctly spelled word from the words in parentheses
and write it on the line.

_____ 1. In this setting, even (prosaic, proseic, prossaic) remarks
were listened to carefully.

_____ 2. George had few friends because of his (cynicall, cinical,
cynical) outlook on life.

_____ 3. Coach Lin said that it was the team's (lasitude, lassitude,
lassetude) that lost the game.

_____ 4. The best fishing hole is usually in some (obsure, obskewer, obscure) section of the lake.

_____ 5. Jane's feisty behavior comes from her (pugnacious, pugnatious, pugnashus) attitude.

_____ 6. All of the dark clouds made the day (drearie, dreary, drearry).

_____ 7. Rita did not study for the test; (subsequently, subsaquently, subcequently) she failed.

_____ 8. One should always (indevor, endeaver, endeavor) to do one's very best.

_____ 9. In a fire drill, the people in charge try to (simuelate, simulate, simmulate) a real fire.

_____ 10. Failure to learn about the rest of the world and its ways will make a very (provincill, provinshall, provincial) person out of you.

Number correct _____ (total 10)

Part C *Related Word Reinforcement*

Using Related Words

Sentence Completion Write the related word from the list below that best completes each sentence.

aristocracy	deduced	extrapolation	moderate	province
catastrophes	endurance	infusion	prosaic	simulation

1. Exlorers Meriwether Lewis and William Clark showed

   great _____ as they traveled from St. Louis to the Pacific Northwest and back charting unknown territory.

2. World War I and World War II were worldwide _____ that must never be repeated.

3. An _____ of cash will be necessary to keep the business from going bankrupt.

4. If you know that a single spider web weighs 1/27,000 of a pound, you can

   make the _____ that 27,000 spiders are required to spin one pound of web.

5. The _____ of Saskatchewan uses the symbol of a farmer and his tractor to indicate that Saskatchewan is Canada's breadbasket.

6. One member of the English _____, King George I, couldn't speak English. His native tongue was German, and he spoke to his English cabinet in French.

7. The average reader would find most of the 327 miles of books in the Library of Congress dull and _____ .

8. The make-believe world of Hollywood can make a _____ of reality for almost anything. The original King Kong movie was filmed using a model that was actually only eighteen inches high.

9. By putting facts and guesswork together, astronomers have _____ that there are 100 billion galaxies in the universe besides our own.

10. Even a _____ tidal wave has tremendous force; many are thirty to forty feet high and can destroy almost anything they strike.

Number correct _____ (total 10)

Reviewing Word Structures

Forming Words Use the word parts from the list to complete the review words below. Then write the part of speech of the completed word in the blank following. Use your dictionary if necessary.

civ	*con-*	*en-*	*ment*	*sub-*
col-	*de-*	*ex-*	*poly-*	*un-*
com-	*duc*	*in-*	*pon*	*ver*

1. pose _____

2. tortion _____

3. civilized _____

4. jecture _____

5. fuse _____

6. ilization _____

7. portment _____

8. glot _____

9. tra _____

10. de _____

11. aug _____

12. lide _____

13. sequently _____

14. durance _____

15. com _____

Number correct _____ (total 15)

Number correct in Unit _____ (total 115)

Vocab Lab 2

Ex Libris

FOCUS ON: **Foreign Words and Phrases**

Even if you never studied a foreign language, you probably already know many foreign words and phrases. To increase your vocabulary, study those listed below and complete the exercise that follows.

coup d'état (ko͞o dā tä′) [French, literally, "stroke of state"] a sudden show of political force, especially the overthrow of a government. • The military staged a *coup d'état* and installed the commander of the army as head of the government.

en masse (en mas′; French, än mäs′) [French, literally, "in mass"] in a group or as a whole. • First one member of the audience began to clap, followed by another and another until everyone was applauding *en masse.*

esprit de corps (es prē′ də kôr′) [French] group spirit and pride. • As the volleyball team worked together, the players developed an *esprit de corps* that contributed to their improvement and success.

et cetera (usually abbreviated *etc.*) (et set′ər ə, -set′ rə) [Latin] and others; and so forth. • Please clear the table, wash the dishes, put the food away, *et cetera.*

eureka (yoo rē′kə) interj. [Greek] I have found (it): an exclamation of triumphant achievement. • When Archimedes learned how to determine the proportion of base metal in King Hiero's golden crown, he cried out, *"Eureka!"*

ex libris (eks lē′bris, lī′-) [Latin] from the library of: an inscription on bookplates. • All of my grandmother's books have book plates that say *ex libris.*

faux pas (fō′ pä′) [French, literally, "false step"] a social blunder or error in etiquette. • Paul committed a *faux pas* in wearing sandals to a formal wedding.

nolo contendere (nō′ lō kən ten′ də rē) [Latin, "I do not wish to contest (it)."] a legal plea in which the defendant makes no defense but does not admit guilt. • Although most people assumed that the defendant was guilty of the charges, he pleaded *nolo contendere.*

nom de plume (näm′ də plo͞om′) [French] pen name; pseudonym. • Mark Twain is the *nom de plume* of Samuel Clemens.

persona non grata (pər sō′nə nän grät′ ə, grät′ ə) [Latin] an unacceptable or unwelcome person. • Because of the unacceptable human rights practices of his country, the diplomat was labeled *persona non grata* and was asked to leave the host country.

potpourri (pō′ po͞o rē′, pät po͞or′ē) n. [French] a miscellaneous collection. • The trunk in the attic contained a *potpourri* of objects from the 1950's.

savoir-faire (sav′wär fer′) n. [French, literally, "to know how to do"] social poise and tact. • Everyone envies Marcia's *savoir-faire* and lack of self-consciousness in any social situation.

tête-à-tête (tāt′ə tät′, tet′ a tet′) n., adj., adv. [French, literally, "head-to-head"] a private conversation between two people. • Sam's teacher decided to have a *tête-à-tête* with him to discuss his grades.

verbatim (vər bāt′əm) adv., adj. [Latin] word for word. ● The news story quoted the witness's testimony *verbatim*.

vice versa (vī′sē vur′sə, vī′sə; vīs′) [Latin] the other way around; conversely. ● You can water the plants and then mow the lawn, or *vice versa*.

Exercise Match each foreign word or phrase from the list with the example below. Write the term in the blank.

_____ 1. Grant neglected to offer his seat to his grandfather; later, he wondered why everyone was staring at him.

_____ 2. The supply center has everything you need for gardening: topsoil, seedlings, pots, fertilizer, and so forth.

_____ 3. Because of Jessica's rude behavior at the last party, her friend decided not to invite her to the next one.

_____ 4. Sharon copied the advertising claims directly from the box so that she could prove that the product did not work.

_____ 5. "Aha!" Orin shouted with glee when he discovered the answer before the rest of us.

_____ 6. We won our personal-injury suit because the driver of the other car pleaded "no defense."

_____ 7. The entire girls' basketball team went to the principal's office to protest the firing of their coach.

_____ 8. The leader of the Central American country had been ousted overnight by a small group of military officers.

_____ 9. Cory loves his science-fiction books and makes sure his name is inscribed in them before he lends them to anyone.

_____ 10. Nineteenth-century novelist Mary Ann Evans knew that people would pay little attention to a woman's work, so she wrote her books under the name George Eliot.

_____ 11. My little sister's box of treasures includes a huge blue marble, several dried flower petals, the first tooth she lost, a doll's head, and a dozen bottle caps.

_____ 12. Tony would rather eat before we see the movie, but we could eat afterwards if you'd prefer.

_____ 13. After the rave reviews on opening night, the cast felt a renewed sense of cooperation and enthusiasm.

_____ 14. The principal and the superintendent have been meeting behind closed doors all morning.

_____ 15. At the large party, Angela was able to converse easily with both her friends and her parents' friends.

Number correct _____ (total 15)

FOCUS ON: *Mnemonics*

Some psychologists believe that everything you have ever learned or experienced is stored somewhere in your brain. The trick, of course, is to discover exactly how to find the information you want to remember when you need to know it. One way to do this is to devise memory cues that will help you retrieve what you have learned. There are several strategies and specific types of memory aids—mnemonics—that can help.

A basic fact about learning and memory is that the more motivated you are to remember something, the more likely you will be to remember it. Therefore, before you get started, always remind yourself why the information you are trying to memorize is important to you.

Much of the general information, and certainly most of the academic material that you know you learned through reading. However, just reading and rereading information is more likely to bore you than to help you learn. Memory research indicates that the more ways you can learn a new piece of information, the easier it will be to remember it. A simple four-step approach can help you use several different senses and ways of learning to fix information in your memory. The acronym of the plan—SWAP—itself is a mnemonic device that will help you remember the steps you must follow:

> **S** ay it
> **W** rite it
> **A** ssociate it
> **P** lay with it

Say It

Review the information you are trying to learn out loud with a friend, or tape-record it and listen to the tape. In repeating the information aloud, you are creating two important sensory links that will help you remember it: the muscular movements you make in speaking and the sounds of the words themselves.

Write It

Take notes, rewrite information in your own words, or draw a diagram that illustrates or incorporates the information. In addition to helping you organize your thoughts and understand the material, writing also creates sensory connections that aid memory. When you try to remember information you have written down, you will have a memory of the physical act of writing as well as a memory of how the words or diagrams look on the page.

Associate It

Create connections between the information you are trying to learn and what you already know. These links provide additional anchors and ways of accessing what you have learned. For example, if you want to remember the year the Roman legions conquered Britain—A.D. 43—you might link it to your birthday (April 3 or 4/3), your mother's age, or the last two digits of your telephone number—facts you are unlikely to forget.

Play with It

There are many ways you can use your imagination to come up with entertaining and effective mnemonics. Several types and examples are listed below:

Acronyms

SWAP (Say it, Write it, Associate it, Play with it)
ROY G BIV (Red, Orange, Yellow, Green, Blue, Indigo, Violet)
HOMES (Huron, Ontario, Michigan, Erie, Superior)

Rhymes

Thirty days hath September, April, June, and November. . . .
In fourteen hundred and ninety-two, Columbus sailed the ocean blue.
i before *e* except after *c*.

Mental Images

picture a man shaving his head—helps you remember Mr. Barber, the very thin,
    bald man you just met
picture a person gobbling his or her food with a fork—helps you remember the
    German word for fork, *gabel*, which sounds like the English word *gobble*

There are no right or wrong mnemonics, only ones that help or don't help you remember certain types of information. So try several different approaches, and SWAP forgetfulness for a better memory.

Creating Mnemonic Devices   Create two different types of mnemonics to help you remember each of the following facts.

The Greek goddess of memory, Mnemosyne (from whose name we get the word *mnemonic*), is the mother of the nine muses—Calliope, Clio, Erato, Euterpe, Melpomene, Polyhymnia, Terpsichore, Thalia, and Urania.

1. _____

On December 17, 1903, Orville and Wilbur Wright flew the first power-driven, heavier-than-air machine at Kitty Hawk, North Carolina.

2. _____

The eight forms of the verb *to be* are *be, am, is, are, was, were, being*, and *been*.

3. _____

The scientific classifications of living things are kingdom, phylum, class, order, family, genus, and species.

4. _____

The three steps in cardiopulmonary resuscitation are opening the airway, restoring breathing, and promoting circulation.

5. _____

Number correct _____ (total 5)

Number correct in Vocab Lab _____ (total 20)

Special Unit: Taking Standardized Vocabulary Tests

As you know, many standardized tests, such as employment tests, placement tests, and college entrance examinations, contain questions relating to vocabulary comprehension. Such questions are designed to measure your basic skills, or aptitude, in language.

Many people believe that your scores on these standardized tests reflect the success you will have in future endeavors, such as college and career. Therefore, it is to your advantage to prepare yourself for these tests in order to do as well as you possibly can.

Because standardized aptitude tests cover skills or learning gained over a long period of time, intensive studying right before these tests is an ineffective method of preparation. The best way to prepare for these tests is to concentrate on improving your language skills throughout the year. Work hard in your English classes. Make it a practice to read more and to develop a keen awareness of how you and others use language in everyday life.

Another effective method of preparation is to learn more about the different types of test questions you are likely to encounter in standardized tests. In the area of vocabulary, these include questions based on **antonyms**, **analogies**, and **sentence completion**.

As you have probably realized by now, this book furnishes extensive practice in these areas of vocabulary study. In addition, the following special unit provides important strategies that will help you prepare for standardized test taking.

Part A   Antonyms

As you know, **antonyms** are words that are opposite in meaning. Standardized test questions covering antonyms are answered by selecting the choice most opposite in meaning to a given word. A typical antonym problem looks like this:

> _____ UNDERSTAND: (A) deliver   (B) comprehend   (C) communicate
> (D) answer   (E) misunderstand

To complete an antonym problem, use the following strategies:

1. Remember that you must find a word that is opposite in meaning. Do not be thrown off by *synonyms*—words similar in meaning—that are included among the possible answers.

2. Decide whether the given word is positive or negative, and then eliminate all possible choices that are in the same category as the given word.

3. Remember that many words have more than one meaning. If no word seems to fit your sense of the opposite meaning, think about other meanings for the given word.

4. If you do not know the meaning of the given word, try to analyze its prefix, suffix, or base word in order to define the word.

Exercise Using the strategies listed above, complete the following practice exercise.

_____ 1. HOSTILE: (A) mean   (B) friendly   (C) militant   (D) hospitable   (E) contrary

_____ 2. ADVANCE: (A) reveal   (B) promote   (C) intervene   (D) retreat   (E) advise

_____ 3. TYRANNY: (A) despotism   (B) monarchy   (C) chaos   (D) freedom   (E) republicanism

_____ 4. VISIBLE: (A) partial   (B) present   (C) hidden   (D) visual   (E) judgmental

_____ 5. DELIBERATE: (A) accidental   (B) planned   (C) delectable   (D) possible   (E) ridiculous

_____ 6. SIMILAR: (A) simian   (B) alike   (C) delightful   (D) different   (E) equal

_____ 7. PRIMITIVE: (A) historical   (B) primary   (C) hysterical   (D) aesthetic   (E) modern

_____ 8. PACIFY: (A) rectify   (B) stimulate   (C) soothe   (D) pardon   (E) sleep

_____ 9. REMOTE: (A) farthest   (B) distant   (C) future   (D) near   (E) automatic

_____ 10. INGENIOUS: (A) genetic   (B) uncreative   (C) clever   (D) intelligent   (E) sincere

Number correct _____ (total 10)

Part B   Analogies

Analogies, as you will recall, are pairs of words that are related to each other. In many analogy problems, you are first given two words that are related to each other in some way. Your job is to find from among the five possible choices the pair of words that shows the same relationship. A typical analogy problem on a standardized test looks like this:

> _____ RING : JEWELRY ::   (A) bell : chimes   (B) boat : cargo   (C) pencil : pen   (D) fir : tree   (E) drink : milk

To complete an analogy problem, use the following strategies:

1. First, recognize the many types of relationships expressed in analogies. Refer to the chart on page 56 for a listing of the most common of these relationships.

2. Second, determine the relationship between the first pair of words given. Then, create a sentence that contains both words and that shows the relationship between them. The first pair of words in the sample problem can be expressed as follows:

A *ring* is a type of *jewelry*.

3. Third, find the pair of words among the answer choices that can replace the first pair in your sentence.

A *fir* is a type of *tree*.

The correct answer is *(D) fir : tree*.

Exercise Using the strategies listed above, complete the following practice exercise.

_____ 1. MUSHROOM : FUNGUS ::   (A) seed : plant   (B) geese : flock   (C) bee : hive   (D) mouse : rodent   (E) tree : forest

_____ 2. FORESIGHT : HINDSIGHT ::   (A) vision : glasses   (B) past : future   (C) future : past   (D) seeing : believing   (E) future : present

_____ 3. PUERTO RICO : ISLAND ::   (A) peninsula : strait   (B) tunnel : mountain   (C) Australia : continent   (D) star : constellation   (E) Canada : United States

_____ 4. INVALID : VALID ::   (A) valid : legitimate   (B) deflated : flat   (C) expired : outdated   (D) undignified : dignified   (E) illegitimate : unlawful

_____ 5. SKILLFUL : CLUMSY ::   (A) agile : awkward   (B) nimble : handy   (C) clumsy : breakable   (D) warring : hostile   (E) brittle : fragile

_____ 6. CHEMIST : FORMULA ::   (A) pitcher : catcher   (B) musician : score   (C) artist : gallery   (D) apprentice : master   (E) farmer : agriculture

_____ 7. MYTH : MYTHOLOGY ::   (A) history : fact   (B) Greek : gods   (C) water : hydrology   (D) myth : reality   (E) belief : uncertainty

_____ 8. MASK : DISGUISE ::   (A) helmet : protection   (B) ghost : sheet   (C) costume : mask   (D) sword : shield   (E) identity : concealment

_____ 9. TELESCOPE : ASTRONOMER ::   (A) circus : lion tamer   (B) plot : author   (C) stethoscope : doctor   (D) restaurant : manager   (E) engine : engineer

_____ 10. ORANGE : FRUIT ::   (A) red : stoplight   (B) carrot : vegetable   (C) food : calorie   (D) banana : pear   (E) cow : calf

Number correct _____ (total 10)

Part C *Sentence Completion*

Sentence completion problems test your ability to use vocabulary words and to recognize relationships among the parts of a sentence. You are given a sentence in which one or two words are missing. You must then choose the word or words that best complete the sentence. A typical sentence completion problem looks like this:

_____ The argument __?__ but Tyrone felt his anger __?__
(A) proceeded . . . grow (B) followed . . . swell
(C) diminished . . . fade (D) escalated . . . increase
(E) continued . . . diminish

To perform sentence completion problems, use the following strategies:

1. Read the entire sentence carefully, noting key words. Pay particular attention to words that indicate contrast (*but, however*) or similarity (*and, another*). For example, the word *but* in the sample problem gives you a clue that the correct word pair will contain words that are opposite in meaning. The correct answer is, therefore, *(E) continued . . . diminish.*

2. Try each of the choices in the sentence. Eliminate those choices that make no sense or those that contradict some other part of the statement.

3. Look for grammatical clues within the sentence. Does the space call for a verb, an adjective, a noun? If the answer is a verb, in what tense must the verb be written in order to correspond with the rest of the sentence? Asking such questions may help you eliminate some incorrect answers.

Exercise Using the strategies listed above, complete the following practice exercise.

_____ 1. As a token of his __?__, Jim gave his mother a(an) __?__ necklace.
(A) hatred . . . ugly (B) indifference . . . beautiful (C) affection . . . exquisite (D) ignorance . . . diamond (E) brother . . . family

_____ 2. Louise did not know the __?__ of the rumor, but she __?__ that Sam had started it.
(A) source . . . wishes (B) reason . . . knew (C) star . . . decided
(D) levity . . . saw (E) origin . . . suspected

_____ 3. The detective made a(an) __?__ as to the __?__ surrounding the burglary.
(A) request . . . jewels (B) inquiry . . . circumstances (C) exhibit . . . reason (D) suspect . . . criminal (E) guess . . . charges

_____ 4. When Phil found the __?__ puppy, he __?__ his confidence in his little sister by giving her the responsibility of caring for it.
(A) lonely . . . refused (B) gigantic . . . elated (C) abandoned . . . demonstrated (D) Spaniel . . . ignored (E) whining . . . accused

_____ 5. Diane's _?_ provided a(an) _?_ part of the news story.
(A) ignorance . . . important   (B) lies . . . useful   (C) research . . .
integral   (D) ego . . . large   (E) brother . . . imaginary

_____ 6. Chad's younger brother _?_ him and tries to do everything he does.
(A) ignores   (B) idolizes   (C) blames   (D) locates   (E) questions

_____ 7. The lecture was _?_, and I could not _?_ on what the speaker was saying.
(A) stimulating . . . focus   (B) interminable . . . concentrate   (C)
revealing . . . focus   (D) canceled . . . expand   (E) symbolic . . . rely

_____ 8. Known for his large contributions to charity, the humanitarian deserved
_?_ for his _?_.
(A) recognition . . . folly   (B) blame . . . insincerity   (C) reward . . .
thriftiness   (D) admonishment . . . wastefulness   (E) credit . . . generosity

_____ 9. We could not believe Fred's story because it was filled with _?_.
(A) inconsistencies   (B) treasures   (C) desire   (D) statistics
(E) distinction

_____ 10. Sonia was quite apprehensive about the _?_ task she had to complete.
(A) pleasant   (B) previous   (C) effortless   (D) formidable   (E) boastful

Number correct _____ (total 10)

Part D   General Strategies

No matter what type of question you are solving, certain strategies can be applied to any part of a standardized test. Keep the following guidelines in mind.

Basic Strategies for Taking Standardized Tests

1. **Read and listen to directions carefully.** This advice may seem obvious, but many students do poorly on tests because they misunderstand the directions.

2. **Most standardized tests are timed.** Budget your time carefully. It is important that you do not spend too much time on any single item.

3. **Complete the test items you know, skipping over the ones that are a problem for you.** Then go back and tackle the more difficult items.

4. **Most standardized tests make use of computerized answer sheets.** Students are required to fill in a circle corresponding to the correct answer in the test booklet, as follows:

When using such computerized answer sheets, follow these guidelines:

a. Always completely fill in the circle for the correct answer.
b. Periodically check your numbering on the answer sheet.
c. Never make notes or stray marks on the answer sheet. These could be misread as wrong answers by the scoring machine. Instead, write on the test booklet itself or on scratch paper, as indicated in the directions for the test.

5. **Be aware of distractors.** Distractors are answer choices that may seem correct at first glance but are actually wrong.   For example:

_____ HOT : COLD ::   (A) water : ice   (B) good : bad   (C) fat : obese
(D) first : second   (E) warm : lukewarm

Two choices, *(A) water : ice* and *(E) warm : lukewarm,* are distractors. Both relate to temperature, as does *hot : cold.* You may be tempted to choose one of these as the correct answer. However, neither of these choices presents the same relationship as *hot : cold.* The correct answer, *(B) good : bad,* shows the relationship of opposites, as does *hot : cold.*

6. **Random guessing is unlikely to improve your score.** In fact, on some standardized tests, points are deducted for incorrect answers. Therefore, guessing is not a good idea. However, if you can eliminate one or more of the choices, then your chance of guessing the correct answer is increased.

These strategies can help you increase your chances of success on standardized tests. Remember, too, that a good mental attitude, plenty of sleep the night before a test, and the ability to relax can be important factors.

UNIT 9

Part A Target Words and Their Meanings

1. anguish (aŋ′gwish) n.
2. authoritative (ə thôr′ə tāt′ iv, -thär′-) adj.
3. falter (fôl′tər) v.
4. hauteur (hō tur′; *Fr.* ō tër′) n.
5. insight (in′sīt′) n.
6. interrelated (in′tər ri lāt′id) adj.
7. intuitive (in too′i tiv, -tyoo′-) adj.
8. objective (əb jek′tiv, äb-) n., adj.
9. omission (ō mish′ən) n.
10. perception (per sep′shən) n.
11. privation (prī vā′shən) n.
12. provocative (prə väk′ə tiv) adj.
13. ramify (ram′ə fī′) v.
14. ruminate (roo′mə nāt′) v.
15. sympathetic (sim′pə thet′ik) adj.
16. tamp (tamp) v.
17. taut (tôt) adj.
18. utter (ut′ər) adj.
19. virtue (vur′choo) n.
20. vitality (vī tal′ə tē) n.

Inferring Meaning from Context

For each sentence write the letter of the word or phrase that is closest to the meaning of the word or words in italics. Use context clues to help you determine the correct answer. (For information about context clues, see pages 1-5.)

_____ 1. Imagine yourself as a victim of the Armenian earthquake of 1988, and you can imagine the terrible *anguish* people experienced from losing homes, possessions, and loved ones.

a. illness   b. grief   c. curiosity   d. dissatisfaction

_____ 2. A college or university catalog, which is assembled by the administrators of a particular institution is the *authoritative* source of information on class schedules, degree requirements, courses available, and costs.

a. most used   b. most recent   c. official   d. most unusual

_____ 3. In 490 B.C. a young Greek ran twenty-four miles from Marathon to Athens to announce a Greek military victory; he shouted, "Rejoice! We have won!", then *faltered* and died.

a. resumed running   b. stumbled   c. celebrated   d. apologized

_____ 4. Life is filled with contrasts: The person who looks on you with *hauteur* today may be begging money from you tomorrow.

a. gentleness   b. love   c. concern   d. arrogance

_____ 5. *Insights* that came to him in his dreams guided Scottish author Robert Louis Stevenson in creating many of his characters, including Dr. Jekyll and Mr. Hyde.

a. secrets   b. theories   c. in-depth understandings   d. memory lapses

_____ 6. We are not isolated beings; each one of us is *interrelated* by our language, our knowledge, our hopes, and our fears.

a. linked to others   b. distinguished from others   c. aware of others
d. antagonized

_____ 7. It is not possible to prove that generous people are happier people; such knowledge is *intuitive*.

a. obtained without conscious reasoning   b. obtained only with great effort   c. unnecessary   d. best

_____ 8. One legend states that when Pascal invented the roulette wheel, his *objective* was to study perpetual motion.

a. disadvantage   b. acculturation   c. purpose   d. interpretation

_____ 9. *Omission of* water in one's diet would have serious effects; ten days is about as long as anyone can go without it.

a. Drinking too much   b. Leaving out   c. Drinking impure
d. Realizing the need for

_____ 10. Bees have five eyes—three on top of the head and two in the front—which must make their *perception of* the world much different from ours.

a. attitude toward   b. dread of   c. concern about
d. understanding of

_____ 11. Not until we suffer *privation* of clean air and natural resources will we come to appreciate these necessary elements.

a. adequacy   b. understanding   c. loss   d. aggregation

_____ 12. The biographer Boswell tells us that writer Samuel Johnson found his meetings at the "Club" *provocative*; his exchanges with friends always produced new ideas and caused him to try new things.

a. thought producing   b. too prolonged   c. expensive   d. painful

_____ 13. This morale problem may seem simple now, but if it is not addressed it may *ramify* into other areas, such as finance and customer relations.

a. shrivel   b. reconcile   c. initiate   d. branch

_____ 14. To distract yourself as you sit in the dentist's chair, *ruminate on* the lemon shark, who cuts all new teeth every two weeks.

a. simulate   b. sneer at   c. experiment on   d. think about

_____ 15. It is somewhat surprising how *sympathetic* many nineteenth-century Americans were toward Susan B. Anthony's campaign to give women the right to vote. Indeed, Ms. Anthony herself may have been occasionally pleased and surprised.

a. grieved   b. hostile   c. supportive   d. indifferent

_____ 16. To be sure that each new seedling was well anchored, the gardener carefully *tamped* the soil around each plant.

a. removed   b. loosened   c. fertilized   d. packed down

_____ 17. In a real tug of war, with each side pulling its hardest, the rope will be *taut*, forming a straight line between the two opposing sides.

    a. nearly invisible   b. bow-shaped   c. tight   d. strong

_____ 18. Today, the price paid for the Louisiana Purchase— about four cents an acre—is viewed with *utter* amazement.

    a. implausible   b. subsequent   c. total   d. conservative

_____ 19. Dependability is the *virtue* that many employers admire most in their employees.

    a. fashion   b. insight   c. flaw   d. characteristic

_____ 20. The U.S. Constitution, which is more than two hundred years old, still shows amazing *vitality*, serving as a revered guide to democracy.

    a. worthlessness   b. aspiration   c. learning   d. endurance

Number correct _____ (total 20)

Part B   Target Words in Reading and Literature

You should now have a general idea of the meaning of each target word. Refine your understanding by examining the shades of meaning these words have in the following excerpt.

Her Mother's Daughter

Marilyn French

In this excerpt the author explores the weight and impact words can have. If cruel peers tag you with a term, does that word become part of your self-concept? Do adults always choose their words accurately? The following incident explains why the author came to "suspect words."

A bunch of the rougher girls from my class came running down the street behind me, and I shrank into myself, terrified. I thought they were chasing me, and they were much taller and heavier than I, being two years older and considerably more developed. As they came nearer, I tried to disguise my fear, both out of pride and out of some **intuitive** awareness that fear is **provocative**,   5 and I held my neck **taut**, my chin high, and plastered my face with **hauteur**. But they were simply playing some—to me—rough game, and passed me laughing, until one turned around and pointed, crying in great gasps of laughter—"Look at Dabrowska! Oh, conceited!" And the others turned then too, and laughed, brayed at me, "Conceited! Conceited!"   10

. . . I did not tell my mother about the girls. I don't know why. Although I told her many things other children would conceal, I concealed much, very selectively. I would have been ashamed to tell her about the girls: I wanted to appear in control of my away-from-home life. I waited on the threshold as she finished the last swipes with the ugly mop. "If you take off your shoes, Anastasia, you can   15 walk over to the table and I'll give you some milk and cookies," she said kindly. I set my books on the table, which was near the back door, and removed my hated shoes, and did as she said. She brought me a glass of milk and some Oreos, and then sank into the chair opposite me, sighing. She lit a cigarette and crossed her legs: she was in her stocking feet.   20

"How was school today?"

"Fine. I got a hundred in the spelling test, and ninety-nine in the math test. It wasn't my fault that I got ninety-nine. The teacher thought my seven was a one on one problem. I told her it wasn't, but she said it was okay."

She smiled. "That's very good, Anastasia."   25

"And in recess, we danced in a circle and I got picked three times." This was an **utter** lie. I was almost never picked when danced in a circle, and I knew it was because of my ugly high shoes. But I also knew that those shoes cost my parents a great deal of money they couldn't afford, and that they sacrificed to buy them for me so my flat feet would grow straight. . . .   30

We fell into silence then. I finished my cookies and swept the crumbs into a little pile. Mother rose and got a dishcloth and wiped them up.

"Is it okay if I walk on the floor now?"

"Yes." She **tamped** her cigarette out and sighed again. "I'm so tired." I glanced at her **sympathetically**. She was always tired. I knew her life was very   35
hard.

"Mommy?" I turned to get my books. "What does *conceited* mean?"

She was standing at the sink, running hot water over the mophead. "It means someone who thinks they're good. Better than other people."

I stood still. "Oh."   40

She turned her head slightly. "Why?"

'Oh, some girls were calling that name—at Rhoda Moore—today. At recess." I had used the name of the only girl in the class I envied, a tall, beautiful girl with long blond hair and big blue eyes. "They said she was conceited."

"Is she?"   45

"I don't know," I **faltered**. "She's the pretty one."

"She probably thinks she's prettier than the others, then," Mother explained.

I left the room so she would not see my hot face, my **anguish** at slandering poor Rhoda Moore, and deceiving my mother, and even worse, concealing my own true nature. For the moment she said it, I knew it was true. I was conceited, I did think I was better than the others. I ran upstairs to my room and threw myself on my bed. I could feel my pulse throbbing in my head, as if I had a fever. I felt utterly alone, without **virtue**. I wished I could disappear, just die there on the spot, just blow away, like some crinkled dried-up brown leaf.

I *was* conceited, I did think I was better than the others. But I *was* better than the others. I was clean and they mostly were not; I was smarter than any of them, in all subjects. They were ignorant and ill-spoken and their manners were bad and they were loud. I felt they were another order of being from me, another species even. And this was true: this was **objectively** true, I felt that I was better in these ways, and that my superiority was recognized by the teachers, even the principal . . . . I lay there in an anguish that was to become familiar to me over the years. What I was was good, and made some people like me but others hate me. I did not enjoy my isolation from other children, but I did not want to stop being superior either. Doing things—the things I could do—doing them well was practically my only source of pleasure.

I don't know what words I used to think about this. I do know it **ramified** far beyond itself, into something so complicated and **interrelated** with other things that it felt overwhelming. . . . There was no way to be oneself and to be good and to be loved. Whatever one chose, one sacrificed the rest. "For matter is never lacking **privation**. . . ." It was too hard for me.

Of course I went on, as one does, and even managed sometimes to forget this old **insight**. But I continued to suspect words. So when a woman said to me that my mother was strong, when others said "Your mother is a lovely woman," I'd simply smile and nod. If you question such statements, people look at you as if they have suddenly discovered you are retarded. Years ago, I would go off by myself and **ruminate** on such statements: *Is* she strong? What does that mean? How does it show? *Is* she lovely?

I took such judgments as **authoritative**, and believed they were based on profound **perception**. I did not then understand that people were in the habit of running around in the world making judgments on all sides without really thinking about what they were saying. I was a very serious child, and believed the state of adulthood was blessed with knowledge and awareness from which I was cut off. I saw adulthood as a special state, people sitting in a brilliantly lit room laughing and talking and nodding their heads, while I stand in the shadows just outside the room unable to understand why they are talking so animatedly about the weather or the traffic, knowing from their **vitality** and amusement that beneath their ordinary words was a world of hidden meaning, that language was a code known only to the initiate—adults. Oh, in time I learned to read the silences and pauses, learned what the **omissions** in conversation meant—sex or shame, money or scandal. But I still have trouble with the words.

Refining Your Understanding

For each of the following items, consider how the target word is used in the passage. Write the letter of the word or phrase that best completes each sentence.

_____ 1. "*Intuitive* awareness" (line 5) is knowledge that is   a. proven   b. felt   c. factual.

_____ 2. If indeed "fear is *provocative*" (line 5), it would mean that fear   a. could cause further difficulties   b. is a sign of superiority   c. is a way to prevent conflict.

_____ 3. An antonym of *hauteur* (line 6) is   a. anger   b. pride   c. humility.

_____ 4. For something to be "*objectively* true" (line 59), it must be recognized as true by   a. someone involved in the situation   b. someone who has a stake in the outcome   c. a nonjudgmental outsider.

_____ 5. When the author would "*ruminate* on such statements" (line 76), she would   a. reject them   b. accept them   c. give careful thought to them.

Number correct _____ (total 5)

Part C   Ways to Make New Words Your Own

By now you are familiar with the target words and their meanings. This section presents reinforcement activities that will help you make these words part of your permanent vocabulary.

Using Language and Thinking Skills

True-False Decide whether each statement is true or false. Write **T** for True and **F** for False.

_____ 1. If there is an *omission* in a sentence, the sentence is complete.

_____ 2. You can *ramify* a business by building more outlets.

_____ 3. A tightrope walker likes a *taut* wire to walk on.

_____ 4. If an engine *falters*, it runs smoothly.

_____ 5. When you *tamp* something, you press it down firmly.

_____ 6. Lethargy is not a *virtue*.

_____ 7. When you pass a test, you feel *anguish*.

_____ 8. If you show *hauteur*, you will usually have a loyal and large following of friends.

_____ 9. A person who survives eight days alone in a lifeboat demonstrates *vitality*.

_____ 10. A millionaire suffers from *privation*.

Number correct _____ (total 10)

Practicing for Standardized Tests

Analogies Write the letter of the pair of words that best expresses a relationship similar to that expressed in the original pair.

_____ 1. DICTATOR : AUTHORITATIVE :: (A) president : equal (B) boss : methodical (C) fighter : pugnacious (D) politician : corrupt (E) banker : magnanimous

_____ 2. CATASTROPHE : ANGUISH :: (A) attainment : satisfaction (B) exponent : opponent (C) plight : interaction (D) argument : reconciliation (E) lyric : prose

_____ 3. TAUT : TIGHT :: (A) tense : dejected (B) loose : lax (C) benevolent : sinister (D) initial : next (E) barbaric : aristocratic

_____ 4. FALTER : STOP :: (A) categorize : unify (B) rectify : destroy (C) eject : initiate (D) suggest : interject (E) decide : act

_____ 5. ATTAIN : OBJECTIVE :: (A) ramify : decision (B) account : finances (C) imitate : ape (D) lose : contest (E) analyze : chemist

_____ 6. UTTER : ABSOLUTE :: (A) economic : social (B) prosaic : tactical (C) political : conservative (D) mundane : ordinary (E) solar : lunar

_____ 7. UNDERSTANDING : INSIGHT :: (A) coercion : benevolence (B) heritage : wealth (C) compromise : disunity (D) prophecy : future (E) passion : ardor

_____ 8. PRIVATION : AFFLUENCE :: (A) equality : inequality (B) policy : aspect (C) deprivation : poverty (D) endurance : will (E) aspiration : power

_____ 9. VITALITY : YOUTH :: (A) plight : aged (B) equality : ethnicity (C) inspiration : animation (D) words : polyglot (E) studiousness : scholar

_____ 10. VIRTUE : VICE :: (A) integrity : insight (B) articulation : stutter (C) component : part (D) consensus : vote (E) health : vitality

Number correct _____ (total 10)

Synonyms Write the letter of the word whose meaning is closest to that of the capitalized word.

_____ 1. FALTER: (A) interject (B) rally (C) enliven (D) hesitate (E) proceed

_____ 2. HAUTEUR: (A) arrogance (B) lowliness (C) dreariness (D) moderation (E) coercion

_____ 3. INTUITIVE: (A) deductive (B) instinctive (C) prosaic (D) sinister (E) infused

_____ 4. OMISSION: (A) extrapolation (B) inclusion (C) oversight (D) pollution (E) augmentation

112

_____ 5. PERCEPTION: (A) void (B) consensus (C) diversification (D) impression (E) permanence

_____ 6. PRIVATION: (A) anguish (B) solitude (C) neediness (D) destruction (E) modification

_____ 7. PROVOCATIVE: (A) stimulating (B) irritating (C) incipient (D) rectifying (E) convulsive

_____ 8. RUMINATE: (A) mediate (B) contemplate (C) radiate (D) articulate (E) agitate

_____ 9. SYMPATHETIC: (A) neutral (B) civilized (C) indifferent (D) composed (E) compassionate

_____ 10. TAMP: (A) toil (B) dig (C) pack (D) eject (E) relate

Number correct _____ (total 10)

Spelling and Wordplay

Word Maze Find and circle each target word in this maze.

```
A   C   I   T   E   H   T   A   P   M   Y   S   I
N   U   O   M   I   S   S   I   O   N   A   X   N
G   V   T   H   G   I   S   N   I   S   I   Q   T
U   I   D   H   A   U   T   E   U   R   T   Y   E
I   T   W   Q   O   Y   K   X   C   Z   N   O   R
S   A   M   V   I   R   T   U   E   O   P   R   R
H   L   I   N   T   U   I   T   I   V   E   E   E
R   I   O   B   J   E   C   T   I   V   E   T   L
E   T   Y   F   I   M   A   R   A   O   K   T   A
T   Y   G   L   P   V   P   M   A   T   A   U   T
L   R   U   M   I   N   A   T   E   F   I   B   E
A   P   E   R   C   E   P   T   I   O   N   V   D
F   K   P   R   O   V   O   C   A   T   I   V   E
```

anguish
authoritative
falter
hauteur
insight
interrelated
intuitive
objective
omission
perception
privation
provocative
ramify
ruminate
sympathetic
tamp
taut
utter
virtue
vitality

Part D Related Words

A number of words are closely related to the target words you have studied. Use your knowledge of the target words and of word parts to determine the meanings of these words. (For information about word parts analysis, see pages 6-12.) If you are unsure of any definitions, use your dictionary. Learning these related words expands your vocabulary and helps you learn the target words more thoroughly.

1. authoritarian (əthôr′ə ter′ē ən, -thär′-) adj.
2. deprivation (dep′rə vā′shən) n.
3. haughtiness (hôt′ē nis, -nəs) n.
4. haughty (hôt′ē) adj.
5. insightful (in′sīt′fəl, f′l) adj.
6. intuition (in′too wish′ ən, -tyoo-) n.
7. omit (ō mit′) v.
8. pathos (pa′thäs, -thôs) n.
9. perceptive (per sep′tiv) adj.
10. provoke (prə vōk′) v.
11. ramification (ram′ə fi kā′shən) n.
12. revitalize (ri vīt′′l īz′) v.
13. rumination (r$\overline{oo}$′mə nā′shən) n.
14. utterly (ut′ ər lē) adv.
15. utterance (ut′ ər əns, ut′rəns) n.
16. virtuous (vʉr′choo wəs) adj.
17. vital (vīt′′l) adj.
18. vitalize (vīt′′l īz′) v.

Understanding Related Words

Sentence Completion Write the word from the Related Words list that best completes each sentence.

1. _____ of vitamin C will lead to a deficiency disease known as scurvy.

2. Some cities have built public housing in an effort to _____ their slum areas.

3. Mrs. Ortega decided not to put up with Manuel's constant whimpering, so she said, "I do not want to hear one more _____ from you for the rest of this hour."

4. In addition to being chivalrous and brave, a medieval knight was expected to live a _____ life.

5. Ellie spent hours in _____ , contemplating every little detail before making a decision.

6. If you _____ any of the requested information, your application cannot be processed.

7. Jill's _____ caused kids to nickname her S.U. behind her back, which stood for "stuck-up."

114

8. An _____ about which particular stock prices will go up could prove very profitable.

9. Ms. Ling, our substitute biology teacher, had such an _____ manner that the class didn't try any of the tricks they usually try with substitutes.

10. Never _____ a watchdog; the result can be very dangerous.

Number correct _____ (total 10)

Analyzing Word Parts

The Latin Root *vita* In Latin *vita* means "life." Match the *vita* words from this unit with their definitions below, and place the word's part of speech in the parentheses.

1. to give vigor or animation to: _____ (v.)

2. necessary to life: _____ (adj.)

3. physical or intellectual energy and vigor: _____ (n.)

4. to bring back after a decline: _____ (v.)

Number correct _____ (total 4)

Turn to **The Prefix *in-*** on pages 205-206 of the **Spelling Handbook**. Read the rule and complete the exercises provided.

The Latin Root *path* The related word *pathos* comes from the Greek root *path*, meaning "feeling." The English words *pathetic*, *sympathy*, *empathy*, and *antipathy* all come from this same root. Match each of the preceding *path* words with its definition below. Then write two sentences, using one *path* word in each sentence. Consult a dictionary if necessary.

1. the ability to share in another's feelings: _____

2. pitifully unsuccessful: _____

3. pity or compassion for another's feelings: _____

4. a strong dislike: _____

5. Sentence _____

6. Sentence _____

_____

Number correct _____ (total 6)

Number correct in Unit _____ (total 75)

Word's Worth: *ruminate*

What does the process of thinking something over have in common with a cow eating? More than you might imagine! Cows, and several other cud-chewing animals, are *ruminants*; that is, they have a stomach with four chambers. A ruminant's food is chewed only slightly and then stored as softened masses called *cuds* in the rumen, or first stomach. As the animal rests, the cuds are sent back to the mouth for further chewing. Sometime during the sixteenth century, a connection was made between a cow's chewing its cud and a person's ruminating, or pulling thoughts back into the mind to be reconsidered. Although *ruminate* still means to "chew the cud," its more common meaning is "to ponder or consider."

The Last Word

Writing

Write a short essay on *virtue*, using the following format:

1. Define the word *virtue* as you perceive it.
2. State a *virtue* you believe to be extremely important.
   a. Define your choice.
   b. Provide an example.
   c. Explain why it is important.
3. Describe how one might go about acquiring or enhancing this *virtue*.

Speaking

Prepare a short speech on one of the following topics.

1. The most *authoritative* person I know
2. My main *objective* in life
3. A situation I consider *provocative*

Group Discussion

Homelessness is a national problem in America. In small groups or in the class as a whole, discuss the *ramifications* of the problem by considering the following:

1. Where is the *privation* in your area?
2. Has there been a specified cause, or has the cause been one of *omission*?
3. How is homelessness in your area *interrelated* with the national problem?
4. What can people do besides being *sympathetic*?
5. To solve the problem, what should be the main *objective*?
   a. locally?
   b. regionally?
   c. nationally?

UNIT 10

Part A   Target Words and Their Meanings

1. apprehensiveness (ap′rə hen′siv nes) n.
2. ascribe (ə skrīb′) v.
3. diabolical (dī′ə bäl′i k'l) adj.
4. embark (im bärk′) v.
5. foreboding (fôr bōd′ iŋ) adj., n.
6. incoherent (in′ kō hir′ ənt) adj.
7. induce (in dōōs′, -dyōōs′) v.
8. issue (ish′ōō) n., v.
9. melancholy (mel′ən käl′ē) adj., n.
10. peremptory (pə remp′tər ē) adj.
11. perturbation (pur′tər bā′shən) n.
12. recur (ri kur′) v.
13. seclusion (si klōō′zhən) n.
14. solemn (säl′əm) adj.
15. transition (tran zish′ən, -sish′-) n.
16. vicariously (vī ker′ē əs lē, vi-) adv.
17. vindictive (vin dik′tiv) adj.
18. vocation (vō kā′shən) n.
19. warranty (wôr′ən tē, wär′-) n.
20. whimsical (hwim′ zi k'l, wim′) adj.

Inferring Meaning from Context

For each sentence write the letter of the word or phrase that is closest to the meaning of the word or words in italics. Use context clues to help you determine the correct answer. (For information about context clues, see pages 1-5.)

_____ 1. The dynamite factory near the town caused *apprehensiveness*.

a. understanding   b. lethargy   c. radiation   d. fearfulness

_____ 2. In his tribute, David *ascribed* qualities of selflessness and perseverance to the previous class president.

a. implicated   b. attributed   c. denied   d. wished

_____ 3. The mystery writer was well known for her chilling stories of *diabolical* terror and suspense.

a. vociferous   b. tedious   c. fiendish   d. absurd

_____ 4. Georgette made a thorough study of the job market before *embarking on* a career in banking.

a. getting started on   b. simulating   c. financing   d. prolonging

_____ 5. Hal's nightmare about his upcoming trip left him with a strange *foreboding*.

a. sense of future misfortune   b. feeling of utter regret   c. realization of fulfillment   d. sense of serenity

_____ 6. After two nights without sleep, Mariana couldn't think clearly. In fact, she didn't even make sense; her speech was *incoherent*.

a. mundane   b. disorganized   c. provocative   d. hostile

117

_____ 7. Mr. Butler *induced* us to buy a new TV by offering us a discount.
      a. persuaded b. pleaded with c. warned d. forced

_____ 8. A torrent of water *issued* from the broken pipe and began filling the basement.
      a. flowed b. exceeded c. departed d. dripped

_____ 9. Ann's *melancholy* mood seemed odd at the joyous celebration.
      a. magnanimous b. modified c. gloomy d. vociferous

_____ 10. The day supervisor was a gentle, quiet person, while the night supervisor barked orders in a *peremptory* manner.
      a. dejected b. commanding c. civilized d. magnanimous

_____ 11. The *perturbation* aboard the subway was caused when someone's pocket was picked.
      a. disturbance b. indifference c. diversion d. propulsion

_____ 12. Heavy storms *recur* every few months in this climate; people are accustomed to them.
      a. delineate b. ramify c. occur repeatedly d. diminish

_____ 13. Jake always goes into *seclusion* when he works on a project; no one sees him for days.
      a. tranquility b. isolation c. mediation d. extrapolation

_____ 14. During the party, the host displayed a strangely *solemn* expression.
      a. friendly b. joyful c. serious d. volatile

_____ 15. The *transition* from high school to college is difficult for some.
      a. passing b. resistance c. diversion d. inference

_____ 16. When Suzanne accepted her award with tears in her eyes, we experienced her joy *vicariously*, as if it were happening to us, too.
      a. temporarily b. reluctantly c. through another d. whimsically

_____ 17. Senator Rosemount felt betrayed by his colleagues and henceforth acted in a *vindictive* manner toward them as his way of getting even.
      a. prosaic b. beneficent c. vengeful d. lethargic

_____ 18. After much thought, Christy decided on law for *a vocation*.
      a. a temperament b. a production c. a career d. an attainment

_____ 19. Most appliances come with *a warranty* against defects in workmanship.
      a. a justification b. a guarantee c. an absolution d. a deterioration

_____ 20. Kris was out of shape, so when he asserted that he would not only go out for track but would also win the one-hundred-yard dash, we took it as merely *a whimsical* notion.
      a. a fanciful b. a dishonest c. an intuitive d. a contemptuous

Number correct _____ (total 20)

Part B Target Words in Reading and Literature

You should now have a general idea of the meaning of each target word. Refine your understanding by examining the shades of meaning these words have in the following excerpt.

Ahab

Herman Melville

In this excerpt from the nineteenth-century novel Moby Dick, *the narrator has joined the crew of a whaling ship. It is here that he gathers his first impressions of the mysterious Captain Ahab.*

For several days after leaving Nantucket, nothing above hatches was seen of Captain Ahab. The mates regularly relieved each other at the watches, and for aught[1] that could be seen to the contrary, they seemed to be the only commanders of the ship; only they sometimes **issued** from the cabin with orders so sudden and **peremptory**, that after all it was plain they but commanded   5
vicariously. Yes, their supreme lord and dictator was there, though hitherto unseen by any eyes not permitted to penetrate into the now sacred retreat of the cabin.

Every time I ascended to the deck from my watches below, I instantly gazed aft to mark if any strange face were visible; for my first vague disquietude[2]   10
touching the unknown captain, now in the **seclusion** of the sea became almost a **perturbation**. This was strangely heightened at times by the ragged Elijah's **diabolical incoherences** uninvitedly **recurring** to me, with a subtle energy I could not have before conceived of. But poorly could I withstand them, much as in other moods I was almost ready to smile at the **solemn whimsicalities** of that   15
outlandish prophet of the wharves. But whatever it was of **apprehensiveness** or uneasiness—to call it so—which I felt, yet whenever I came to look about me in the ship, it seemed against all **warranty** to cherish such emotions. For though the harpooners, with the great body of the crew, were a far more barbaric,

---

[1] aught: anything whatever
[2] disquietude: disturbed or uneasy condition; restlessness; anxiety

heathenish,[3] motley[4] set than any of the tame merchant-ship companies which 20
my previous experiences had made me acquainted with, still I **ascribed**
this—and rightly ascribed it—to the fierce uniqueness of the very nature of that
wild Scandinavian **vocation** in which I had so abandonly **embarked**. But it was
especially the aspect of the three chief officers of the ship, the mates, which was
more forcibly calculated to allay these colorless misgivings, and **induce** confi- 25
dence and cheerfulness in every presentment[5] of the voyage. . . . Now, it being
Christmas when the ship shot from out her harbor, for a space we had biting
Polar weather, though the time running away from it to southward; and by every
degree and minute of latitude which we sailed, gradually leaving that merciless
winter, and all its intolerable weather behind us. It was one of those less 30
lowering, but still grey and gloomy enough mornings of the **transition**, when with
a fair wind the ship was rushing through the water with a **vindictive** sort of
leaping and **melancholy** rapidity, that as I mounted to the deck at the call of the
forenoon watch, so soon as I levelled my glance toward the taffrail,[6] **foreboding**
shivers ran over me. Reality outran apprehension; Captain Ahab stood upon his 35
quarterdeck.[7]

---

[3] heathenish: resembling or characteristic of heathens; uncivilized
[4] motley: mixed; composed of many elements not usually grouped
[5] presentment: idea; mental picture
[6] taffrail: the rail around the stern of a ship
[7] quarterdeck: the section of the upper deck to the rear of the mainmast

Refining Your Understanding

For each of the following items, consider how the target word is used in the passage. Write the letter of the word or phrase that best completes each sentence.

_____ 1. If the three mates "commanded *vicariously*" (lines 5-6), then
a. someone else must have been giving the orders   b. they were giving commands they had no right to give   c. no one really paid attention to orders.

_____ 2. Melville describes Elijah's talks as *incoherences* (line 13), indicating that Elijah.   a. was accurate   b. made no sense   c. was crafty.

_____ 3. Which of the following sayings illustrates the narrator's statement "for my first vague disquietude touching the unknown captain . . . became almost a *perturbation*" (lines 10-12)?   a. what you don't know won't hurt you   b. fear of the unknown is the greatest fear of all   c. knowledge is power.

_____ 4. The "wild Scandinavian *vocation*" (line 23) is   a. whaling   b. the merchant marine   c. service on a passenger ship.

_____ 5. The ship's "rushing through the water with a *vindictive* sort of leaping" (lines 32-33) would create a feeling of   a. confidence   b. curiosity   c. fear.

Number correct _____ (total 5)

Part C *Ways to Make New Words Your Own*

Using Language and Thinking Skills

Understanding Multiple Meanings Each word in this exercise has two or more definitions. Read the definitions and read the sentences using the word. Then choose the definition that fits each sentence.

---

issue
a. a point or matter under dispute (n.)
b. a set of things published at the same time (n.)
c. to go, pass, or flow out (v.)
d. to put forth (v.)

_____ 1. A thin but fiery stream of lava *issued* from the volcano.

_____ 2. The government *issued* emergency aid to the tornado victims.

_____ 3. Do you think the senator will refuse to debate the *issues*?

_____ 4. Do you have the April *issue* of the magazine about astronomy?

---

transition
a. a passing from one condition to another (n.)
b. a word, phrase, or sentence that smoothly connects one topic or paragraph to a succeeding one (n.)
c. a modulation from one key to another in music (n.)

_____ 5. The jazz trumpeter gracefully made a *transition* from B-flat to E-flat.

_____ 6. The pronoun served as a *transition* by referring to the person in the preceding paragraph.

_____ 7. Fido seemed to make the *transition* from puppy to adult dog overnight.

_____ 8. Two common *transitions* used by writers are *therefore* and *consequently*.

---

melancholy
a. sadness and depression of spirits (n.)   b. gloomy (adj.)

_____ 9. Joan suffered from *melancholy* for days after her cat died.

_____ 10. The flutist played a *melancholy* melody.

Number correct _____ (total 10)

Finding Examples Write the letter of the situation that best illustrates the meaning of each word.

_____ 1. **solemn**

   a. A comedian entertains a crowd.
   b. A funeral is held for an important person.
   c. A ghost descends a winding staircase.

_____ 2. **apprehensiveness**

   a. A baseball team cheers its winning run.
   b. An applicant waits to hear if she was given the summer job.
   c. A small child awaits Christmas morning.

_____ 3. **peremptory**

   a. Emily always makes decisions without consulting others.
   b. Peter always has a kind word for everyone.
   c. Dorothy always arrives early, before everyone else.

_____ 4. **seclusion**

   a. A group of teen-agers plays volleyball on the beach every Saturday.
   b. Some students study for a test by meeting together for review.
   c. My uncle says he needs quiet so he is working on his novel in our attic.

_____ 5. **foreboding**

   a. Dad cheerfully waved us off to camp.
   b. A friend warned me not to take the flight to Denver today.
   c. The tour began with a welcoming party in the hotel lobby.

_____ 6. **diabolical**

   a. The thief devised a scheme to steal the prized necklace.
   b. The doorman assisted the lady in the wheelchair.
   c. One car dealer offers a cash rebate, but the other has a lower interest rate.

_____ 7. **whimsical**

   a. Jerome has fancifully suggested that he might run off to Alaska.
   b. Some brokers were philosophical about their losses in the stock market.
   c. Monday is reason enough to be melancholy.

_____ 8. **vocation**

   a. Gina plans to travel to Rome this summer.
   b. Aunt Ellen started as the youngest attorney in the law office.
   c. I can never seem to stick to a diet.

_____ 9. **incoherent**

   a. The speech was unorganized and barely understandable.
   b. The shuttle became disengaged from the larger craft.
   c. Puerto Rico is not part of the United States but it is a commonwealth.

_____ 10. **vindictive**

   a. A criminal cannot be tried twice for the same crime.
   b. In some science-fiction it is difficult to distinguish fantasy from reality.
   c. Captain Ahab spent most of his life trying to get revenge on Moby Dick.

Number correct _____ (total 10)

Practicing for Standardized Tests

Antonyms Write the letter of the word that is most nearly *opposite* in meaning to the capitalized word.

_____ 1. WHIMSICAL: (A) witty (B) serious (C) lyric (D) sensitive (E) volatile

_____ 2. DIABOLICAL: (A) scornful (B) coercive (C) angelic (D) evil (E) cultured

_____ 3. INCOHERENT: (A) articulate (B) impetuous (C) insightful (D) disorganized (E) argumentative

_____ 4. EMBARK: (A) falter (B) commence (C) eject (D) return (E) start

_____ 5. PEREMPTORY: (A) perceptive (B) prime (C) grave (D) wary (E) indecisive

_____ 6. APPREHENSIVE: (A) fearless (B) free (C) wan (D) vocal (E) apt

_____ 7. FOREBODING: (A) favorable (B) ominous (C) sinister (D) supple (E) coy

_____ 8. INDUCE: (A) coax (B) infuse (C) enlarge (D) hinder (E) register

_____ 9. PERTURBATION: (A) peril (B) calmness (C) ardor (D) clamor (E) rumination

_____ 10. MELANCHOLY: (A) gloom (B) lethargy (C) joy (D) fear (E) privation

Number correct _____ (total 10)

Analogies Write the letter of the word pair that best expresses a relationship similar to that expressed in the original pair.

_____ 1. GENERAL : PEREMPTORY :: (A) leader : vociferous (B) admiral : authoritative (C) benefactor : evil (D) ally : neutral (E) nurse : careless

_____ 2. FUNERAL : SOLEMN :: (A) wedding : joyful (B) picnic : crowded (C) election : provincial (D) game : combative (E) concert : mundane

_____ 3. ARDOR : ZEAL :: (A) aspect : endeavor (B) virtue : lethargy (C) anguish : catastrophe (D) passion : enthusiasm (E) endurance : lassitude

_____ 4. PERSIST : RECUR :: (A) wither : flourish (B) govern : mediate (C) endure : change (D) test : toil (E) simulate : copy

_____ 5. TEACHING : VOCATION :: (A) boxing : ring (B) farming : crops (C) thinking : insight (D) vice : virtue (E) hobby : avocation

_____ 6. PROTECTION : WARRANTY :: (A) whole : segment (B) enlightenment : insight (C) want : luxury (D) ardor : need (E) excess : moderation

_____ 7. EMBARK : VOYAGE :: (A) return : journey (B) endure : tour (C) board : room (D) begin : cruise (E) record : adventure

_____ 8. INDUCE : PERSUADE ::   (A) influence : motivate   (B) rectify : consent   (C) mediate : augment   (D) agitate : simulate   (E) infer : refer

_____ 9. PERTURB : PERTURBATION ::   (A) new : renew   (B) agitate : agitated   (C) sympathy : sympathetic   (D) anguish : anguishing   (E) endure : endurance

_____ 10. FEAR : APPREHENSIVE ::   (A) pen : pensive   (B) success : melancholy   (C) awareness : blind   (D) ardor : fiery   (E) seclusion : sinister

Number correct _____ (total 10)

Spelling and Wordplay

Crossword Puzzle

ACROSS

1. Taking the place of another
9. First person singular, present indicative, of *to be*
11. Third person singular, present indicative, of *to be*
12. Formal or serious
13. Poison _ _ _
14. Abbr. *Nova Scotia*
15. Abbr. *Cent*
16. Not out
17. Title used by Benito Mussolini meaning "the leader"
20. Not bright
22. Abbr. *Id Est* ("that is")
23. A strong dislike
25. Devilish
27. A sticky, brown or black liquid used to surface roads
29. A female deer
30. An upper limb of the human body
33. An indefinite article
34. Any trade or profession
36. Abbr. *Aid to Dependent Children*
37. To begin a journey
38. Poetic for *before*
40. Also
41. A word of choice
42. Distance, measured in degrees; freedom
48. One of two equal parts
49. A guarantee

DOWN

1. Vengeful; unforgiving
2. To pass; to put forth
3. To go up
4. To decay
5. Abbr. *Illinois*
6. Abbr. *Old English*
7. Abbr. *University of Minnesota*
8. Chemical symbol for tin
9. Abbr. *Avenue*
10. Possessive form of *I*
13. To persuade
18. A small, flat loop or strap
19. Past participle of *to hold*
21. Sadness and depression of spirits
23. The sound of a laugh
24. Homonym of 40 Across
26. Abbr. *I Owe You*
28. To happen again and again
30. Past tense of *to eat*
31. An edge
32. A disorderly and lawless crowd
33. A public announcement of something for sale
35. Abbr. *North America*
38. A period of time
39. A small fairy
40. The number following nine
41. A word of exclamation
43. Author Mark _ _ ain
44. Abbr. *Iowa*
45. Abbr. *Treasurer*
46. A vase: _ _ n
47. Abbr. *District Attorney*

Part D   Related Words

Use your knowledge of the target words and of word parts to determine the meanings of these related words. If you are unsure of any definitions, use your dictionary.

1. apprehend (ap′rə hend′) v.	11. transcribe (trans skrīb′) v.
2. apprehension (ap′rə hen′shən) n.	12. transfuse (trans fyōōz′) v.
3. coherence (kō hir′əns) n.	13. transgress (trans gres′, tranz-) v.
4. diabolic (dī′ə bäl′ik) adj.	14. transitory (tran′sə tôr′ē, -zə-) adj.
5. inducement (in dōōs′mənt, -dyōōs′-) n.	15. vicarious (vī ker′ē əs, vi-) adj.
6. induct (in dukt′) v.	16. vindication (vin′də kā′shən) n.
7. perturb (pər turb′) v.	17. vocational (vō kā′shən'l) adj.
8. recurrence (ri kur′əns) n.	18. warrant (wôr′ənt, wär′-) n., v.
9. seclude (si klōōd′) v.	19. whimsy (hwim′ zē, wim′-) n.
10. solemnity (sə lem′nə tē) n.	

Understanding Related Words

Sentence Completion Write the related word that best completes each sentence.

1. Scholars worked for years trying to _____ the hieroglyphics on the Rosetta stone into English.

2. The community college provides _____ counseling to help students make career choices.

3. As an _____ to shoppers with children, the local shopping center offers a free child-care center.

4. The defending attorney entered a plea of "not guilty" and expects total _____ for his client.

5. Their romance was just a _____; it lasted for only a week.

6. The central figure in *Phantom of the Opera* _____ himself in an underground area beneath the city.

7. The club constitution states that the outgoing president is to _____ the newly elected members.

8. The police could not search the house without a _____ .

9. The _____ of unexplainable disappearances of ships and planes has made the Bermuda Triangle famous.

10. Frankenstein's monster was not _____ but compassionate.

Number correct _____ (total 10)

Turn to **Doubling the Final Consonant** on pages 212-213 of the **Spelling Handbook.** Read the rule and complete the exercise provided.

The Prefix *trans*- This prefix means "on or to the other side," "over," "across," "through," or "so as to change completely." Keeping this in mind, match each *trans-* word with its appropriate definition. Write the word in the answer blank.

transcribe   transfuse   transgress   transitory   transport

_____ 1. (v.) to transfer by causing to flow

_____ 2. (v.) to carry from one destination to another; (n.) a
                           vehicle used for carrying things

_____ 3. (v.) to change from one medium to another, such as to
                           turn shorthand into typed copy

_____ 4. (adj.) of a passing or changing nature; not lasting

_____ 5. (v.) to overstep or break a law

Number correct _____ (total 5)

The Latin Roots *cur, duct, scribe, turb,* and *voc* Several of the target and related words come from these common Latin roots. Study each root and its definition below. Then list the words from the Target or Related Words list that are formed from that root. Finally, choose one word from each root and use it in a sentence.

1. cur ("run") _____

2. (sentence) _____

3. duct ("to lead") _____

4. (sentence) _____

   _____

5. scribe ("to write") _____

6. (sentence) _____

   _____

7. turb ("confusion") _____

8. (sentence) _____

9. voc ("voice" or "call") _____

10. (sentence) _____

Number correct _____ (total 10)

Number correct in Unit _____ (total 90)

Word's Worth: *melancholy*

Melancholy, of Greek origin, takes us back to the times when medical people believed that one's health was determined by the mixtures of the four "humors" in the body—blood, yellow bile, black bile, and phlegm. *Melancholia* was the Greek term for an overabundance of black bile, which caused depression or habitual unhappiness. The word *malyncoly* appeared in English in the fourteenth century with the same basic meaning as in the original Greek. Medical science rejected the theory of the four humors years ago, of course, but the word *melancholy* remained. It no longer describes a medical condition but instead characterizes a down or black mood.

The Last Word

Writing

Use a thesaurus to look up synonyms for five words introduced in this unit. Note whether there are shades of meaning that distinguish each word from its synonyms. For example, is *apprehension* a stronger feeling than *terror*, or vice versa? How does *solemn* differ from *serious*? Write sentences for each synonym you find. Make sure each sentence illustrates the appropriate shade of meaning.

Speaking

Relate an instance in which you had a *vicarious* experience. For example, you may choose to describe a movie you saw during which you identified strongly with a particular character or felt that you experienced the adventure of the story.

Group Discussion

Discuss what *vocation* each student in your class has chosen or would choose if he or she could do anything possible. Each student should give reasons for his or her choice.

UNIT 11

Part A Target Words and Their Meanings

1. contour (kän′toor) n., v., adj.
2. counterbalance (koun′tər bal′əns) n., v.
3. delinquency (di liŋ′kwən sē) n.
4. deviousness (dē′vē əs nes) n.
5. devise (di vīz′) v.
6. duplicity (doo plis′ə tē, dyoo-) n.
7. emancipation (i man′sə pā′shən) n.
8. escalate (es′kə lāt′) v.
9. faculty (fak′′l tē) n.
10. idealism (ī dē′əl iz′m) n.
11. integrity (in teg′rə tē) n.
12. mode (mōd) n.
13. morality (mə ral′ə tē, mô-) n.
14. neurosis (noo rō′sis, nyoo-) n.
15. paternalistic (pə tʉr′n′l is′tik) adj.
16. prerequisite (pri rek′wə zit) adj., n.
17. prevail (pri vāl′) v.
18. recompense (rek′əm pens′) n., v.
19. repress (ri pres′) v.
20. strive (strīv) v.

Inferring Meaning from Context

For each sentence select the word or phrase that is closest to the meaning of the italicized word or phrase.

_____ 1. The *contour* of the mountains was created thousands of years ago when small tributaries of the river eroded the land, creating gullies.

   a. shape b. construction c. peak d. deforestation

_____ 2. Country A's spying efforts on Country B are often *counterbalanced* by Country B's spying on Country A.

   a. enhanced b. studied c. offset d. prophesied

_____ 3. People were irritated by Thomas's *delinquency* in paying his debt, which was due in part to his inability to save money.

   a. anguish b. negligence c. contempt d. extrapolation

_____ 4. Most people trust Jake, but I have always found him to be guilty of *deviousness*.

   a. deceitfulness b. articulating c. moderation d. vindication

_____ 5. To *devise* a foolproof system will require much thought; it's never been done before.

   a. unite b. invent c. eject d. augment

_____ 6. When Agent Samuels was found to be a counterspy, his *duplicity* shocked everyone.

   a. ardor b. serenity c. deceptiveness d. solemnity

_____ 7. Believing that they were jailed unjustly, the political prisoners vociferously demanded their *emancipation*.

    a. freedom b. confinement c. deportation d. privation

_____ 8. The minor argument between the two friends *escalated* into a major conflict, causing them to reject any claims of previous friendship.

    a. condensed b. surfaced c. decreased d. expanded

_____ 9. The poet's ability lay in his talent for blank verse, but he had no *faculty* whatsoever for rhyme.

    a. teacher b. outlet c. aptitude d. shortcoming

_____ 10. Many people criticized Joni for her unfailing *idealism*, but she saw no reason to give up hope of achieving her goals.

    a. kindness b. pessimism c. laziness d. optimism

_____ 11. When the housing development was begun, the bulldozers cut through the wildflowers and destroyed the ecological *integrity* of the meadow.

    a. placement b. soundness c. simulation d. economics

_____ 12. Only a century ago, our primary *mode of* overland transportation was the railroad; the automobile was little more than a possibility.

    a. problem of b. reason for c. augmentation of d. method of

_____ 13. Dirty political campaigns show a poor sense of *morality*—on the part of both the politicians who campaign dishonestly and the voters who elect them.

    a. endurance b. right and wrong c. acculturation d. temperament

_____ 14. He was not physically ill, but his *neurosis* caused him to lose sleep.

    a. mental disorder b. curiosity c. stomachache d. inability to dream

_____ 15. The president of the company had *a paternalistic* attitude toward his employees; he treated them as if they were children.

    a. a pathetic b. a remote c. an aristocratic d. a fatherlike

_____ 16. In order to enroll in the advanced-composition class, you must have completed *the prerequisite*, a course in basic composition.

    a. something required after b. something required before
    c. unification d. vocation

_____ 17. Even in his absence, Mr. Martinez's rules on conduct *prevailed*. Students were indeed well-behaved.

    a. remained strong b. were ignored c. faltered d. transgressed

_____ 18. When a tree fell on our car, the insurance-company claims adjuster determined that some form of *recompense* was due our family.

    a. warning b. simulation c. reconstruction d. payment

_____ 19. Although we were quite hungry, we had to *repress* our appetites until dinner time.

    a. imitate b. satisfy c. hold back d. initiate

_____ 20. Don Quixote's goal was to *strive against* injustice in the fight for right.
a. surrender to   b. falter against   c. struggle against   d. postulate about

Number correct _____ (total 20)

Part B   *Target Words in Reading and Literature*

You should now have a general idea of the meaning of each target word. Refine your understanding by examining the shades of meaning these words have in the following excerpt.

The Female Eunuch

Germaine Greer

Germaine Greer, an Australian feminist, is the author of The Female Eunuch. *One topic Greer discusses is stereotypes, such as "woman's intuition" and the greater sensibility and creativity of the female mind. In the following excerpt Greer also warns against women's adoption of traditionally male behaviors and roles that would spell defeat.*

The **prevailing** criticism of the female soul can best be explained by the male battle to **repress** certain **faculties** in their own mental functioning. Women possessed in abundance those qualities which civilized men **strove** to repress in themselves, just as children and savages did. The value of such criticism is in the degree to which it reveals the severity of the **contouring** of the ideal   5
personality; that is to say, male criticism of the female mind is revealing only of the male himself. Men in our culture crippled themselves by setting up an impossible standard of **integrity**; women were not given the chance to fool themselves in this way. Women have been charged with **deviousness** and **duplicity** since the dawn of civilization, so they have never been able to pretend   10
that their masks were anything but masks. It is a slender case, but perhaps it does mean that women have always been in closer contact with reality than men; it would seem to be the just **recompense** for being deprived of idealism.

If women understand by **emancipation** the adoption of the masculine role, then we are lost indeed. If women can supply no **counterbalance** to the   15
blindness of male drive, the **aggressive** society will run to its lunatic extremes at ever-**escalating** speed.

Womanpower means the self-determination of women, and that means that all the baggage of **paternalistic** society will have to be thrown overboard. Women must have room and scope to **devise** a **morality** that does not disqualify her   20
from excellence and a psychology that does not condemn her to the status of a spiritual cripple. The penalties for such **delinquency** may be terrible, for she must explore the dark without any guide. It may seem at first that she merely exchanges one **mode** of suffering for another, one **neurosis** for another.

However, she may at least claim to have made a definite choice which is the first **prerequisite** of moral action. She may never herself see the ultimate goal, for the fabric of society is not unraveled in a single lifetime, but she may state it as her belief and find hope in it.

25

Refining Your Understanding

For each of the following items, consider how the target word is used in the passage. Write the letter of the word or phrase that best completes each sentence.

_____ 1. A *"prevailing* criticism" (line 1) is one that is   a. invalid   b. frequently heard   c. powerful.

_____ 2. Greer's use of *strove* (line 3) suggests that for men to repress was a   a. struggle   b. natural feeling   c. character-building experience.

_____ 3. *Recompense* (line 13) is synonymous with.   a. punishment   b. compensation   c. praise.

_____ 4. The need for women to create a *counterbalance* (line 15) suggests that the male drive is   a. creative   b. inadequate   c. harmful.

_____ 5. By *delinquency* (line 22) the author means   a. dishonesty   b. adolescent behavior   c. nonconformity to standard customs.

Number correct _____ (total 5)

Part C Ways to Make New Words Your Own

By now you are familiar with the target words and their meanings. This section presents a variety of reinforcement activities that will help you make these words part of your permanent vocabulary.

Using Language and Thinking Skills

True-False Decide whether each statement is true or false. Write **T** for True and **F** for False.

_____ 1. If you *strive* for a goal, you usually have no interest in achieving it.

_____ 2. The *contour* of your shadow would change if you gained weight.

_____ 3. A *prerequisite* for putting on your socks is tying your shoes.

_____ 4. Inventors *devise* new ways to accomplish tasks.

_____ 5. *Neurosis* is an example of good mental health.

_____ 6. We look for people who lack *deviousness* when we look for friends.

_____ 7. A ten-dollar check is fair *recompense* for a totally destroyed car.

_____ 8. Talking calmly is the best way to *escalate* an argument.

_____ 9. Deviousness and *morality* go hand in hand.

_____ 10. The skills of a professional basketball player would *prevail* over those of an amateur player.

Number correct _____ (total 10)

Practicing for Standardized Tests

Antonyms Write the letter of the word that is most nearly *opposite* in meaning to the capitalized word.

_____ 1. DEVIOUSNESS: (A) neglect (B) honesty (C) haughtiness (D) slyness (E) carelessness

_____ 2. DUPLICITY: (A) insight (B) deceit (C) perception (D) tactic (E) straightforwardness

_____ 3. EMANCIPATION: (A) rumination (B) freedom (C) enslavement (D) privation (E) moderation

_____ 4. ESCALATE: (A) ascend (B) tamp (C) diminish (D) increase (E) ramify

_____ 5. FACULTY: (A) inability (B) talent (C) college (D) component (E) issue

_____ 6. IDEALISM: (A) barbarianism (B) optimism (C) provincialism (D) pessimism (D) lyricism

_____ 7. INTEGRITY (A) virtue (B) vitality (C) equality (D) objectiveness (E) dishonesty

_____ 8. PATERNALISTIC: (A) authoritative (B) intuitive (C) fatherly (D) maternalistic (E) luxurious

_____ 9. REPRESS: (A) encourage (B) impress (C) provoke (D) revitalize (E) falter

_____ 10. STRIVE: (A) toil (B) traverse (C) endeavor (D) transfuse (E) give up

Number correct _____ (total 10)

Spelling and Wordplay

Word Maze Find and circle each target word in this maze

```
P  S  S  E  R  P  E  R  Y  T  I  L  A  R  O  M     contour
E  T  P  L  R  E  C  O  M  P  E  N  S  E  Y  E     counterbalance
C  I  E  M  A  N  C  I  P  A  T  I  O  N  T  T     delinquency
N  D  E  V  I  O  U  S  N  E  S  S  C  Z  I  I     deviousness
A  K  C  I  B  I  N  T  E  G  R  I  T  Y  C  S     devise
L  E  L  D  O  S  A  T  A  C  T  D  E  A  I  I     duplicity
A  T  I  E  R  O  G  O  S  S  I  E  L  R  L  U     emancipation
B  A  C  L  T  R  O  I  I  T  S  A  R  O  P  Q     escalate
R  L  N  I  A  V  S  L  V  R  T  L  V  T  U  E     faculty
E  A  E  N  I  O  A  L  I  I  B  I  S  L  D  R     idealism
T  C  U  Q  R  N  Z  D  E  V  I  S  E  K  E  E     integrity
N  S  Q  U  R  Q  M  A  M  E  N  M  T  Y  R  R     mode
U  E  E  E  N  T  O  U  R  L  I  A  V  E  R  P     morality
O  N  T  N  P  H  D  L  R  D  S  T  R  I  V  E     neurosis
C  A  F  C  R  A  E  M  C  O  N  T  O  U  R  A     paternalistic
P  W  U  Y  T  L  U  C  A  F  S  O  S  T  I  C     prerequisite
```

contour
counterbalance
delinquency
deviousness
devise
duplicity
emancipation
escalate
faculty
idealism
integrity
mode
morality
neurosis
paternalistic
prerequisite
prevail
recompense
repress
strive

Turn to **The Suffix _-ion_** and **The Letter _c_** on pages 213 and 217 of the **Spelling Handbook.** Read the rules and complete the exercises provided.

Part D Related Words

A number of words are closely related to the target words you have studied. Use your knowledge of the target words and of word parts to determine the meanings of these words. (For information about word parts analysis, see pages 6-12.) If you are unsure of any definitions, use your dictionary. Learning these related words expands your vocabulary and helps you learn the target words more thoroughly.

1. compress (käm′pres) n. (kəm pres′) v.
2. delinquent (di liŋ′kwənt) adj.
3. deviation (dē′vē ā′shən) n.
4. devious (dē′ vē əs) adj.
5. duplication (dōō′plə kā′shən) n.
6. duplicitous (dōō plis′ə təs, dyōō-) adj.
7. emancipate (i man′sə pāt′) v.
8. escalation (es′kə lā′shən) n.
9. express (ik spres′) adj., n., v.
10. idealistic (ī′dē ə lis′tik, ī dē′ə-) adj.
11. impress (im′pres) n. (im pres′) v.
12. integral (in′tə grəl, in teg′rəl) adj.
13. neurotic (nōō rät′ ik, nyōō-) adj., n.
14. paternalism (pə tur′n'l iz′m) n.
15. prevalent (prev′ə lənt) adj.
16. repression (ri presh′ən) n.
17. requisite (rek′wə zit) adj., n.
18. requisition (rek′wə zish′ən) n., v.
19. suppress (sə pres′) v.

Understanding Related Words

Matching Study the list of related words. Match the correct related word with its appropriate definition below. Write the word in the blank.

_____ 1. something necessary for a special circumstance or purpose

_____ 2. to free from oppression or bondage; to release

_____ 3. existing widely; generally practiced

_____ 4. behaving as if things are as they should be or as one would wish them to be

_____ 5. the act of copying or reproducing

_____ 6. a rapid increase; a rising; an expansion

_____ 7. a person who is excessively fearful or worried

_____ 8. a system of controlling a country, a group of people, etc., like that used by a father in dealing with his children

_____ 9. a turning aside from the correct or prescribed course

_____ 10. a formal request, as for supplies; a requiring, as by authority

Number correct _____ (total 10)

Word's Worth: duplicity

Two of something is not always better than one. Think of expressions such as *double trouble, double talk, double-cross, two-faced,* and *two-timer.* Or think of the bookkeeper who keeps two sets of books. As you can see, these words suggest *duplicity,* which comes from the Latin *duplex,* meaning "double" or "twofold." The original word in English, *duplycyte,* meant "deceitfulness." However, not all words in English that mean "double" are negative. Word-family relatives such as *duplicate,* "a replica," and *duplex,* "two houses or living quarters joined together," are quite harmless.

Analyzing Word Parts

The Latin Root *press* The target word *repress* comes from the Latin word *premere,* meaning "to press." The following words also come from this same Latin word:

compress (n., v.)   express (adj., v.)   impression (n.)
suppress (v.)   impress (n., v.)   repression (n.)

Consult a dictionary and note the meanings for the parts of speech of the words listed above. Fill in the blanks in the sentences below with the appropriate words.

1. Psychiatrists hold that the constant _____ of anger and stress can contribute to health problems such as high blood pressure and ulcers.

2. Putting a hot _____ on the swelling will reduce the inflammation and pain.

3. The 4:35 P.M. train is _____; it stops at only three stations.

4. Even though the cake was for the party, I couldn't _____ the urge to stick my finger in the icing and taste it.

5. The diving instructor wanted to _____ the class with the importance of checking equipment before each dive.

6. Paul Revere's work bears an _____ on the bottom of each piece of silver that identifies it as his.

7. So far, the military junta has been able to _____ any uprisings.

8. Can you _____ your ten-minute introductory remarks into five minutes?

9. The U.S. Constitution guarantees the right to _____ our ideas about government, even if those ideas are negative.

10. Did the magician's disappearing act _____ you?

Number correct _____ (total 10)

Number correct in Unit _____ (total 65)

The Last Word

Writing

Write a short description of the most *idealistic* person you know. Include information about the person's beliefs and goals. Also include your own opinion of the person's *idealism*. Do you think idealism makes sense in today's world?

Speaking

Prepare a speech in which you discuss one of the following concepts:

morality   emancipation   paternalism   delinquency
suppression   repression

Group Discussion

As a class, compile a list of the *prevalent* attitudes of the 1960's. Compare and contrast these attitudes with those that prevail today. Discuss why these changes might have occurred.

UNIT 12: Review of Units 9-11

Part A Review Word List

Unit 9 Target Words

1. anguish
2. authoritative
3. falter
4. hauteur
5. insight
6. interrelated
7. intuitive
8. objective
9. omission
10. perception
11. privation
12. provocative
13. ramify
14. ruminate
15. sympathetic
16. tamp
17. taut
18. utter
19. virtue
20. vitality

Unit 9 Related Words

1. authoritarian
2. deprivation
3. haughtiness
4. haughty
5. insightful
6. intuition
7. omit
8. pathos
9. perceptive
10. provoke
11. ramification
12. revitalize
13. rumination
14. utterly
15. utterance
16. virtuous
17. vital
18. vitalize

Unit 10 Target Words

1. apprehensiveness
2. ascribe
3. diabolical
4. embark
5. foreboding
6. incoherent
7. induce
8. issue
9. melancholy
10. peremptory
11. perturbation
12. recur
13. seclusion
14. solemn
15. transition
16. vicariously
17. vindictive
18. vocation
19. warranty
20. whimsical

Unit 10 Related Words

1. apprehend
2. apprehension
3. coherence
4. diabolic
5. inducement
6. induct
7. perturb
8. recurrence
9. seclude
10. solemnity
11. transcribe
12. transfuse
13. transgress
14. transitory
15. vicarious
16. vindication
17. vocational
18. warrant
19. whimsy

Unit 11 Target Words

1. contour
2. counterbalance
3. delinquency
4. deviousness
5. devise
6. duplicity
7. emancipation
8. escalate
9. faculty
10. idealism
11. integrity
12. mode
13. morality
14. neurosis
15. paternalistic
16. prerequisite
17. prevail
18. recompense
19. repress
20. strive

Unit 11 Related Words

1. compress
2. delinquent
3. deviation
4. devious
5. duplication
6. duplicitous
7. emancipate
8. escalation
9. express
10. idealistic
11. impress
12. integral
13. neurotic
14. paternalism
15. prevalent
16. repression
17. requisite
18. requisition
19. suppress

Inferring Meaning from Context

For each sentence write the letter of the word or phrase that is closest to the meaning of the word or words in italics.

_____ 1. The author *ascribed* her writing ability to the training she received from her grade-school teachers.
a. aspired b. coordinated c. attributed d. reconciled

_____ 2. Because the *contour* of the land was uneven, it was unsuitable for farming.
a. sand b. value c. shape d. recurrence

_____ 3. Kevin was known for his *duplicity*; even his friends began to distrust him.
a. melancholy b. cleverness c. foreboding d. underhandedness

_____ 4. If you *embark on* your trip on July 31, will you return in time for our Labor Day party?
a. plan b. continue c. get back from d. leave on

_____ 5. Carmen has an amazing *faculty* for doing impressions of other people.
a. disregard b. ability c. virtue d. absurdity

_____ 6. The *hauteur* that we encountered in Club Elite persuaded us not to join.
a. snobbery b. foreboding c. melancholy d. morality

_____ 7. The qualities most people remembered when they thought of Grandfather Warner were decency and *integrity*.
a. disgust b. evasion c. humor d. honesty

_____ 8. Coach Anderson said that Randy's *intuitive* sense of ball awareness made him a natural basketball player.
a. conservative b. impressive c. compulsive d. instinctive

_____ 9. The darkness of the shortened days of winter always leaves me with a feeling of *melancholy*.
a. equality b. serenity c. vitality d. sadness

_____ 10. Deloris was in her frugal *mode* and spent hours counting costs and pinching pennies.
a. manner b. whimsy c. costume d. faculty

_____ 11. We all hoped that Jack's good sense would *prevail* over his initial rude outburst.
a. radiate b. ruminate c. predominate d. extrapolate

_____ 12. Sol likes to be with people when he is relaxing, but when he works he goes into *seclusion*.
a. isolation b. retirement c. privation d. moderation

_____ 13. After we set the fence posts, we *tamped* the soil firmly around the base.
a. contoured b. counterbalanced c. packed d. escalated

_____ 14. Ms. Jones says that it is an *utter* impossibility to get her flu-stricken team
ready by tomorrow.
   a. whimsical   b. total   c. methodical   d. vindictive

_____ 15. Career statistics indicate that the prevailing reason for choosing *a
vocation* is not money, but personal satisfaction.
   a. an endeavor   b. to toil   c. a career   d. a deduction

Number correct _____ (total 15)

Using Review Words in Context

Using context clues, determine which word from the list below best completes
each sentence in the story. Write the word in the blank. Each word is used once.

ascribed	idealism	perception
authoritative	integral	prerequisite
counterbalance	interrelated	prevail
devise	issues	privation
foreboding	morality	recur

Ecological Stewardship

The all-day conference was entitled "Ecological Problems of the 1990's." It was
to focus on the preservation and reasonable use of the earth's viable land. The
topics under discussion reflected very little optimistic _____ ; in fact,
they were somewhat ominous.

The first speaker created a feeling of _____ in the audience as
she portrayed a picture of widespread _____ as a result of famine in
the years to come. Famine, she predicted, will _____ again and
again if we continue to overburden the land and in so doing create semiarid,
desertlike areas that can no longer be farmed. She concluded by pointing out that
when the future of our food supply is at stake, the use of the land becomes a
matter of _____ .

A geneticist, who addressed the conference in an _____ ,
businesslike manner, then presented a grim _____ of farming in the
future. He pointed out that today's farming practices deplete the gene pool of
plant varieties and make us dependent on fewer crops. He also _____
blame to the practices of overgrazing and overfertilizing that are
_____ to the creation of useless farm land.

A third speaker discussed several other important _____ , such as
overpopulation and the stresses that result from overcrowding. He emphasized
the need to _____ an education program that will alert people to
these specific dangers.

The final speaker looked not to a single answer but to several closely

_____ situations as possible solutions. She told us that the principal

_____ in finding answers to these problems is to change people's

attitudes about the use of the earth's resources. She also stated that nations must

_____ upon their citizens to forget their differences and work

together. She seemed to believe that these measures would help to even up and

_____ part of the harm that has already been done. However, we

inferred from the tone of her voice that she did not think that such cooperation

was likely to take place in the near future.

Number correct _____ (total 15)

Part B   Review Word Reinforcement

Using Language and Thinking Skills

Finding Examples Write the letter of the situation that best demonstrates the
meaning of each word.

_____ 1. **faculty**

    a. Teachers are often underpaid.
    b. Many dams provide hydroelectric power.
    c. The power to reason is one aspect of intelligence.

_____ 2. **morality**

    a. Patience is considered a virtue.
    b. Your favorite team wins the championship.
    c. Every society has some kind of a code of ethics.

_____ 3. **perturbation**

    a. Over millions of years a piece of wood becomes as hard as stone.
    b. Some planets exhibit an irregularity of orbit.
    c. You find the remarks of a friend are upsetting.

_____ 4. **provocative**

    a. Mrs. Hamilton's lectures are always stimulating and offer new ways of
       viewing a subject.
    b. No matter how grim the situation, Alan always comes up with a joke.
    c. The first debater yielded to the arguments of the other side.

_____ 5. **vicariously**

    a. A deputy sheriff issues an arrest warrant.
    b. Parents often take great pleasure in seeing their children accomplish
       things that they themselves were not able to achieve.
    c. Some investors seem to have an intuition about which stocks to buy.

Number correct _____ (total 5)

Practicing for Standardized Tests

Antonyms Write the letter of the word that is most nearly opposite in meaning to the capitalized word.

_____ 1. ANGUISH: (A) relief (B) temper (C) sorrow (D) dejection
(E) dreariness

_____ 2. APPREHENSIVENESS: (A) foreboding (B) contempt (C) fear
(D) calmness (E) forthrightness

_____ 3. DUPLICITY: (A) diversion (B) treachery (C) guile
(D) deviousness (E) forthrightness

_____ 4. ESCALATE: (A) ascend (B) diminish (C) falter (D) intensify
(E) assimilate

_____ 5. HAUTEUR: (A) disdain (B) superciliousness (C) modesty (D) pride
(E) whimsy

_____ 6. INCOHERENT: (A) provocative (B) disorganized (C) mundane
(D) muddled (E) articulate

_____ 7. MELANCHOLY: (A) gaiety (B) deduction (C) deportment
(D) gloom (E) obstinacy

_____ 8. OMISSION: (A) intuition (B) blank (C) obscurity (D) inclusion
(E) seclusion

_____ 9. PRIVATION: (A) loss (B) deprivation (C) abundance
(D) aggregation (E) loneliness

_____ 10. SOLEMN: (A) sinister (B) spirited (C) sympathetic
(D) suppressive (E) serious

Number correct _____ (total 10)

Synonyms Write the letter of the word whose meaning is closest to that of the capitalized word.

_____ 1. COUNTERBALANCE: (A) delineate (B) offset (C) collide
(D) countersign (E) overbalance

_____ 2. EMANCIPATION: (A) freedom (B) endurance (C) pugnacity
(D) enslavement (E) luxuriance

_____ 3. FALTER: (A) compose (B) collide (C) infuse (D) hesitate
(E) facilitate

_____ 4. INDUCE: (A) ramify (B) reconcile (C) restrain (D) convulse
(E) motivate

_____ 5. INSIGHT: (A) intuition (B) vitality (C) whimsy (D) ardor
(E) singularity

_____ 6. RUMINATE: (A) mediate (B) contemplate (C) extrapolate (D) ruin (E) simulate

_____ 7. STRIVE: (A) agitate (B) succumb (C) toil (D) initiate (E) bolster

_____ 8. TRANSITION: (A) change (B) aspect (C) permanence (D) moderation (E) deportment

_____ 9. VINDICTIVE: (A) vicarious (B) vocational (C) seamy (D) barbaric (E) vengeful

_____ 10. WARRANTY: (A) arrest (B) objective (C) guarantee (D) satisfaction (E) prerequisite

Number correct _____ (total 10)

Analogies Write the letter of the word pair that best expresses a relationship similar to that expressed in the original pair.

_____ 1. DEVISE : PLAN :: (A) concoct : recipe (B) induce : pressure (C) commit : act (D) relay : message (E) study : strategy

_____ 2. ISSUE : MAGAZINE :: (A) universe : planet (B) benefit : need (C) puzzle : piece (D) chapter : book (E) millennia : era

_____ 3. ANGUISH : SORROW :: (A) despair : grief (B) endeavor : failure (C) dejection : elation (D) joy : celebration (E) garden : vegetation

_____ 4. PREREQUISITE : REQUISITE :: (A) privation : deprivation (B) aspiring : aspiration (C) adjustment : alteration (D) moderate : moderation (E) preconception : conception

_____ 5. PERSUADE : INDUCE :: (A) motivate : ignore (B) simulate : originate (C) request : consent (D) smolder : blaze (E) infer : conclude

_____ 6. PREMONITION : INTUITIVE :: (A) poetry : prosaic (B) integrity : virtuous (C) deduction : solemn (D) barbarian : aristocratic (E) extortion : legal

_____ 7. RELATIVES : INTERRELATED :: (A) extras : extrapolated (B) family : civilized (C) temperament : temperamental (D) categories : categorized (E) objectives : objectionable

_____ 8. PACK : TAMP :: (A) stroll : race (B) strive : accomplish (C) falter : stumble (D) express : suppress (E) embark : travel

_____ 9. ACQUITTAL : VINDICATION :: (A) lassitude : vitality (B) annoyance : perturbation (C) condensation : moisture (D) accusation : defense (E) trial : verdict

_____ 10. VOCATION : CAREER :: (A) contour : interior (B) conjecture : deduction (C) ethnicity : food (D) warranty : guarantee (E) job : skill

Number correct _____ (total 10)

Spelling and Wordplay

Proofreading Find the ten misspelled words in the following letter and write them correctly on the lines below the letter.

The Dude Ranch

Dear Folks,

I begin this letter with some aprehension because my poor spelling often makes my meaning almost incoherent. But I will repress my fears because of my prevailing need to tell you the news. I rode a horse today.

The horse was big and looked forbodeing, but the head ranch hand, who is very paternallistic, told me in an authoratative manner that my faculty for riding is excellent. Although it didn't seem so at first, it turned out that he was very intuitive.

It was a solem moment when I climbed the ladder to get on Diobolical—that is the horse's name—and prepared to embark on my ride. We started at a nice trot, and then he escallated into a gallop. I tried to hold the reins taut, but as we went through a ditch, the horse faultered. I lost my grip on the reins, and that induced me to grab his mane. As I slipped off his back, I realized that I was not cut out for the vocation of jockey.

But the good news is that I got over my meloncalley mood and I have regained my vitality. Ben, the head ranch hand, has been very sympathetic. He told me that the only way to emansipate myself from fear is to get on that horse again tomorrow. Ben said that he would teach me to ride, as well as to jockey, for only fifty dollars. Would you send me a check?

Love,
Verna

1. _____
2. _____
3. _____
4. _____
5. _____

6. _____
7. _____
8. _____
9. _____
10. _____

Number correct _____ (total 10)

Part C   Related Word Reinforcement

Using Related Words

Sentence Completion Write the related word from the following list that best completes each sentence.

deprivation	emancipate	provoked	revitalize	transitory
duplicitous	prevalent	ramification	suppress	utterance

1. The _____ found in the slums only encouraged Europe's bubonic plague of 1347 to permeate the cities.

2. Donations from sympathetic television viewers around the world helped the Armenians _____ their cities following the earthquake on December 7, 1988.

3. The subcommittee was investigating the senator because they suspected him of _____ behavior.

4. The outbreak of World War I _____ America into recruiting pilots; before that time, the U.S. Air Force consisted of only fifty men.

5. One _____ of industrial development is the pollution of our environment.

6. No _____ was heard from the prisoners, yet unspoken words seemed to fill the air.

7. Unfortunately, Grandmother's seeming return to good health was only _____ ; a week later she was back in the hospital.

8. France did not begin to _____ her female citizens until 1944, when French women were finally given the right to vote.

9. In an effort to _____ the leakage of vital information about American troop and ship movement during World War II, all mail sent by military personnel was censored.

10. Dumbwaiters, devices to transport food or dishes from one floor to another, were _____ in large Victorian homes around the turn of the century.

Number correct _____ (total 10)

Reviewing Word Structures

Prefixes and Roots On the lines below, write a word formed from the prefix-root combination.

	press	cur	duce

1. **re-** _____

2. **im-/in-** _____

3. **com-/con** _____

Write six sentences. Use one of the newly formed words in each.

1. _____

_____

2. _____

_____

3. _____

_____

4. _____

_____

5. _____

_____

6. _____

_____

Number correct _____ (total 15)

Number correct in Unit _____ (total 100)

145

Vocab Lab 3

FOCUS ON: **Economics**

Economics is the science dealing with the production, distribution, and consumption of goods and services. Study the following terms relating to the field of economics, and complete the exercise that follows.

asset (as′et) n. anything that has an exchange value on the market, including intangible items such as a skill or a good reputation. • The value of the Moores' *assets* increased dramatically when they received their Ph.D. degrees and bought a new home.

capitalism (kap′ə t'l iz′m) n. an economic system in which private individuals and businesses own most of the resources. • Under *capitalism*, people can make, or lose, great sums of money.

consumer (kən sōō′ mər, -syōō′-) n. a person who buys goods and services. • Providers of goods and services spend vast amounts of money in order to convince *consumers* to choose their products.

cost of living (kôst uv liv′iŋ) n. the average cost of essential goods and services at a specific place and time. • A worker will be able to save money only if her income exceeds her *cost of living*.

demand (di mand′) n. the desire for a specific product or service. • A company that sells a product that is not in *demand* may go out of business.

depreciation (di prē′shē′ ā′shən) n. a reduction in the cost or value of something. • Unlike most consumer goods, which undergo *depreciation* as they age, collector's items such as fine art, antiques, and vintage automobiles increase in value.

depression (di presh′ən) n. a period of sluggish business activity, falling prices and wages, and severe unemployment. • In a *depression*, people must adjust their life styles to the reduced economic circumstances.

gross national product (grōs nash′ə n'l präd′əkt) n. the total value of a nation's annual production of goods and services. • A rise in the *gross national product* generally is a sign of a healthy economy.

income (in′kum) n. money or other gain received for goods or services. • Although Marina's new job in Boston offered her an increase in *income*, the gain was offset by her increased cost of living.

inflation (in flā′shən) n. a reduction in the value of money and a rise in prices due to an excess of currency in circulation. • During a recent period of *inflation*, prices rose more than 50 percent in less than six months.

interest (in′ trist, -tər ist) n. the charge for borrowing or the payment for lending money. • In an attempt to attract customers, the bank lowered the rate of *interest* on home-mortgage and automobile loans.

monopoly (mə näp′ə lē) n. the complete control of a commodity or service in a particular market. • If one supplier has a *monopoly* on a product, the supplier will not be forced to keep prices low, because it has no competitors.

national debt (nash′ə n'l det) n.   the amount of money owed by the federal government.   • Occasionally, the government raises taxes to help pay off the *national debt*.

recession (ri sesh′ən) n.   a period of reduced economic activity.   • A *recession* is a temporary economic slump that is not as serious as a depression.

supply (sə plī′) n.   the amount of a particular product or service available for purchase.   • When the *supply* of portable calculators increased, the prices decreased.

Finding Examples   Match each economic term from the list with the appropriate example below.   Write the term in the blank.

_____ 1. When the steel mill closed down, automobile factories across the country could not continue to operate and shut their doors, leaving thousands of people out of work.

_____ 2. The price of corn is 10 percent less than it was last year.

_____ 3. The federal government informed the telephone company that it must split up into several smaller companies.

_____ 4. The increase in the total value of all goods and services produced in the United States last year indicated that the economy was booming.

_____ 5. The Green Thumb Lawn-Mowing Company owns two trucks, eight lawn mowers, and six edge trimmers, and the owner is a trusted member of the community.

_____ 6. Airline companies in the United States are privately owned.

_____ 7. Darnell's annual salary for his part-time job at the grocery store is five thousand dollars.

_____ 8. The school store has a total of one thousand rulers to sell.

_____ 9. Several local companies had difficulty during the first half of the year, but now business is thriving.

_____ 10. Leo made a detailed list of his expenses to determine if the income from his job was sufficient to cover them.

_____ 11. The price of beef went up 20 percent in one week.

_____ 12. Bookstores often run out of a best-selling book.

_____ 13. The U.S. government had to take out a huge loan in order to pay the salaries of armed-service personnel.

_____ 14. Bill just bought a new electric guitar and amplifier.

_____ 15. The landlord returned Sam's security deposit and paid him 5 percent of that amount for the use of the money.

Number correct _____ (total 15)

FOCUS ON: *Semantic Change*

So far in this vocabulary book you have learned the meanings of almost 350 words. Eventually, however, many of those words will not mean what they mean today. This evolution of word meanings—**semantic change**—occurs because words are arbitrary labels, meaning only what people agree that they mean. As people and the world they live in change, the meanings of the words they use also change.

Consider the word *tattle*. In the fifteenth century, that verb meant "to speak hesitantly or stammer." It later came to mean "to chat" or "to gossip." Today, *tattle* means "to tell other people's secrets." *Hogwash* once referred to what was fed to hogs, but now it means "nonsense." A *shindig* once was a kick in the shins from someone at a dance; now it denotes a party or other social occasion. Although no one can predict exactly if, when, or how a particular word meaning will change, if and when it does, the change will fall into one of four categories: **degeneration, elevation, generalization,** or **specialization.**

Degeneration and Elevation

Words that undergo **degeneration** start out with respectable meanings but over time acquire a "bad reputation." In addition to *tattle*, which underwent degeneration to acquire the negative connotation it has today, many other word meanings changed in this way. For example, you probably can't imagine that a present-day farmer would want to hire a villain, yet at one time, *villain* merely meant "farmhand." Once, you were expected to act silly in a place of worship, since *silly* meant "holy" or "innocent." Today, however, such behavior is more appropriate in a playground. At one time, a crafty person was admired because he or she was adept at a craft, whereas today, when *crafty* means "sly," such a person is regarded with caution. Likewise, *cunning*, which once meant "wise" or "knowledgeable," today suggests skill in deception.

The degeneration of word meanings does not suggest that our language is deteriorating or our civilization is declining. Words with negative connotations just as often undergo **elevation** and become more respectable as time passes. At one time, for example, describing someone as *nice* would not have been complimentary, since *nice* meant "ignorant." *Marshall*, which now designates a person with a respected position in the armed forces or in the local law-enforcement ranks, once referred to someone who worked in a stable. Once, a *pioneer* was a low-ranking foot soldier, whereas a pioneer today is respected as a person at the frontiers of knowledge.

Generalization and Specialization

Words meanings can also change by becoming more inclusive—through generalization—or exclusive—through specialization. For example, *virtue* originally meant "manliness" and referred only to masculine qualities. After undergoing **generalization,** it has come to refer to any moral excellence. The word *hazard*, which once was the name of a game of dice, has been generalized to mean any kind of risk. *Barn*, which was once the name of a building for storing barley, today refers to a storage place for any kind of grain or livestock.

Other words undergo **specialization** to acquire more narrow meanings. For example, whereas *deer* once referred to any beast, it now designates a very specific type of animal. The word *undertaker*, which once referred to a person who "undertook" to do anything, now refers solely to someone who prepares the dead for burial. *Wedlock*, which now refers to a very specific commitment, once meant any kind of pledge.

Word meanings evolve continually. This constant change requires that everyone—readers, writers, and speakers, language students, and publishers of vocabulary texts and dictionaries—must also continue to change and grow. Anyone who uses language must become a *pioneer* in both this word's former and current senses—a foot soldier diligently keeping in step with advancing knowledge.

Semantic Sleuthing Look up the following words in an unabridged dictionary. Indicate the type of semantic change each has undergone—degeneration, elevation, generalization, or specialization.

1. arrive _____

2. awful _____

3. boor _____

4. censure _____

5. enthusiasm _____

6. governor _____

7. hound _____

8. liquor _____

9. lust _____

10. minister _____

11. pastor _____

12. shrewd _____

13. smirk _____

14. starve _____

15. throw _____

Number correct _____ (total 15)

Number correct in Vocab Lab _____ (total 30)

UNIT 13

Part A Target Words and Their Meanings

1. aloof (ə lōōf′) adj., adv.
2. aphorism (af′ə riz′m) n.
3. austere (ô stir′) adj.
4. bisect (bī sekt′, bī′sekt) v.
5. casual (kazh′ōō wəl) adj.
6. demeanor (di mēn′ər) n.
7. domain (dō mān′, də-) n.
8. elegance (el′ə gəns) n.
9. enigmatic (en′ig mat′ik, ē′nig-) adj.
10. exemplify (ig zem′plə fī′) v.

11. explicitly (ik splis′it lē) adv.
12. impose (im pōz′) v.
13. inscribe (in skrīb′) v.
14. magnetism (mag′n tiz′m) n.
15. obliterate (ə blit′ə rāt′, ō-) v.
16. prime (prīm) adj., n., v.
17. profound (prə found′) adj.
18. reactionary (rē ak′shə ner′ē) adj., n.
19. rigor (rig′ər, rī′gôr) n.
20. tantamount (tan′tə mount′) adj.

Inferring Meaning from Context

For each sentence write the letter of the word or phrase that is closest to the meaning of the word or words in italics. Use context clues to help you determine the correct answer. (For information about how context helps you understand vocabulary, see pages 1–5.)

_____ 1. Although the other children joined in the party games, the painfully shy boy stood *aloof* at the edge of the room.

    a. proudly b. defiantly c. relaxed d. apart

_____ 2. Ben Franklin collected many American *aphorisms* in his *Poor Richard's Almanac*, such as "A stitch in time saves nine" and "The early bird gets the worm."

    a. sayings b. sentences c. sentiments d. myths

_____ 3. The financial planner recommended *an austere* budget that would cover only absolute necessities and eliminate all frills and luxuries.

    a. a balanced b. a strict c. a large d. a planned

_____ 4. Rachel *bisected* the apple and gave half to each of the boys.

    a. paid for b. carefully washed c. selected d. cut in two

_____ 5. At the summer home we wore *casual* attire: shorts, sandals, and tank tops.

    a. elegant b. stylish c. informal d. sloppy

_____ 6. Although Jennifer is outgoing and friendly, Juanita's *demeanor* is quiet and modest; she does not like to draw attention to herself in public.

    a. heritage b. conduct c. plight d. attire

_____ 7. Alaska was part of Russia's *domain* in 1863, when it was purchased by the United States.

a. ethnicity b. emancipation c. consensus d. realm

_____ 8. The splendid and ornate furnishings in the royal palace reflect the French taste for *elegance*.

a. grandeur b. economy c. comfort d. moderation

_____ 9. The child's *enigmatic* behavior puzzled his teacher, his parents, and even his friends; no one could understand it.

a. mean b. mysterious c. nervous d. mischievous

_____ 10. According to the Arthurian legends, the noble actions of the knights of the Round Table *exemplified* the ideals of chivalry, courage, and courtesy, which were cherished in the Middle Ages.

a. defied b. discussed c. demonstrated d. criticized

_____ 11. The clerk at the Traveler's Aid desk gave directions so *explicitly* that everyone understood them and easily found his or her destination.

a. precisely b. loudly c. quickly d. cheerfully

_____ 12. After the judge found the man guilty of hunting without a license, he *imposed* a fine of five hundred dollars, the maximum penalty.

a. assessed b. canceled c. suspended d. explained

_____ 13. The jeweler said that he could easily *inscribe* the names of the bride and groom and the date of their wedding on their wedding rings.

a. engrave b. order c. paint d. leave out

_____ 14. Kris's *magnetism* made her a leader among her schoolmates; people were readily drawn to her and enjoyed her company.

a. energy b. powerful intelligence c. wit
d. power to attract or charm

_____ 15. The heavy, pounding rainstorm eventually *obliterated* all the sand castles we made on the beach.

a. damaged b. isolated c. destroyed d. dampened

_____ 16. Senator Solarz promised her constituents that her *prime* objective would be to lower the tax rate, because she believed that lower taxes were absolutely essential for economic progress.

a. chief b. last c. secondary d. solemn

_____ 17. When Russ heard the unexpected news about the death of his favorite uncle, he experienced a *profound* sense of grief.

a. brief b. surprising c. temporary d. very deep

_____ 18. The governor called his opponent *a reactionary* who wanted to reverse progress and abolish the major reforms of the last twenty years.

a. an ultraconservative b. a progressive c. a moderate
d. an agitator

_____ 19. During the Revolutionary War, many soldiers died as a result of the *rigor* of the long, cold New England winters.
   a. anguish   b. dreariness   c. length   d. severity

_____ 20. The mayor's popularity dropped drastically because people saw his refusal to deny the charges against him as *tantamount to* an admission of guilt.
   a. much worse than   b. almost the same as   c. unrelated to
   d. better than

Number correct _____ (total 20)

Part B *Target Words in Reading and Literature*

You should now have a general idea of the meaning of each target word. Refine your understanding by examining the shades of meaning these words have in the following excerpt.

Gauss

Ian Stewart

Carl Friedrich Gauss was a leading German mathematician of the late eighteenth and early nineteenth centuries. Born into humble circumstances, he exhibited his mathematical genius at an early age. In this excerpt the author discusses Gauss and reveals a significant discovery he made—at the age of eighteen!

"Mathematics is the queen of the sciences," Carl Friedrich Gauss once said, and his own career **exemplified** that **aphorism**. Generally considered to rank with Archimedes and Newton as one of the ablest mathematicians of all time, Gauss was interested in both theory and application, and his contributions range from the purest number theory to practical problems of astronomy, 5
magnetism, and surveying. In all the branches of mathematics in which he worked, he made **profound** discoveries, introduced new ideas and methods, and laid the foundations of later investigations. It is a measure of his abilities that, on the 200th anniversary of his birth, many of his ideas are still bearing fruit. 10

Gauss was in many ways an **enigmatic** and contradictory personality. The only son of working-class parents, he rose to become the leading mathematician of his age, yet he lived modestly and avoided public notice. His **demeanor** was mild, yet he was an **aloof**, politically **reactionary**, and often unyielding man who asked only that he be allowed to continue his creative work undisturbed. He 15
was prepared to recognize mathematical ability wherever he found it, in spite of contemporary prejudices, but his **casual** neglect of some of the best young mathematicians of his time, notably Janos Bolyai, one of the pioneers of non-Euclidean geometry, had unfortunate consequences.

A particularly striking aspect of Gauss's character was his refusal to present any of his work until he believed it had been polished to the point of perfection. No result, however important, was published until he deemed it to be complete. He reworked his mathematical proofs to such an extent that the path whereby he had obtained his results was all but **obliterated**. His published work has a quality of classical grace and **elegance, austere** and unapproachable. Many of his best ideas do not appear **explicitly** in print and have to be inferred by retracing the steps by which his discoveries must have been made. As a result, important concepts did not see the light of day until they were discovered independently by others.

When Gauss left the Collegium Carolinum in October 1795 to study at the University of Göttingen, he was torn between mathematics and his other great love: the study of ancient languages, at which he was equally brilliant. On March 30, 1796, however, his mind was made up by one of the most suprising discoveries in the history of mathematics.

To provide some background for this discovery, let us go back two millennia to classical Greece. The main Greek contribution to mathematics was the flourishing school of geometry associated with the names of Pythagoras, Eudoxus, Euclid, Apollonius, and Archimedes. The Greeks were probably the first to recognize the importance of **rigor** in proofs, and in search of such rigor they had **imposed** a number of restrictions. One of them was that in geometric constructions, only a straightedge and a compass were to be used. In effect, the only curves allowed were the straight line and the circle.

Euclid showed that it was possible to construct regular polygons with three, four, five, and fifteen sides, together with the polygons derived by the repeated **bisecting** of these sides, with a straightedge and a compass. Such polygons, however, were the only ones the Greeks could construct; they knew of no way to make polygons with, for example, seven, nine, eleven, thirteen, fourteen, and seventeen sides. For the next 2,000 years no one appears to have suspected that it might be possible to construct any of these other polygons. Gauss's achievement was to find a construction for a regular polygon of seventeen sides, which he **inscribed** within a circle using only a straightedge and a compass. Moreover, he explained exactly which polygons could be so constructed: the number of sides must be any power of 2 (2^n) or 2 multiplied by one or more

different odd **prime** numbers of the type known as Fermat primes (after Pierre de Fermat, who discovered them). A prime number is, by definition, a number that cannot be divided evenly by any number except itself and 1; a Fermat prime has the additional requirement of being one greater than 2 to a power of 2, or $2^{2n}+1$. The only known Fermat primes are 3, 5, 17, 257, and 65,537. Thus, we have the remarkable result that although regular seventeen-sided polygons can be constructed with a straightedge and a compass, regular polygons with seven, nine, eleven, thirteen, and fourteen sides cannot be.

Gauss proved this theorem (at the age of 18) by combining an algebraic argument with a geometric one. He showed that constructing a seventeen-sided polygon is **tantamount** to solving the equation $X^{16}+X^{15}+xxx+x+1=0$. Because 17 is prime and 16 is a power of 2, it turns out that this equation can be reduced to a series of quadratic[1] equations (expressions of the form $ax^2+bx+c=0$, where a, b, and c are given numbers and x is to be found). Since it had already been proved that quadratic equations can be solved with a straightedge-and-compass construction, the proof was complete. Apart from the proof's importance in inducing Gauss to take up mathematics as a career, it is the first real instance (beyond Descartes's introduction of coordinates) of a technique that has since become one of the most useful in mathematics: moving a problem from one **domain** (in this case geometry) to another (algebra) and solving it there.

55

60

65

70

---

[1] quadratic: involving a quantity or quantities that are squared, but none that are raised to a higher power

Refining Your Understanding

For each of the following items, consider how the target word is used in the passage. Write the letter of the word or phrase that best completes each sentence.

_____ 1. The meaning of *profound* (line 7) apparently intended by the author is a. very low   b. intellectually deep   c. intensely felt.

_____ 2. The opposite of an *enigmatic* person (line 11) would be a person who is a. easy to understand   b. easy to get along with   c. foolish.

_____ 3. Gauss's "*casual* neglect" (line 17) of some young mathematicians suggests that he   a. carefully guarded his leisure time   b. feared giving credit to younger mathematicians   c. sometimes did not pay serious attention to other mathematicians.

_____ 4. If the processes behind Gauss's proofs were "all but *obliterated*" (line 24), those proofs would be   a. difficult to understand due to his wordy writing style   b. difficult to trace   c. mathematically valid.

_____ 5. If many of Gauss's ideas "do not appear *explicitly* in print" (line 26), they apparently are   a. stated indirectly   b. inadequately developed c. vague and undeveloped.

Number correct _____ (total 5)

Part C Ways to Make New Words Your Own

Using Language and Thinking Skills

Matching Ideas In the blank write the word that best describes the idea expressed in each sentence.

austere	elegance	impose	magnetism	profound
casual	enigmatic	inscribe	obliterate	reactionary

_____ 1. The architects planned to build a beautiful marble staircase with brass railings in the new library.

_____ 2. There were neither telephones nor electricity in the Amish village.

_____ 3. Ben spent most of his time in a secret hiding place. Not even his brother knew what Ben was up to.

_____ 4. Mr. Kolson loves dropping in on his neighbors unexpectedly and staying for dinner.

_____ 5. At the impromptu barbecue, everything from bathing suits to shorts was acceptable attire.

_____ 6. The famous author sat for hours in the bookstore, signing his autograph in the customers' books.

_____ 7. Some houses and restaurants on the waterfront were completely destroyed by the hurricane.

_____ 8. Although Plato and Aristotle wrote thousands of years ago, their thinking continues to challenge today's students.

_____ 9. Grandfather has always been resistant to change, especially about women. He believes that women should neither go to college nor work outside the home.

_____ 10. Michael is bright, athletic, musical, friendly, and understanding. His personality appeals to everyone.

Number correct _____ (total 10)

Practicing for Standardized Tests

Synonyms Write the letter of the word whose meaning is closest to that of the capitalized word.

_____ 1. AUSTERE: (A) plain (B) foreboding (C) showy (D) gloomy (E) ostentatious

_____ 2. BISECT: (A) duplicate (B) augment (C) unify (D) divide (E) deduct

_____ 3. DEMEANOR: (A) morality   (B) vindication   (C) ethnicity   (D) heritage
(E) manner

_____ 4. ENIGMATIC: (A) instant   (B) mysterious   (C) shriveled
(D) automatic   (E) inanimate

_____ 5. EXEMPLIFY: (A) communicate   (B) ruminate   (C) represent
(D) induce   (E) ridicule

_____ 6. EXPLICITLY: (A) ambiguously   (B) obscurely   (C) clearly
(D) absurdly   (E) provocatively

_____ 7. IMPOSE: (A) force   (B) deduce   (C) infuse   (D) request   (E) soften

_____ 8. PROFOUND: (A) ideal   (B) deep   (C) whimsical   (D) coercive
(E) productive

_____ 9. RIGOR: (A) severity   (B) morality   (C) virtue   (D) pugnacity
(E) provincialism

_____ 10. TANTAMOUNT: (A) unequal   (B) lustrous   (C) equal   (D) inanimate
(E) attractive

Number correct _____ (total 10)

Analogies Each item below consists of a related pair of words. Write the letter of
the pair of words that best expresses a relationship similar to that of the original pair.

_____ 1. MAGNETISM : ATTRACTION ::   (A) aviation : airplane   (B) faculty :
principal   (C) train : truck   (D) intuitive : insight   (E) taut : tamp

_____ 2. OBLITERATE : DAMAGE ::   (A) toil : rest   (B) scorn : tease
(C) accelerate : hurry   (D) cry : moan   (E) endure : prevail

_____ 3. AMBIGUOUSLY : EXPLICITLY ::   (A) quietly : silently   (B) privately :
publicly   (C) subsequently : later   (D) obstinately : stubbornly
(E) reasonably : moderately

_____ 4. EMPIRE : DOMAIN ::   (A) nation : country   (B) state : city
(C) government : anarchy   (D) city : county   (E) politician : politics

_____ 5. ELEGANCE : CRUDENESS ::   (A) sympathy : virtue   (B) integrity :
honesty   (C) destruction : war   (D) morning : night   (E) vacation : rest

_____ 6. INSCRIBE : STONE ::   (A) write : pencil   (B) jog : jogger   (C) print :
paper   (D) type : typewriter   (E) act : theater

_____ 7. ALOOF : FRIENDLY ::   (A) solemn : serious   (B) weak : sickly
(C) luxurious : extravagant   (D) perceptive : dense   (E) agitated : upset

_____ 8. INFORMAL : CASUAL ::   (A) thoughtful : whimsical   (B) supportive :
antagonistic   (C) animated : lively   (D) spontaneous : deliberate
(E) medical : healthy

_____ 9. REACTIONARY : LIBERAL :: (A) science : physics (B) snow : precipitation (C) poetry : prose (D) perception : insight (E) contradiction : confusion

_____ 10. TANTAMOUNT : EQUAL :: (A) plastic : wooden (B) first : second (C) sympathetic : indifferent (D) best : better (E) final : last

Number correct _____ (total 10)

Spelling and Wordplay

Crossword Puzzle

ACROSS
1. Outward behavior
11. To erase
12. Abbr. *Notary Public*
14. Abbr. *Missouri*
15. Abbr. *Obstetrician*
16. Conjunction meaning "in order that"
17. Indefinite article
18. Abbr. *Horsepower*
20. Abbr. *International Business Machines*
23. Chemical symbol for chlorine
24. One who resists change
27. Abbr. *Irish*
28. To excavate
29. Abbr. *Attorney General*
30. To view
33. A vagrant or wanderer
34. To move, as a liquid
35. Preposition meaning "to" or "until"
36. Prefix meaning "in"
37. A word of choice
38. The sound of a laugh
39. Abbr. *Alcoholics Anonymous*
41. To perform an action
42. Tasteful luxury
47. Following
48. Unadorned

DOWN
1. Territory under one government
2. Poetic form of *ebony*
3. Abbr. *Middle Latin*
4. One or the other
5. Preposition for "on," "in," "near," or "by"
6. Prefix meaning "new" or "recent"
7. The path of a heavenly body
8. Chemical symbol for radium
9. To put in place
10. To mark or engrave
13. A closed plane figure with more than four sides
19. Ma's spouse
21. Prefix meaning "having two"
22. Used for washing floors
24. Extreme hardness or severity
25. Informal
26. Fuss
29. Distant in sympathy or interest
31. Suffix meaning "to become" or "to cause to be"
32. Latin abbreviation for *and so forth:* — — c.
38. That girl
39. An insect that lives in a colony
40. A playing card with a numerical value of one
41. Abbr. *District Attorney*
43. Abbr. *Each*
44. Abbr. *Guam*
45. Adverb meaning "equally"
46. A word of hesitation

Turn to **The Letter c** on pages 217–218 of the **Spelling Handbook.** Read the rules and complete the exercises provided.

Part D Related Words

A number of words are closely related to the target words you have studied. Use your knowledge of the target words and of word parts to determine the meanings of these words. If you are unsure of any definitions, use your dictionary.

1. aloofness (ə loof′nes) n.
2. austerity (ô ster′ə tē) n.
3. casually (kazh′ oo wəl ē) adv.
4. casualty (kazh′əl tē, -oo wəl-) n.
5. dissect (di sekt′, dī-) v.
6. dominate (däm′ə nāt′) v,
7. elegant (el′ə gənt) adj.
8. enigma (ə nig′mə) n.
9. exemplary (ig zem′plə rē) adj.
10. implicit (im plis′it) adj.
11. imposition (im′pə zish′ən) n.
12. magnetic (mag net′ik) adj.
13. obliteration (ə blit′ə rā′shən) n.
14. primeval (prī mē′v′l) adj.
15. primitive (prim′ə tiv) adj.
16. profundity (prə fun′də tē) n.
17. reaction (rē ak′shən) n.
18. rigorous (rig′ər əs) adj.

Understanding Related Words

Finding Examples In the blank write the letter of the situation that best demonstrates the meaning of each word.

_____ 1. **dominate**

a. The police detective systematically questioned all of the suspects.
b. The Mustangs won the last ten games against their cross-town rivals.
c. The club officers voted to accept or reject each new member.

_____ 2. **dissect**

a. The biologist cut the worm into segments and examined each part.
b. The insects caused great damage to the tomato crop.
c. The speaker advocated a new way of looking at the problem.

_____ 3. **casually**

a. Tina created a relaxed, informal atmosphere for the company picnic.
b. Deliberate neglect had created hazardous working conditions.
c. The two roommates had been close friends for years.

_____ 4. **imposition**

a. The Petersons go out to dinner at least once a week.
b. Dave asked to stay for dinner even though we hadn't invited him.
c. The controversial athlete released a statement to the press.

_____ 5. **primitive**

a. The Museum of Contemporary Art held an exhibition last week.
b. The cave paintings at Lascaux, France, provide outstanding displays of prehistoric art.
c. Scientists are still expanding their knowledge of tornadoes.

Number correct _____ (total 5)

Sentence Completion Complete each sentence with the correct word from the list below.

aloofness   magnetic
austerity   primeval
casualty   profundity
enigma   reaction
implicit   rigorous

1. When the coach loosened his tie, it was a(n) _____ sign that he felt confident of victory.

2. Olympic contenders must undergo _____ training and discipline.

3. The riddle of the Sphinx was a famous _____ that was solved by Oedipus.

4. The doctor carefully observed her patient's _____ to the new medication.

5. Sometimes children are capable of astonishing _____ , which surprises us only because we vastly underestimate their mental capacity.

6. Some people mistakenly thought that Isaiah's _____ was due to disdainful pride, but it really was a sign of extreme shyness.

7. In its _____ state, the earth was a fiery, glowing ball.

8. A _____ force can either attract an object or repel it.

9. The biography revealed the extreme poverty and _____ of the hermit's life.

10. The only _____ of the accident was my straw hat, which lay crushed on the sidewalk.

Number correct _____ (total 10)

Word's Worth: austere

Have you ever heard your parents or grandparents talk about *austerity* programs during World War II? Various items, such as gasoline, sugar, and car tires, were rationed because the supply of these products "dried up." *Austerity* comes from the Greek root *austeros*, "to make the tongue dry." In its original English meaning, *austere* simply referred to foods with a sharp or bitter taste, such as unripened fruit. Gradually, the meaning expanded to include anything that made life more harsh or severe.

Analyzing Word Parts

The Latin root *scrib* The Latin root *scrib*, from the word *scribere*, meaning "to write," is found in the target word *inscribe* as well as in many other English words. Match each of the following words based on this root with its definition. Use a dictionary to check your work.

_____ 1. transcribe   a. to write out

_____ 2. circumscribe   b. a written document

_____ 3. scripture   c. any sacred writing or book

_____ 4. inscription   d. to trace a line around; to encompass

_____ 5. script   e. something engraved, as on a coin

Number correct _____ (total 5)

Number correct in Unit _____ (total 75)

The Last Word

Writing

An *aphorism* is a pithy statement, or proverb, that offers wise advice about life. Ben Franklin collected many American aphorisms in *Poor Richard's Almanac*. Here are some of the more famous ones:

"Early to bed and early to rise makes a man healthy, wealthy, and wise."
"Don't throw stones at your neighbors if your windows are glass."
"Lost time is never found again."

Compile a list of other aphorisms that you have heard, perhaps about such topics as love, sports, or success. You may find it useful to enlist the help of your family or friends. Then create your own aphorism to add to the list.

Speaking

Prepare a speech in which you describe the *demeanor* of a famous person whose identity you do not divulge. Make sure the famous person is someone with whom most members of the class would be familiar, perhaps a well-known comedian, sports celebrity, or politician. Class members should attempt to guess whom you have described.

Group Discussion

As a class, jointly compile a list of personality traits. Then members of the class should offer the names of public figures who *exemplify* one or more of these traits. After discussion, try to narrow the list down to the two men and two women who have most of the traits on the list.

UNIT 14

Part A Target Words and Their Meanings

1. advent (ad′vent) n.
2. capital (kap′ə t′l) adj., n.
3. desolation (des′ə lā′shən) n.
4. domestic (də mes′tik) adj., n.
5. foresight (fôr′sīt′) n.
6. gaunt (gônt) adj.
7. hale (hāl) adj.
8. manifest (man′ə fest′) v., adj.
9. misanthrope (mis′ ən thrōp′, miz′-) n.
10. peevish (pē′vish) adj.
11. perseverance (pur′sə vir′əns) n.
12. pious (pī′əs) adj.
13. reserved (ri zurvd′) adj.
14. resolution (rez′ə lōō′shən) n.
15. sentiment (sen′tə mənt) n.
16. solicit (sə lis′it) v.
17. soliloquize (sə lil′ə kwīz′) v.
18. solitary (säl′ə ter′ē) adj.
19. tumult (tōō′mult, tyōō′-) n.
20. wince (wins) v.

Inferring Meaning from Context

For each sentence write the letter of the word or phrase that is closest to the meaning of the word or words in italics. Use context clues to help you determine the correct answer. (For information about context clues, see pages 1-5.)

_____ 1. Each year when the crocuses bloom, signaling the *advent* of spring, we put away our boots and snow shovels.
   a. peak b. recollection c. arrival d. conclusion

_____ 2. The local performance of the play was *capital*, just as enjoyable and exciting as the acclaimed performance by the Broadway company.
   a. profitable b. competent c. first-rate d. different

_____ 3. The documentary revealed the *desolation* of a steel-mill town by vividly portraying the overwhelming problems caused by the closing of the mill.
   a. generosity b. dismalness c. pride d. determination

_____ 4. Although Elaine works long hours as an attorney, when she is away from the office she enjoys *domestic* endeavors such as cooking and sewing.
   a. secretarial b. casual c. household d. dreary

_____ 5. Although we were saddened to learn of Aunt Esther's death, we were relieved that she had shown excellent *foresight*; the life-insurance policy she purchased will provide well for her family.
   a. discipline b. willpower c. perception d. planning for the future

_____ 6. The *gaunt* faces of the famine victims reflected the hunger and suffering they had endured.

   a. thin   b. angry   c. reflective   d. tired

_____ 7. Grandpa boasted that, at eighty, he still had a *hale* body and a sharp mind.

   a. soft   b. large   c. weak   d. healthy

_____ 8. After having been totally indifferent to every sport the school had to offer, Jack finally *manifested* an interest.

   a. displayed   b. devised   c. invented   d. arranged

_____ 9. The hermit was a *misanthrope*; he could not tolerate others and avoided human contact whenever possible.

   a. philosopher   b. sickly person   c. hater of humankind   d. miser

_____ 10. Vanessa was *a peevish* child who enjoyed very few activities and always found something to complain about.

   a. a special   b. an irritable   c. a young   d. a fearful

_____ 11. The runner showed great *perseverance* after his disabling knee injury; through a rigorous rehabilitation and exercise program, he eventually regained his championship form.

   a. discouragement   b. perceptivenss   c. pain   d. persistence

_____ 12. The Camptons were *pious*, attending church twice a week and participating in many religious retreats.

   a. attentive   b. aloof   c. devout   d. busy

_____ 13. Because Danny is so *reserved* and quiet, he does not make friends easily.

   a. cynical   b. cowardly   c. foolish   d. aloof

_____ 14. Because Allen kept his *resolution* to get up early and run at least five miles each day, he was able to complete his first marathon this summer.

   a. methodical notation   b. threatened promise   c. simple deduction
   d. determined decision

_____ 15. When Charles Dickens read his novels aloud, audiences were often moved to tears by the tender *sentiments* he expressed.

   a. characters   b. feelings   c. predictions   d. faculties

_____ 16. To *solicit* business for the new pizza parlor, the owners sent out fliers offering a free pizza to the first hundred customers.

   a. seek   b. limit   c. conduct   d. estimate

_____ 17. The director explained that when everyone else left the stage, the main character would be left alone to *soliloquize* about his dilemma, thinking aloud about his possible options.

   a. fantasize   b. tell others   c. talk to himself   d. complain

_____ 18. The assistant coach voiced *solitary* opposition to the game strategy, but he eventually convinced the head coach and players to change their minds and try his approach.

    a. mistaken b. fierce c. isolated d. hesitant

_____ 19. The speaker at the pep rally could not quiet the *tumult* of the crowd; students continued to yell, scream, and stamp their feet in anticipation of a great victory.

    a. uproar b. temperament c. panic d. anger

_____ 20. By the way Jeremy *winced* when the doctor inspected his infected knee, we could tell that he was in great pain, even before he said anything.

    a. shouted b. flinched c. cried d. grinned

Number correct _____ (total 20)

Part B *Target Words in Reading and Literature*

You should now have a general idea of the meaning of each target word. Refine your understanding by examining the shades of meaning these words have in the following excerpt.

Wuthering Heights

Emily Brontë

Wuthering Heights *is one of the most famous English novels of the nineteenth century. In the following excerpt, taken from the beginning of the novel, the narrator of the story meets Heathcliff, his prospective landlord, at a remote rural location.*

1801—I have just returned from a visit to my landlord—the **solitary** neighbour that I shall be troubled with. This is certainly a beautiful country! In all England, I do not believe that I could have fixed on a situation so completely removed from the stir of society. A perfect **misanthropist's** Heaven—and Mr. Heathcliff and I are such a suitable pair to divide the **desolation** between us. A **capital** fellow!   5
He little imagined how my heart warmed towards him when I beheld his black eyes withdrawn so suspiciously under their brows, as I rode up, and when his fingers sheltered themselves, with a jealous **resolution** still further in his waistcoat, as I announced my name.

"Mr. Heathcliff?" I said.   10

A nod was the answer.

"Mr. Lockwood your new tenant, sir. I do myself the honour of calling as soon as possible, after my arrival, to express the hope that I have not inconvenienced you by my **perseverance** in **soliciting** the occupation of Thrushcross Grange[1]; I heard, yesterday, you had some thoughts—"   15

"Thrushcross Grange is my own, sir," he interrupted **wincing**, "I should not allow any one to inconvenience me, if I could hinder it—walk in!"

The "walk in," was uttered with closed teeth and expressed the **sentiment**, "Go to the Deuce!"[2] Even the gate over which he leant[3] **manifested** no sympathizing movement to the words; and I think that circumstance determined me to accept the invitation: I felt interested in a man who seemed more exaggeratedly **reserved** than myself.

When he saw my horse's breast fairly pushing the barrier, he did pull out his hand to unchain it, and then sullenly preceded me up the causeway,[4] calling, as we entered the court:

"Joseph, take Mr. Lockwood's horse; and bring up some wine."

"Here we have the whole establishment of **domestics**, I suppose," was the reflection, suggested by this compound order, "No wonder the grass grows up between the flags, and cattle are the only hedge-cutters."

Joseph was an elderly, nay, an old man, very old, perhaps, though **hale** and sinewy.

"The Lord help us!" he **soliloquised**[5] in an undertone of **peevish** displeasure, while relieving me of my horse: looking, meantime, in my face so sourly that I charitably conjectured he must have need of divine aid to digest his dinner, and his **pious** ejaculation[6] had no reference to my unexpected **advent**.

Wuthering Heights is the name of Mr. Heathcliff's dwelling. "Wuthering" being a significant provincial adjective, descriptive of the atmospheric **tumult** to which its station is exposed, in stormy weather. Pure, bracing ventilation they must have up there, at all times, indeed: one may guess the power of the north wind, blowing over the edge, by the excessive slant of a few, stunted firs at the end of the house; and by a range of **gaunt** thorns all stretching their limbs one way, as if craving alms of the sun. Happily, the architect had **foresight** to build it strong: the narrow windows are deeply set in the wall; and the corners defended with large jutting stones.

---

[1] Thrushcross Grange: the name of the house the narrator wants to rent
[2] Deuce: the devil
[3] leant: same as *leaned*
[4] causeway: a raised path or road, as across a marsh
[5] soliloquise: Bronte has used the British spelling of the word *soliloquize*
[6] ejaculation: exclamation

Refining Your Understanding

For each of the following items, consider how the target word is used in the passage. Write the letter of the word or phrase that best completes each sentence.

_____ 1. A "*misanthropist's* Heaven" (line 4) would especially appeal to people who   a. enjoy parties   b. prefer rural living   c. wish to separate themselves from others.

_____ 2. You would expect "a *capital* fellow" (line 5) to be   a. execellent   b. wealthy   c. in politics.

_____ 3. In "*soliciting* the occupation of Thrushcross Grange" (line 14), Lockwood was   a. defending his right to visit Thrushcross Grange   b. informing Heathcliff that the army would occupy Thrushcross Grange   c. asking to live at Thrushcross Grange.

_____ 4. The fact that Heathcliff *winced* (line 16) when he responded to Lockwood suggests that what Lockwood said caused him to be   a. pleased   b. confused   c. upset.

_____ 5. Joseph was "the whole establishment of *domestics*" (line 27) at Thrushcross Grange because he was the only   a. spouse   b. servant   c. polite person.

Number correct _____ (total 5)

Part C. *Ways to Make New Words Your Own*

By now you are familiar with the target words and their meanings. This section presents a variety of reinforcement activities that will help you make these words part of your permanent vocabulary.

Using Language and Thinking Skills

Finding the Unrelated Word Write the letter of the word that is not related in meaning to the other words in the set.

_____ 1. a. insolent   b. isolated   c. alone   d. solitary

_____ 2. a. sociable   b. reserved   c. neighborly   d. amiable

_____ 3. a. destruction   b. desolation   c. barrenness   d. fertility

_____ 4. a. prudence   b. caution   c. carelessness   d. foresight

_____ 5. a. conceal   b. manifest   c. hide   d. cover

_____ 6. a. virtue   b. persistence   c. determination   d. perseverance

_____ 7. a. time   b. resolution   c. duration   d. term

_____ 8. a. discuss   b. debate   c. soliloquize   d. argue

_____ 9. a. request   b. solicit   c. ask   d. demonstrate

_____ 10. a. sentiment   b. fact   c. opinion   d. feeling

Number correct _____ (total 10)

Practicing for Standardized Tests

Antonyms Write the letter of the word that is most nearly opposite in meaning to the capitalized word.

_____ 1. ADVENT: (A) domain   (B) conclusion   (C) aspect   (D) arrival
(E) escalation

_____ 2. CAPITAL: (A) unimportant   (B) economic   (C) prime
(D) authoritarian   (E) urbane

_____ 3. DOMESTIC: (A) housekeeper   (B) clerk   (C) serf   (D) citizen
(E) master

_____ 4. GAUNT: (A) lean   (B) diabolical   (C) plump   (D) hard
(E) reactionary

_____ 5. HALE: (A) elegant   (B) healthy   (C) aloof   (D) sick   (E) rigorous

_____ 6. MANIFEST: (A) prove   (B) defeat   (C) hide   (D) exemplify
(E) show

_____ 7. PEEVISH: (A) pleasant (B) solemn (C) coercive (D) dreary
(E) irritable

_____ 8. PIOUS: (A) devout (B) profound (C) hypocritical (D) enigmatic
(E) irreverent

_____ 9. RESERVED: (A) cautious (B) formal (C) uninhibited (D) annoyed
(E) agitated

_____ 10. TUMULT: (A) ardor (B) destruction (C) commotion
(D) tranquility (E) disease

Number correct _____ (total 10)

Spelling and Wordplay

Word Maze Find and circle each target word in this maze.

D	M	I	S	A	N	T	H	R	O	P	E	A	advent
P	G	A	U	N	T	E	C	N	I	W	P	T	capital
R	E	P	T	N	E	V	D	A	S	I	M	S	desolation
S	E	R	R	L	A	T	I	P	A	C	F	E	domestic
O	T	S	S	E	J	O	E	Q	I	E	O	F	foresight
L	N	U	O	E	S	E	U	T	V	T	R	I	gaunt
I	E	O	N	L	V	E	S	O	P	X	E	N	hale
T	M	I	G	I	U	E	R	Y	Z	K	S	A	manifest
A	I	P	S	O	M	T	R	V	A	P	I	M	misanthrope
R	T	H	E	O	S	X	I	A	E	L	G	Q	peevish
Y	N	C	D	E	L	A	H	O	N	D	H	G	perseverance
D	E	S	O	L	A	T	I	O	N	C	T	L	pious
H	S	O	L	I	L	O	Q	U	I	Z	E	M	reserved
B	S	O	L	I	C	I	T	L	U	M	U	T	resolution

advent
capital
desolation
domestic
foresight
gaunt
hale
manifest
misanthrope
peevish
perseverance
pious
reserved
resolution
sentiment
solicit
soliloquize
solitary
tumult
wince

Turn to **The Final Silent _e_** on pages 209-211 of the **Spelling Handbook.**
Read the rule and complete the exercises provided.

Part D Related Words

A number of words are closely related to the target words you have studied. Use your knowledge of the target words and of word parts to determine the meanings of these words. (For information about word parts analysis, see pages 6-12.) If you are unsure of any definitions, use your dictionary. Learning these related words expands your vocabulary and helps you learn the target words more thoroughly.

1. capitalism (kap'ə t'l iz'm) n.
2. desolate (des'ə lit) adj., (-lāt') v.
3. domesticity (dō'mes tis'ə tē) n.
4. domicile (däm'ə sīl', -sil; dō' mə-) n., v.
5. foresee (fôr sē') v.
6. hindsight (hīnd'sīt') n.
7. manifestation (man'ə fes tā'shən, -fəs-) n.
8. peeve (pēv) n., v.
9. persevere (pʉr'sə vir') v.
10. piety (pī' ə tē) n.
11. reservation (rez'ər vā'shən) n.
12. resolute (rez'ə lōōt') adj.
13. resolve (ri zälv', -zôlv') v., n.
14. sentimentality (sen'tə men tal'ə tē) n.
15. solicitous (sə lis'ə təs) adj.
16. soliloquy (sə lil'ə kwē) n.
17. solitude (säl' ə tōōd', -tyōōd') n.
18. tumultuous (tōō mul'choo wəs) adj.

Understanding Related Words

True-False Decide whether each statement is true or false. Write **T** for True and **F** for False.

_____ 1. It would be unusual for a priest, rabbi, or minister to display *piety*.

_____ 2. People who live in *desolate* areas should expect many visitors.

_____ 3. A fortuneteller might claim that she can *foresee* the future.

_____ 4. When you *persevere* in a project, you do not give up in the face of difficulty.

_____ 5. A *peeve* can be an unexpected delight.

_____ 6. In a *soliloquy*, two characters face the audience and explain the meaning of the play.

_____ 7. If you had just *resolved* a major problem in your life, you would probably be happy or relieved.

_____ 8. Most parents are much more *solicitous* of their children than of strangers.

_____ 9. A *tumultuous* celebration would not be noticed by many people.

_____ 10. You would expect a *resolute* person to change his or her opinions frequently.

Number correct _____ (total 10)

Finding Examples In the blanks write the word that is the best example for the situation.

desolate   domicile   manifestation   reservation   soliloquy
domesticity   hindsight   peeve   sentimentality   tumultuous

_____ 1. Myra was moved to tears by the haunting oboe music.

_____ 2. My mother hates it when I turn up the stereo.

_____ 3. The young couple loved to spend their evenings relaxing at home.

_____ 4. The coach later realized what she should have done during the game.

_____ 5. Ron's uncle lives by himself in the remote wilderness.

_____ 6. The driver sat alone in her car complaining to herself about the hopelessness of the morning traffic situation.

_____ 7. The roar of the crowd echoed off the arena walls, making an incredible racket.

_____ 8. Rena called ahead to make sure that we could get a table at our favorite restaurant.

_____ 9. Her smile was an unmistakable sign of the pleasure she took in her work.

_____ 10. The college admissions form asked for my permanent address.

Number correct _____ (total 10)

Analyzing Words Parts

The Latin Root _sol_ The target words _desolation_, _solitary_, and _soliloquize_ all contain the Latin root _sol_, meaning "alone." The following words also come from this Latin word:

desolate   solace   sole   soliloquy   solitude

Use each word above in one of the following sentences. If needed, look up the meanings in your dictionary.

1. Lorenzo hoped that his old car would not break down on the

   _____ stretch of road, where no help would be available.

2. The little girl found _____ in the companionship of her stuffed bear.

3. Brutus's _____ in Shakespeare's _Julius Caesar_ reveals a great deal about the character's motivations.

4. After his mother died, Richard became the _____ heir to her fortune.

5. Henry David Thoreau learned a great deal about self-reliance from his life

of _____ at Walden Pond.

Number correct _____ (total 5)

Number correct in Unit _____ (total 70)

Word's Worth: capital

Capital has many different meanings, all of which can be traced to the Latin word *caput*, meaning "the human head." You can refer to the capital of a state (the "head" of government), a capital letter (which stands at the "head" of a word), or capital punishment (which used to involve the beheading—de*cap*itation—of the offender). In architecture, the top part, or head, of a column is called the capital. In business, capital refers to the money and/or property that is needed to stay ahead of the competition. Clearly, *capital* is a word that stands head and shoulders above the pedestrian crowd.

The Last Word

Writing

Hindsight is the ability to see, after an event, what should have been done. This ability enables us to learn from our experiences so that we do not repeat past mistakes. Write a short essay in which you describe how hindsight from one experience enabled you to have foresight for another.

Speaking

Comedians often draw upon the little nuisances of life for their humor. Make a list of your own pet *peeves*—the kinds of things that annoy and irritate you. Prepare a humorous speech in which you decribe one of these pet peeves and propose a way of abolishing it from the face of the earth.

Group Discussion

Every year millions of Americans make New Year's *resolutions*, promises to themselves that they will change their behavior or attitudes in the coming year. Discuss the idea of resolutions with your classmates. Here are some questions to consider. Why do people feel compelled to make resolutions on New Year's Eve? Why do so many people break their resolutions? What does this reveal about human character?

UNIT 15

Part A   Target Words and Their Meanings

1. archaism (är′ kē iz′m) n.
2. bravado (brə vä′ dō) n.
3. cliché (klē shā′) n.
4. congeal (kən jēl′) v.
5. ebullience (i bōōl′ yəns) n.
6. emanate (em′ə nāt′) v.
7. embodiment (im bäd′ ē mənt) n.
8. engaging (in gāj′ iŋ) adj.
9. macho (mä′ chō) adj.
10. maudlin (môd′ lin) adj.
11. musty (mus′ tē) adj.
12. naive (nä ēv′) adj.
13. redemption (ri demp′ shən) n.
14. repulsive (ri pul′ siv) adj.
15. resonance (rez′ə nəns) n.
16. sheer (shir) adj.
17. simplistic (sim plis′ tik) adj.
18. unspeakably (un spēk′ə blē) adv.
19. unworldliness (un wurld′ lē nes) n.
20. waif (wāf) n.

Inferring Meaning from Context

For each sentence write the letter of the word or phrase that is closest to the meaning of the word or words in italics. Use context clues to help you determine the correct answer. (For information about context clues, see pages 1-5.)

_____ 1. *Thou,* which can be traced to Old English, is *an archaism* no longer used in ordinary conversation.

a. a sign of disrespect   b. a noun   c. a tasteless expression
d. an outdated word

_____ 2. An old photo from 1859 shows Charles Blondin walking across a tightrope stretched 165 feet above Niagara Falls. That look of confidence on his face—was it bravery, or was it mere *bravado*?

a. cowardice   b. pretending to be brave   c. courage   d. curiosity

_____ 3. "Calm, cool, and collected" and "cool as a cucumber" are examples of familiar *clichés*—too familiar, perhaps—that describe tranquility.

a. overused expressions   b. erroneous notions   c. official statements
d. proverbs

_____ 4: In soups containing meat, the fat will often rise to the top, where it will *congeal*. Then the cook can skim it off.

a. solidify   b. mix in   c. bubble   d. evaporate

_____ 5. When Maureen discovered that she had won the contest, she could not contain her *ebullience*; she immediately shouted for joy.

a. surprise   b. vocal cords   c. enthusiasm   d. ignorance

_____ 6. Hot, molten lava still *emanates* from live volcanoes in Hawaii.

       a. condenses b. flows c. evaporates d. flickers

_____ 7. Many medieval people believed witches to be the *embodiment* of evil and persecuted supposed witches mercilessly.

       a. opponent b. victim c. triumph d. visible form

_____ 8. The account of a Dutch boy saving a city from a flood by inserting his finger in the dike is *an engaging* story that people have enjoyed for centuries.

       a. an unpleasant b. a dishonest c. a poorly structured
       d. an appealing

_____ 9. The advertiser developed a campaign around the *macho* image of a tough-looking cowboy with bronzed skin and muscled physique.

       a. masculine b. literary c. caring d. dictatorial

_____ 10. In that *maudlin* movie, the heroine cried through an entire scene, at the end of which she fainted into her lover's arms. Many in the audience wept with her.

       a. colorful b. subtle and restrained c. overly sentimental
       d. philosophical

_____ 11. The windows in the old abandoned barn had not been opened for years, so we were hardly surprised to find that the air inside was *musty*.

       a. invigorating b. pure c. stale d. steamy

_____ 12. The city mouse was sophisticated and knew the ways of the world; the country mouse, on the other hand, was *naive*.

       a. simple b. quiet c. honest d. unfortunate

_____ 13. If you borrow money from a pawnbroker, you must leave something of equal value. The *redemption* of your merchandise can take place only when you pay back the loan.

       a. purchase b. investigation c. loss d. recovery

_____ 14. Some people think that smoking in a restaurant is inconsiderate; others go further and consider it *repulsive* because it ruins their enjoyment.

       a. impolite b. disgusting c. dangerous d. sophisticated

_____ 15. The recording studio was specially designed to maximize the *resonance* of the singers' voices, which resulted in rich and ringing tones.

       a. melody b. vibration c. noise d. harmony

_____ 16. It took *sheer* persistence for Marie Ashton to play the piano for five days and thirteen hours straight in August, 1958, in Blyth, England.

       a. some b. wicked c. absolute d. delicate

_____ 17. To state conclusively that raising taxes will hurt the economy is *simplistic*; too many other factors influence the relationship between taxes and the economy to make such a definite statement.

       a. false b. naive c. incoherent d. cynical

_____ 18. Inspectors found that conditions at the nursing home were *unspeakably* filthy.

a. doubtfully   b. indescribably   c. vicariously   d. casually

_____ 19. Amish farmers display their *unworldliness* by living simple lives and ignoring modern technology.

a. foresight   b. superstition   c. lack of interest in material goods
d. acceptance of new ideas

_____ 20. In the novel *Bleak House*, Charles Dickens tells a heart-rending story about *a waif* named Jo, a young orphan left to fend for himself on the streets of London.

a. an unappreciated child   b. a delinquent child   c. a child without home or friends   d. a child who is unable to get along with others

Number correct _____ (total 20)

Part B   Target Words in Reading and Literature

You should now have a general idea of the meaning of each target word. Refine your understanding by examining the shades of meaning these words have in the following excerpt.

Stallone's *Rocky*

Pauline Kael

The film Rocky *was released in 1976 and became an immediate box-office success. At the time of release, Sylvester Stallone, who wrote the script and played the lead role, was an obscure actor and unknown writer. Pauline Kael, one of the nation's most famous movie critics, reviewed the movie for the* New Yorker *magazine.*

Chunky, muscle-bound Sylvester Stallone looks **repulsive** one moment, noble the next, and sometimes both at once. In *Rocky*, which he wrote and stars in, he's a thirty-year-old club fighter who works as a stong-arm man, collecting money for a loan shark. Rocky never got anywhere, and he has nothing; he lives in a Philadelphia tenement, and even the name he fights under—the Italian Stallion—has become a joke. But the world heavyweight champion, Apollo Creed (Carl Weathers), . . . announces that for his Bicentennial New Year's fight he'll give an unknown a shot at the title, and he picks the Italian Stallion. . . . This small romantic fable is about a palooka gaining his manhood. . . . *Rocky* is a threadbare patchwork of old-movie bits, . . . yet it's **engaging**, and the **naive** elements are emotionally effective. John G. Avildson's directing is his usual strictly-from-hunger approach; he slams through a picture like a poor man's Sidney Lumet.[1] But a more painstaking director would have been too proud to

5

10

---

[1] Sidney Lumet: movie director whose work has been widely praised for its artistry

shoot the mildewed ideas and would have tried to throw out as many as possible and to conceal the others—and would probably have wrecked the movie. *Rocky* is shameless, and that's why—on a certain level—it works. What holds it together is innocence.

In his offscreen **bravado**, Stallone (in Italian *stallone* means stallion) has claimed that he wrote the script in three and a half days, and some professional screenwriters, seeing what a ragtag of a script it is, may think that they could have done it in two and a half. But they wouldn't have been able to believe in what they did, and it wouldn't have got the audience cheering, the way *Rocky* does. The innocence that makes this picture so winning **emanates** from Sylvester Stallone. It's a street-wise, flowers-blooming-in-the-garbage innocence. Stallone plays a **waif**, a strong-arm man who doesn't want to hurt anybody, a loner with only his pet turtles to talk to. Yet the character doesn't come across as **maudlin**. Stallone looks like a big, battered Paul McCartney. There's bullnecked energy in him, smoldering; he has a field of force, like Brando's.[2] And he knows how to use his overripe, cartoon sensuality—the eyelids at half-mast, the sad brown eyes and twisted, hurt mouth. . . . Stallone is aware that we see him as a hulk, and he plays against this comically and tenderly. In his deep, caveman's voice, he gives the most surprising, fresh shadings to his lines. He's at his funniest trying to explain to his boss why he didn't break somebody's thumbs, as he'd been told to; he's even funny talking to his turtles. He pulls the whiskers off the film's **cliché** situations, so that we're constantly charmed by him, waiting for what he'll say next. He's like a child who never ceases to amaze us.

Stallone has the gift of direct communication with the audience. Rocky's naive observations come from so deep inside him that they have a Lewis Carroll[3] enchantment. His **unworldliness** makes him seem dumb, but we know better; we understand what he feels at every moment. Rocky is the **embodiment** of the

out-of-fashion pure-at-heart. His **macho** strut belongs with the ducktails of the fifties—he's a sagging peacock. I'm not sure how much of his **archaism** is thought out, how much is the accidental result of Stallone's overdeveloped, weight lifter's muscles combined with his **simplistic** beliefs, but Rocky represents the **redemption** of an earlier ideal—the man as rock for woman to cleave to. Talia Shire plays Adrian, a shy girl with glasses who works in a pet store. . . . It's **unspeakably musty**, but they put it over; her delicacy (that of a button-faced Audrey Hepburn[4]) is the right counterpoint to his primitivism. It's clear that he's drawn to her because she isn't fast or rough and doesn't make fun of him; she doesn't make hostile wisecracks, like the other woman in the pet store, or talk dirty, like the kids in the street. We don't groan at this, because he's such a tortured macho nice-guy—he has failed his own high ideals. And who doesn't have a soft spot for the teen-age aspirations **congealed** inside this thirty-year-old bum?

Stallone is the picture, but the performers who revolve around him are talented. Carl Weathers, a former Oakland Raiders linebacker, is a real find. His Apollo Creed has the flash and **ebullience** to put the fairy-tale plot in motion; when the champ arrives at the ring dressed as Uncle Sam, no one could enjoy the racial joke as much as he does. Adrian's heavyset brother Paulie is played by Burt Young, who has been turning up in movies more and more frequently in the past three years and still gives the impression that his abilities haven't begun to be tapped. Young, who actually was a professional fighter, has the cracked, mottled voice of someone who's taken a lot of punishment in the sinuses; the **resonance** is gone. As Mickey, the ancient pug who runs a fighters' gym, Burgess Meredith uses the harsh, racking sound of a man who's been punched too often in the vocal cords. . . .

Rocky is the kind of movie in which the shots are underlighted, because the characters are poor and it's wintertime. I was almost never convinced that the camera was in the right place. The shots don't match well, and they're put together jerkily, with cheap romantic music thrown in like cement blocks of lyricism, and **sheer** noise used to build up excitement at the climactic prizefight, where the camera is so close to the fighters that you can't feel the rhythm of the encounter. And the film doesn't follow through on what it prepares. Early on, we see Rocky with the street-corner kids in his skid-row neighborhood, but we never get to see how these kids react to his training or to the fight itself. Even the bull mastiff who keeps Rocky company on his early-morning runs is lost track of. . . .

Stallone can certainly write; that is, he can write scenes and a dialogue. But as a writer he stays inside the character; we never get a clear outside view of Rocky. For that, Stallone falls back on clichés, on an urban primitive myth; at the end, Rocky has everything a man needs—his manhood, his woman, maybe even his dog. . . .

---

[2] Brando: Marlon Brando, an actor known for his portrayal of tough and passionate characters
[3] Lewis Carroll: the author of *Alice in Wonderland*
[4] Audrey Hepburn: actress admired for her delicate beauty

Refining Your Understanding

For each of the following items, consider how the target word is used in the passage. Write the letter of the word or phrase that best completes each sentence.

_____ 1. Rocky is not a *maudlin* (line 27) character, but he could have been because   a. given the rags-to-riches plot, it would have been easy to over sentimentalize   b. other people felt sorry for him   c. he is a strong and likable character.

_____ 2. A *cliché* (line 35) situation is one that   a. has been used so often that it is predictable and stale   b. contains a well-known expression   c. has been poorly acted or directed.

_____ 3. *Redemption* (line 46), as Kael uses the term, suggests a. monetary repayment   b. religious truth   c. reclaiming past values

_____ 4. By describing Rocky's relationship with Adrian as *musty* (line 48), Kael means that the basic story line is a. mythical   b. old and trite   c. inept.

_____ 5. The music that builds up to the climax is described as *sheer* (line 72) noise because   a. it is thin and transparent   b. it suggests steep barriers   c. it is intense sound without musical quality.

Number correct _____ (total 5)

Part C   Ways to Make New Words Your Own

This section presents activities that will help you make the target words part of your permanent vocabulary.

Using Language and Thinking Skills

Finding the Unrelated Word Write the letter of the word that is not related in meaning to the other words in the set.

_____ 1. a. engaging   b. attractive   c. aloof   d. charming

_____ 2. a. simple   b. innocent   c. naive   d. sophisticated

_____ 3. a. feeble   b. macho   c. virile   d. manly

_____ 4. a. victim   b. personification   c. embodiment   d. form

_____ 5. a. stale   b. fresh   c. moldy   d. musty

_____ 6. a. partial   b. thorough   c. sheer   d. complete

_____ 7. a. ebullience   b. exuberance   c. excitement   d. enervation

_____ 8. a. rebel   b. orphan   c. child   d. waif

_____ 9. a. indescribably   b. unspeakably   c. untypically   d. inexpressibly

_____ 10. a. salvation   b. sin   c. redemption   d. deliverance

Number correct _____ (total 10)

Practicing for Standardized Tests

Analogies Write the letter of the word pair that best expresses a relationship similar to that expressed in the original pair.

_____ 1. BRAVADO : HUMILITY ::   (A) courage : war   (B) companion : friend   (C) cynicism : idealism   (D) anguish : discomfort   (E) ardor : fervor

_____ 2. THEE : ARCHAISM ::   (A) loyalty : virtue   (B) irreverence : piety (C) child : parent   (D) go : noun   (E) friend : friendship

_____ 3. RAT : REPULSIVE ::   (A) metal : wooden   (B) cliff : sheer (C) misanthrope : philanthropic   (D) memories : current (E) authority : illegal

_____ 4. UNWORLDLINESS : PRACTICALITY ::   (A) hermit : monk (B) child : orphan   (C) hunger : starvation   (D) spiritual : physical (E) teacher : faculty

_____ 5. EMANATE : ISSUE ::   (A) love : like   (B) whimper : sob (C) soliloquize : daydream   (D) tamp : pack   (E) throw : catch

_____ 6. BOREDOM : EBULLIENCE ::   (A) chaos : control   (B) scholar : teacher   (C) politician : politics   (D) farmer : field   (E) coach : game

_____ 7. SOUND : RESONANCE ::   (A) stalemate : compromise (B) indifference : apathy   (C) actor : actress   (D) light : reflection (E) elegance : refinement

_____ 8. SIMPLISTIC : SOPHISTICATED ::   (A) taut : tight   (B) complete : partial   (C) stingy : generous   (D) shy : reserved   (E) perceptive : insightful

_____ 9. BLOOD : CONGEAL ::   (A) water : freeze   (B) dinner : serve (C) lies : manifest   (D) ice : melt   (E) snow : fall

_____ 10. PLATITUDE : CLICHÉ ::   (A) sympathy : aloofness   (B) utterance : word   (C) sentence : archaism   (D) letter : pen   (E) blank : form

Number correct _____ (total 10)

Word's Worth: cliché

Cliché was originally a technical term used by printers. The word referred to a metal printing plate that duplicated a plate made from less durable material. This process, which was called _stereotyping_, enabled printers to use the same plate repeatedly. In the twentieth century, _cliché_ gradually took on a wider application and now refers to any expression that has been repeated so often that its meaning is trite and commonplace.

Spelling and Wordplay

Crossword Puzzle Read the clues and print the correct answer to each in the proper squares. There are several target words in the puzzle.

ACROSS

1. State or condition of not being worldly-wise
12. Pretended courage
13. A negative word
14. Seldom used word meaning "to hurry or hasten"
16. Told a falsehood
17. Very serious
19. Abbr. *French*
20. A radioactive gas
21. Abbr. *Electronic Proving Ground*
22. Abbr. *Naval Station*
25. Abbr. *Restricted Landing Area*
26. Abbr. *South*
27. Tearfully sentimental
30. Abbr. *Indo-Germanic*
31. Begs
32. Father's nickname
33. Spanish *yes*
34. Abbr. *Each*
36. Abbr. *Standard*
37. An outdated word
41. A swine
42. A building site
43. Abbr. *Id Est* ("that is")
44. Abbr. *Indo-China*
45. French for *friend*
46. Abbr. *Army Reserve*
47. Abbr. *State*
49. To coagulate or jell
52. Abbr. *Alcoholics Anonymous*
53. Abbr. *Light Observation Helicopter*
54. Having a stale, moldy smell
56. The state of being embodied

DOWN

1. Abbr. *Union of Burma*
2. Abbr. *National Research Library*
3. An orphan
4. All done
5. Abbr. *Radius*
6. Abbr. *Learning Disabled*
7. Disney's duck
8. In securely (2 words)
9. Midday
10. Steep
11. Oversimplified
15. Charming and attractive
18. Beyond spoken description
23. Of the sun
24. A shoulder___ ___ ___

27. Very masculine
28. Objective case of *we*
29. Childlike
35. Contraction of *I am*
36. Saliva
38. A trite expression
39. Preposition meaning "on," "in," "near," or "by"
40. Certain
43. Sick
46. Abbr. *Adjutant General*
47. To daze
48. Settles a debt
50. Slang: "the head"
51. Abbr. *American Virgin Islands*
52. Abbr. *Attorney*
54. Objective case of *I*
55. Abbr. *Saint*

Part D   Related Words

A number of words are closely related to the target words you have studied. Use your knowledge of the target words and of word parts to determine the meanings of these words. (For information about word parts analysis, see pages 6-12.) If you are unsure of any definitions, use your dictionary. Learning these related words expands your vocabulary and helps you learn the target words more thoroughly.

1. archaic (är kā′ ik) adj.
2. bravura (brə vyoor′ə) n.
3. ebullient (i bool′ yənt) adj.
4. emanation (em′ə nā′ shən) n.
5. embody (im bäd′ē) v.
6. engage (in gāj′) v.
7. engagement (in gāj′ mənt) n.
8. machismo (mä chēz′ mö′ chô) n.
9. naiveté (nä ēv tā′) n.
10. redeem (ri dēm′) v.
11. redemptive (ri demp′ tiv) adj.
12. repulse (ri puls′) v.
13. resonant (rez′ ə nənt) adj.
14. resonate (rez′ ə nāt′) v.
15. resounding (ri zound′ iŋ) adj.
16. unworldly (un wʉrld′ lē) adj.

Understanding Related Words

Sentence Completion In the blank write the word that best completes the meaning of the sentence.

archaic   engagement
bravura   machismo
ebullient   naiveté
emanation   redeem
embody   repulse

1. The English used by early British writers now seems _____ to us.

2. We were amazed at Carla's _____ ; her comments were so simplistic that they made her sound like a child.

3. Ms. Calderon planned to _____ her coupons at the local supermarket in order to save on her weekly grocery bill.

4. Luis and Sue announced their _____ on the wedding anniversary of Sue's parents.

5. The political expert said that the new candidate would need

    to _____ a new philosophy and vision of the future.

6. The boys were trying to demonstrate their _____ by displaying their muscles and speaking in deep voices.

179

7. Jenny attempted to _____ the menacing dog with her umbrella.

8. The scientists calculated how to stop the _____ of poisonous gases from the abandoned garbage dump.

9. The _____ winning team held their coach aloft and shouted for joy.

10. The flamboyant musician played with passion and _____ .

Number correct _____ (total 10)

True-False Decide whether each statement is true or false. Write **T** for True and **F** for False.

_____ 1. A violin can have a *resonant* tone.

_____ 2. When a pin drops on the floor, it makes a *resounding* noise.

_____ 3. Boxers and football players seldom illustrate the characteristics of *machismo*.

_____ 4. You would expect a monk or a mystic to be *unworldly*.

_____ 5. If you were a singer, you would not want your voice to *resonate*.

Number correct _____ (total 5)

Turn to **The Addition of Prefixes** on page 203 of the **Spelling Handbook.** Read the rule and complete the exercise provided.

Analyzing Word Parts

The Latin Prefixes *en-/em-* and *re-* The prefixes *en-/em-* ("in" or "into") and *re-* ("back" or "backward") are found in many of the target and related words in this unit. Use your knowledge of these words to match the definitions on the left with the correct words on the right. Write the letter in the blank.

_____ 1. to send back sound   a. redeem

_____ 2. to enter into conflict or battle   b. embody

_____ 3. to buy back   c. resound

_____ 4. to make into bodily form   d. engage

_____ 5. the state of being saved from sin   e. redemption

Number correct _____ (total 5)

Number correct in Unit _____ (total 65)

The Last Word

Writing

Sometimes there is a thin line between real bravery and mere *bravado*. Write a brief essay in which you explain the difference between *bravery* and *bravado*. Use examples to illustrate the difference.

Speaking

Working in groups of three, create a plan for a *maudlin* made-for-television movie. Think of a plot and some pathetic characters that will leave the audience misty-eyed. After your planning is complete, one member of your group should describe your movie idea to the whole class.

Group Discussion

A famous critic by the name of Lionel Trilling once said that *clichés* "seem to close for us the possibility of thought and imagination." Discuss what you think Trilling might have meant by this statement. Why such harsh words about harmless everyday expressions? Do *clichés* play a role in our language, or should we strive to eliminate them from our writing and speech?

U N I T **16:**   *Review of Units 13–15*

Part A   *Review Word List*

Unit 13 Target Words

1. aloof
2. aphorism
3. austere
4. bisect
5. casual
6. demeanor
7. domain
8. elegance
9. enigmatic
10. exemplify
11. explicitly
12. impose
13. inscribe
14. magnetism
15. obliterate
16. prime
17. profound
18. reactionary
19. rigor
20. tantamount

Unit 13 Related Words

1. aloofness
2. austerity
3. casually
4. casualty
5. dissect
6. dominate
7. elegant
8. enigma
9. exemplary
10. implicit
11. imposition
12. magnetic
13. obliteration
14. primeval
15. primitive
16. profundity
17. reaction
18. rigorous

Unit 14 Target Words

1. advent
2. capital
3. desolation
4. domestic
5. foresight
6. gaunt
7. hale
8. manifest
9. misanthrope
10. peevish
11. perseverance
12. pious
13. reserved
14. resolution
15. sentiment
16. solicit
17. soliloquize
18. solitary
19. tumult
20. wince

Unit 14 Related Words

1. capitalism
2. desolate
3. domesticity
4. domicile
5. foresee
6. hindsight
7. manifestation
8. peeve
9. persevere
10. piety
11. reservation
12. resolute
13. resolve
14. sentimentality
15. solicitous
16. soliloquy
17. solitude
18. tumultuous

Unit 15 Target Words

1. archaism
2. bravado
3. cliché
4. congeal
5. ebullience
6. emanate
7. embodiment
8. engaging
9. macho
10. maudlin
11. musty
12. naive
13. redemption
14. repulsive
15. resonance
16. sheer
17. simplistic
18. unspeakably
19. unworldliness
20. waif

Unit 15 Related Words

1. archaic
2. bravura
3. ebullient
4. emanation
5. embody
6. engage
7. engagement
8. machismo
9. naiveté
10. redeem
11. redemptive
12. repulse
13. resonant
14. resonate
15. resounding
16. unworldly

Inferring Meaning from Context

For each sentence write the letter of the word or phrase that is closest to the meaning of the word or words in italics.

_____ 1. "What *a capital* idea!" exclaimed Fred.
   a. an excellent   b. a common   c. a profitable   d. a practical

_____ 2. The teacher advised us to avoid *clichés* in our writing.
   a. philosophic statements   b. flowery expressions   c. trite expressions
   d. mistakes in usage

_____ 3. The *desolation* of the vast desert unnerved the tourists.
   a. barrenness   b. dryness   c. heat   d. size

_____ 4. Some film critics regard James Dean as the *embodiment* of youthful rebellion.
   a. victim   b. leader   c. hero   d. personification

_____ 5. The new regulations *imposed* by the factory manager were not popular
     with the employees.
   a. put in place   b. scoffed at   c. defined   d. planned

_____ 6. The city officials said that the new monument would have the names of
     those who died in Vietnam *inscribed* on it.
   a. drawn   b. displayed   c. engraved   d. painted

_____ 7. The movie was so *maudlin* that we were embarrassed by it.
   a. pious   b. sentimental   c. violent   d. trite

_____ 8. Only *a naive* person could believe that a warning would deter a criminal.
   a. a virtuous   b. an unsophisticated   c. a hopeful   d. a silly

_____ 9. The fire *obliterated* the trees on the west side of the mountain.
   a. damaged   b. destroyed   c. illumined   d. threatened

_____ 10. It takes *perseverance* to become successful in business.
   a. intelligence   b. skill   c. persistence   d. patience

_____ 11. She seemed dedicated to the *solitary* life of a scholar.
   a. isolated   b. intellectual   c. quiet   d. reserved

_____ 12. The discovery had *a profound* effect on subsequent research projects.
   a. a discouraging   b. a far-reaching   c. an immediate
   d. a philosophical

_____ 13. The *rigor* of the climb discouraged all but the hardiest mountaineers.
   a. length   b. difficulty   c. height   d. danger

_____ 14. Guy would not reveal his *sentiments* concerning the presidential election.
   a. predictions   b. prejudices   c. feelings   d. fears

_____ 15. Mayumi denounced the plan as *sheer* nonsense.
   a. ridiculous   b. immature   c. thoughtless   d. complete

Number correct _____ (total 15)

Using Review Words in Context

Context Awareness Using context clues, determine which word from the list below best completes each sentence in the story. Write the word in the blank. Each word is used once.

aloof	cliché	explicitly
aphorism	demeanor	foresight
austere	domain	naive
bravado	elegance	reserved
casual	emanating	tumult

Tell It to the Judge

In the late morning on a bright summer day, George walked toward the courthouse. As usual, his mind was pulled in opposite directions. On the one hand, he was relieved that he had had the _____ to wear cool clothing because the temperature had risen at least fifteen degrees since he had left home. On the other hand, he feared that perhaps his clothes might be too _____ for the formal atmosphere of traffic court. George wondered if the _____ of his best suit and tie might help his case, but he convinced himself that it was useless to worry now.

Upon entering the courtroom, George felt as if he were an intruder in a strange _____ . Amid the crowd of lawyers and accused, he became unusually self-conscious and _____ , for he was afraid of drawing attention to himself. He had planned to enter the room with _____ , but now he could not create the _____ of someone with brave confidence. Eventually, he spied an unoccupied chair where he could sit _____ , trying to ignore the intimidating crowd. He sank into the chair, then he proceeded to go over the speech he had prepared for the judge.

George's confidence slowly rose as he reviewed his speech. He was pleased that so many excuses were crammed into his plea for leniency. He envisioned himself _____ describing each unfortunate circumstance that had compelled him to exceed the speed limit by thirty miles an hour. George believed that the judge would respond favorably.

Before long, the judge's entrance was announced by the bailiff, and the _____ of the courtroom was immediately quieted. At the sight of the stern and _____ judge, George lost all confidence. He could actually hear his knees knocking and feel the sweat _____ from every pore in his body.

When his name was called, George's mind went blank. He walked toward the bench as if he were a robot on an assembly line. When asked how he was going to plead, George even lost the power of speech. He couldn't say anything, let alone recall his prepared speech. He felt like a _____ and foolish little boy overwhelmed by the hard realities of an adult world.

George heard a meek little voice say, "Guilty." He slowly came to the realization that it was his voice.

After paying his fine, George trudged down the courthouse steps. Suddenly, all the excuses in his speech for the judge flooded his mind, and he realized the truth of the old _____ "too little, too late." On his way home, George thought about the feebleness of his excuses. Grudgingly, he admitted to himself that his plan was wrong from the start. An _____ that his grandmother was fond of quoting came to mind: "Honesty's the best policy."

Number correct _____ (total 15)

Part B   Review Word Reinforcement

Using Language and Thinking Skills

Understanding Multiple Meanings Read the definitions and the sentences that use the word. Then write the letter of the definition that fits the sentence.

> **manifest**
> a. readily perceived by the senses (adj.)
> b. to make clear; to reveal (v.)
> c. easy to understand; obvious; evident (adj.)

_____ 1. The river boat did not become *manifest* until it rounded the bend.

_____ 2. The lawyer argued that the evidence would clearly *manifest* the innocence of his client.

_____ 3. The *manifest* logic of her statement persuaded us to support her.

> **prime**
> a. first, best, main, or chief (adj.)
> b. the first part of the day, year, life, etc. (n.)

_____ 4. The choreographer said that the dancer was past her *prime*.

_____ 5. As a good customer, Luis got the *prime* choice of seats at the restaurant.

> **sheer**
> a. transparent (adj.)
> b. absolute (adj.)
> c. pure (adj.)
> d. very steep; perpendicular (adj.)
> e. to swerve or turn aside (v.)

_____ 6. The principal told us that our complaint was *sheer* foolishness.

_____ 7. Everette had to *sheer* to the side to avoid a collision.

_____ 8. The mountain climbers had to turn back after they encountered the *sheer* face of the cliff.

_____ 9. The *sheer* nylon stockings did not cover up the bruise on Sadie's leg.

_____ 10. The road was a *sheer* sheet of ice.

Number correct _____ (total 10)

Practicing for Standardized Tests

Antonyms Write the letter of the word that is most nearly opposite in meaning to the capitalized word.

_____ 1. ALOOF: (A) outgoing (B) casual (C) primitive (D) indifferent (E) magnetic

_____ 2. ENGAGING: (A) dominant (B) offensive (C) charming (D) disoriented (E) discouraged

_____ 3. DOMESTIC: (A) native (B) desolate (C) foreign (D) simplistic (E) national

_____ 4. MUSTY: (A) romantic (B) stale (C) fresh (D) healthy (E) crude

_____ 5. MACHO: (A) dispassionate (B) brave (C) feminine (D) masculine (E) intellectual

_____ 6. HALE: (A) robust (B) fresh (C) healthy (D) old (E) weak

_____ 7. PIOUS: (A) austere (B) irreverent (C) devout (D) vindictive (E) transitory

_____ 8. UNWORLDLINESS: (A) sophistication (B) innocence (C) irrelevance (D) stupidity (E) simplicity

_____ 9. REACTIONARY: (A) chemical (B) progressive (C) cautious (D) ordinary (E) agitated

_____ 10. REPULSIVE: (A) loathing (B) primitive (C) alluring (D) offensive (E) indifferent

Number correct _____ (total 10)

Synonyms Write the letter of the word whose meaning is closest to that of the capitalized word.

_____ 1. ADVENT : (A) conclusion (B) season (C) beginning (D) expectation (E) addition

_____ 2. BISECT : (A) study (B) infuse (C) compose (D) divide (E) obliterate

_____ 3. CONGEAL : (A) retain (B) ooze (C) embody (D) react (E) solidify

_____ 4. EBULLIENCE : (A) elegance (B) exuberance (C) defiance (D) gaseousness (E) dreariness

_____ 5. ENIGMATIC : (A) maudlin (B) clear (C) sympathetic (D) simplistic (E) cryptic

_____ 6. WINCE : (A) inflict (B) shrivel (C) refuse (D) shudder (E) imply

_____ 7. MAGNETISM : (A) demeanor (B) repulsion (C) ambition (D) attraction (E) deception

_____ 8. PEEVISH : (A) irritable (B) moderate (C) ugly (D) agreeable (E) cheap

_____ 9. SOLICIT : (A) endure (B) reply (C) request (D) exemplify (E) respond

_____ 10. UNSPEAKABLY : (A) expressively (B) critically (C) silently (D) indescribably (E) resolutely

Number correct _____ (total 10)

Analogies Write the letter of the word pair that best expresses a relationship similar to that expressed in the original pair.

_____ 1. SKINNY : GAUNT :: (A) typical : rare (B) elastic : heavy (C) lukewarm : hot (D) verbal : oral (E) temporary : permanent

_____ 2. CASUAL : FORMAL :: (A) excessive : extreme (B) unsteady : resolute (C) kind : generous (D) wealthy : elegant (E) passionate : feverish

_____ 3. WAIF : ORPHAN :: (A) rhyme : poem (B) writing : speech (C) typing : work (D) sentiment : feeling (E) cliché : expression

_____ 4. PRIEST : PIOUS :: (A) father : maternal (B) justice : arbitrary (C) worker : laborious (D) teacher : educational (E) hermit : solitary

_____ 5. MISANTHROPE : BENEVOLENT :: (A) monster : frightening (B) lawyer : wealthy (C) tyrant : domineering (D) parent : fraternal (E) miser : generous

_____ 6. SOUND : RESONANCE :: (A) conductor : orchestra (B) member : group (C) song : speech (D) politician : politics (E) steel : strength

_____ 7. PERSEVERANCE : ADVERSITY :: (A) bravado : humility (B) loneliness : friendship (C) mammal : reptile (D) sympathy : grief (E) vegetation : vegetable

_____ 8. ERASER : OBLITERATE :: (A) school : read (B) memory : forget (C) chisel : inscribe (D) pencil : paint (E) odor : smell

_____ 9. PUNISHMENT : CAPITAL :: (A) housekeeping : domestic (B) silk : silky (C) smell : musty (D) moderation : extreme (E) biology : zoological

_____ 10. REDEMPTION : SALVATION :: (A) naiveté : experience (B) austerity : flexibility (C) business : education (D) solicitation : request (E) etiquette : society

Number correct _____ (total 10)

Spelling and Wordplay

Middle Message Using the clues on the left, write the correct related words in the blanks to the right. The middle letters will reveal an appropriate toast to you.

1. an issuing forth — — — — — | — | — — —

2. give form to — — — | — | — —

3. severe — — — | — | — — —

4. masculinity — — — | — | — —

5. an appearance — — — — | — | — — — —

6. graceful — — — | — | — —

7. obsolete — — | — | — — — —

8. a mystery — — — — | — |

9. to command | — | — — — — —

10. a talk to oneself — — — — | — | — —

11. childlike innocence — — | — | — —

12. alluring — — — — | — | — —

13. implied — — — — | — | — —

14. demanding — — — — | — | — —

15. wisdom — — — — | — | — —

Number correct _____ (total 15)

Part C Related Word Reinforcement

Using Related Words

Sentence Completion Write the related word that best completes each sentence.

capitalism   dominated   casualty   manifestation   soliloquies

1. In battle, an officer is far more likely to become a _____ than is an enlisted man.

2. A clear _____ of superstition can be found in France, where no homes are ever numbered thirteen.

3. _____ is an economic system that maximizes private incentives.

4. One of Shakespeare's most famous _____ begins with Hamlet saying, "To be, or not to be: that is the question."

5. Property ownership in the United States is _____ by the federal government, which owns 34 percent of all the land.

Number correct _____ (total 5)

Reviewing Word Structures

Latin Roots and Prefixes Using your dictionary, find one new word (*not* a target or a related word) for each of the following prefixes and roots. For each word that you find, write a sentence that uses the word correctly.

1. scrib ("write") _____

_____

2. in- ("in, into") _____

_____

3. en- ("in, into") _____

_____

4. sol ("alone") _____

_____

5. re- ("back, backward, again") _____

_____

Number correct _____ (total 5)

Number correct in Unit _____ (total 95)

Vocab Lab 4

FOCUS ON: *The Law*

Improve your vocabulary by learning the following common legal terms.

appellate (ə pel′it) adj. having to do with an appeal. • *Appellate* courts have the power to reexamine decisions of lower courts.

arraignment (ə rān′mənt) n. the act of bringing someone before a court of law to hear and answer charges. • The suspect was held in jail until his *arraignment*.

deposition (dep′ə zish′ən) n. a written testimony made under oath. • Although the witness was out of town, her *deposition* was admitted as evidence in court.

executor (ig zek′yə tər) n. a person appointed to carry out the provisions of another person's will. • Mr. Jackson named his daughter as *executor* of his will.

habeas corpus (hā′be əs kôr′pəs) [Latin, "you should have the body"] n. written order requiring that a prisoner be brought before a court to decide whether he or she is being held legally. • The writ of *habeas corpus* ensures a person's right of not being imprisoned without just cause.

injunction (in juŋk′shən) n. a court order that someone should or should not do something. • Ms. Smith was served an *injunction* ordering her to vacate her office during the IRS investigation.

libel (lī′b'l) n. a false and malicious written statement that unjustly damages someone's reputation. • The senator sued the newspaper for *libel* after a story was published accusing him of tax evasion.

malfeasance (mal fē′z′ns) n. wrongdoing or misconduct, especially by a public official.

• The county commissioner was charged with *malfeasance* for accepting a bribe.

misdemeanor (mis′di mēn′ ər) n. a minor criminal offense that is punishable by fine or imprisonment for less than a year. • Bill was charged with a *misdemeanor* and fined fifty dollars for careless driving.

mortgage (môr′gij) n. an agreement in which someone borrowing money gives the lender claim to property as a pledge that the loan will be repaid. • Before obtaining a *mortgage* to buy a house, find the lowest interest rate.

probate (prō′bāt) n. the act of establishing that an official document is genuine. • Aunt Margaret's will was in *probate* to determine whether or not it was valid.

slander (slan′dər) n. an oral falsehood that damages someone's reputation. • Idle gossip can very easily become *slander*.

subpoena (sə pē′nə) n. an official written order directing someone to appear in court. • The witness to the hit-and-run accident was issued a *subpoena* requiring her to testify in court. v. to order to court with such a document.

tort (tôrt) n. a wrongful act, injury, or damage for which a civil lawsuit may be brought. • When Sam cut down his neighbor's tree in a fit of anger, he did not suspect that this act could constitute a *tort*.

writ (rit) n. a written legal document ordering or prohibiting an action. • The *writ* from the judge ordered the psychiatrist to release the patient's records.

Sentence Completion In the blank write the word from the list that completes each sentence.

1. The rock star maintained that the statements of the talk-show host were innuendoes and lies and constituted _____ .

2. The _____ court had to verify the will's authenticity before the heirs could receive their inheritance.

3. Sheriff Olson served Ms. Johnson with a _____ requiring her to testify at the upcoming trial.

4. The judge declared that the act was not serious enough to be considered a _____ , and therefore there was no basis for a lawsuit.

5. The right of _____ protects people against wrongful imprisonment or detention.

6. At his _____ , the robbery suspect heard the judge read the formal charges filed against him.

7. Even though the key witness to the accident had been dead for six months, the _____ he had given more than a year ago was used as evidence in the trial.

8. Because the accused and her attorney did not agree with the verdict of the court, they submitted the case to an _____ court for further consideration.

9. The police enforced the court _____ against mass demonstrations by telling the picketers to disperse and go home.

10. When the police officers came to search the suspect's home, they presented a search warrant and a _____ ordering him to turn over his financial records.

11. Our family attorney served as _____ of my grandmother's estate, as she requested in her will.

12. The mayor was charged with _____ for allegedly using city funds to cover his personal expenses.

13. Alison was charged with disturbing the peace, a _____ that did not involve severe punishment but would nevertheless remain on her record.

14. Ramon took out a _____ on his house so that he could borrow enough money to start a new business.

15. The actor brought a lawsuit against the newspaper for _____ , stating that the malicious gossip printed in the paper had damaged his reputation and made it difficult for him to get work.

Number correct _____ (total 15)

FOCUS ON: *American and British English*

English is English. Or is it Australian, Canadian, American, or something else? To an American on tour in Britain or to an English citizen traveling in America, the answer may be "something else." For example, following directions can present some problems. Would you understand a British cousin who advised going about a kilometer (almost a mile) down the road, just past the chemist's shop (pharmacy) in order to find the cinema (movie theater)? Such differences exist because living languages grow and change in a natural way. A language grows by continually developing new words to meet new situations.

The English that the British colonists brought to America in the seventeenth century began to take on a separate identity almost immediately. Early settlers encountered unknown things and added new words to the language by simplifying the Indian names for these things. Soon American English contained words such as *skunk, raccoon, rattlesnake,* and *possum.* Invention served when there was no name for *jack-in-the-pulpit, spelling bee,* and *landslide.* French and Spanish explorers contributed many place names, and later immigrants from many parts of Europe enriched American English with words from their native tongues. By 1828 Noah Webster spoke out for the need for an American dictionary. In that year he compiled the first *American Dictionary of the English Language.* His philosophy, stated in the preface to the dictionary, reflects not only the need for a separate dictionary, but shows how political independence from England influenced the language:

> It is not only important, but, in a degree necessary, that the people of this country should have an *American Dictionary of the English Language.* . . . Language is the expression of ideas; and if the people of our country cannot preserve an identity of ideas, they cannot retain an identity of language. . . . No person in this country will be satisfied with the English definitions of the words *congress, senate* and *assembly, court,* etc., for although these are words used in England, yet they are applied in this country to express ideas which they do not express in that country.

What's the Difference?

Actually, the differences between American and British English are minor, not much more extensive than those that distinguish various American dialects. These differences are confined to some vocabulary items, a few spellings and grammatical points, and selected pronunciations and speech patterns, such as those listed below.

Vocabulary			Spelling	
American	**British**		**American**	**British**
billion	milliard		cider	cyder
cracker	biscuit		connection	connexion
elevator	lift		curb	kerb
French fries	chips		favor	favour
garbage collector	dustman		jail	gaol
kerosene	paraffin		realize	realise
potato chips	crisps		theater	theatre
private school	public school			

Pronunciation

American		British	
been (bin, ben)	frontier (frun tir′)	(bēn)	(frun′tir)
class (klas)	laboratory (lab′rə tôr′ ē)	(kläs)	(lə bär′ə tər ē)

Household Words Use context clues to determine the meanings of the italicized household words in British English. Write the American English equivalents.

_____ 1. Alice laid the table with her best dishes and silverware and her special linen tablecloth and matching *serviettes*.

_____ 2. The theater manager told the crowd to *queue* up single file in front of the box office.

_____ 3. Mom had to change the baby's *nappy* twice last night.

_____ 4. "The john" is an American euphemism for the *loo*.

_____ 5. Dad likes to take an afternoon nap on the *Chesterfield*.

Number correct _____ (total 5)

Getting the Story Translate the italicized words in the following story from British to American English. Write the American words in the blanks.

Teacher and Student

George Williams had just been named *headmaster* _____ of the new school and decided to move into a *flat* _____ close by.

George borrowed a *lorry* _____ to haul his belongings to the new flat. When the lorry was loaded, he started it up and drove off. He was careful going over the *level crossing* _____ so as not to break anything or be hit by a train. At the *junction* _____ , he looked both ways and pulled onto the *motorway* _____ . Just then he heard a cough from the engine.

George decided to ignore the sound and drove on. He hadn't been driving for five minutes when the lorry coughed again and the engine died. After guiding the lorry onto the *central reservation* _____ between the one-way lanes, he got out and lifted the lorry's *bonnet* _____ . George had no idea what could be wrong.

Just then two *lads* _____ from his school drove up. One of them looked in the cab. "Mr. Williams, look at your gauge. You're out of *petrol* _____ !"

George Williams had learned his first lesson from his students.

Number correct _____ (total 10)

Number correct in Vocab Lab _____ (total 30)

Units 1–8 *Standardized Vocabulary Test*

The following items test your comprehension of words studied in the first half of the book. Test items have been written in a way that will familiarize you with the typical standardized test format. As on most standardized vocabulary tests, test items are divided into the following categories: **antonyms, analogies,** and **sentence completion.**

Antonyms

Each test item below consists of a word in capital letters, followed by five lettered words or phrases. Choose the word or phrase that is most nearly opposite in meaning to the word in capital letters. Because some of the test items require you to distinguish fine shades of meaning, consider all the choices before deciding which is best.

_____ 1. CONTEMPT: (A) hatred (B) temper (C) esteem (D) capacity (E) consent

_____ 2. LETHAL: (A) deadly (B) toxic (C) life-giving (D) medicated (E) colorful

_____ 3. OBSCURE: (A) divert (B) aspire (C) immerse (D) descend (E) reveal

_____ 4. SINGULAR: (A) cynical (B) unique (C) multiple (D) moderate (E) only

_____ 5. LETHARGY: (A) resemblance (B) feature (C) indifference (D) vigor (E) facet

_____ 6. PUGNACIOUS: (A) belligerent (B) unattractive (C) accommodating (D) militant (E) impetuous

_____ 7. IRREVERSIBLE: (A) inanimate (B) changeable (C) helpless (D) irreverent (E) contemptuous

_____ 8. MOBILIZE: (A) organize (B) move (C) coerce (D) disband (E) modify

_____ 9. UNIFY: (A) infuse (B) marry (C) match (D) ameliorate (E) divide

_____ 10. DOMINATE: (A) rule (B) serve (C) benefit (D) mediate (E) govern

_____ 11. VOLATILE: (A) violent (B) angry (C) gaseous (D) stable (E) sinister

_____ 12. AUGMENT: (A) decrease (B) increase (C) change (D) endure (E) compose

_____ 13. EJECT: (A) accept (B) evict (C) deject (D) attain (E) dismiss

_____ 14. CIVILIZED: (A) aristocratic   (B) barbaric   (C) pleasant
(D) talented   (E) cultured

_____ 15. PROVINCIAL: (A) naive   (B) obscure   (C) secluded   (D) lustrous
(E) cosmopolitan

_____ 16. INANIMATE: (A) insensible   (B) lively   (C) senseless   (D) indifferent
(E) incipient

_____ 17. AMELIORATE: (A) improve   (B) dominate   (C) interact
(D) deteriorate   (E) simulate

_____ 18. SHRIVEL: (A) eject   (B) wither   (C) extort   (D) extrapolate
(E) flourish

_____ 19. DREARY: (A) depressing   (B) cheerful   (C) plausible   (D) sinister
(E) costly

_____ 20. AGITATED: (A) prolonged   (B) disturbed   (C) prior
(D) synonymous   (E) tranquil

Number correct _____ (total 20)

Analogies

Each test item below consists of a pair of words or phrases, followed by five lettered pairs of words or phrases. Select the lettered pair that best expresses a relationship similar to that expressed in the original pair.

_____ 1. LUXURIANCE : MODERATION ::   (A) deduction : reduction
(B) excess : temperance   (C) lassitude : lethargy   (D) wealth : money
(E) poverty : privation

_____ 2. AGGREGATION : CROWD ::   (A) barbarian : savage   (B) civilian :
authority   (C) genus : species   (D) virtue : patience   (E) benefactor :
recipient

_____ 3. SEGMENT : WHOLE ::   (A) apple : pie   (B) whole : half   (C) portion :
part   (D) wedge : pie   (E) forest : tree

_____ 4. LASSITUDE : FATIGUE ::   (A) component : building   (B) vacation :
work   (C) postulation : theory   (D) heritage : posterity   (E) abode :
business

_____ 5. SUN : SOLAR ::   (A) star : bright   (B) son : paternal   (C) moon :
lunar   (D) energy : warm   (E) satellite : distant

_____ 6. CONDENSATION : EVAPORATION ::   (A) serenity : disquietude
(B) steam : water   (C) serenity : tranquility   (D) steam : engine
(E) heat : warmth

_____ 7. COERCE : FORCE ::   (A) volunteer : draft   (B) maintain : alter
(C) magnify : glorify   (D) arrest : convict   (E) compel : permit

_____ 8. CORRESPONDENT : WRITE :: (A) descendent : descend
(B) polyglot : speak   (C) benefactor : benefits   (D) employee : employ
(E) contestant : win

_____ 9. SONG : LYRICS :: (A) tune : melody   (B) piano : instrument
(C) sentence : paragraph   (D) music : songs   (E) poem : words

_____ 10. POLYGLOT : MULTILINGUAL :: (A) language : Spanish
(B) polygon : linear   (C) tongue : fluent   (D) aristocrat : genteel
(E) club : international

_____ 11. MILLENNIUM : CENTURY :: (A) falcon : bird   (B) year : birth
(C) century : decade   (D) milestone : age   (E) era : eon

_____ 12. VOCIFEROUS : UNCOMMUNICATIVE :: (A) vigorous : energetic
(B) clamorous : taciturn   (C) talkative : friendly   (D) mute : silent
(E) pious : religious

_____ 13. ARISTOCRAT : ARISTOCRATIC :: (A) barbarian : barbaric
(B) actor : talented   (C) artist : realistic   (D) relative : close
(E) democrat : republican

_____ 14. TACTIC : STRATEGY :: (A) disaster : catastrophe   (B) item :
category   (C) plan : confusion   (D) airplane : airline   (E) pilot : engineer

_____ 15. PLAUSIBLE : IMPLAUSIBLE :: (A) second : third   (B) lost : found
(C) placid : serene   (D) volatile : explosive   (E) credible : believable

Number correct _____ (total 15)

Sentence Completion

Each sentence below has one or two blanks, each blank indicating that
something has been omitted. Beneath the sentence are five lettered words or sets
of words. Choose the word or set of words that best fits the meaning of the
sentence as a whole.

_____ 1. The boys __?__ climbing up the __?__ cliff, but decided it was too
dangerous.
(A) ascended . . . lethal   (B) contemplated . . . sinister (C) endured . . .
mundane   (D) simulated . . . dreary   (E) declined . . . obscure

_____ 2. Due to the __?__ of the fire, the residents of the surrounding homes
were evacuated.
(A) magnitude   (B) consensus   (C) lassitude   (D) deportment
(E) simulation

_____ 3. Sophia lives in a(an) __?__ neighborhood; many people have a
similar __?__ .
(A) prosperous . . . occupation   (B) sinister . . . tactic   (C) remote . . .
mobility   (D) ethnic . . . heritage   (E) economic . . . impression

_____ 4. After studying the clues, Sherlock Holmes __?__ that the butler had committed the murder.
(A) reconciled   (B) endeavored   (C) extrapolated   (D) acquiesced
(E) infused

_____ 5. The accountant, who was commenting on the __?__ state of the company, assured the owner that the business would remain __?__ to the investor.
(A) volatile . . . immersed   (B) civilian . . . extorted   (C) policy . . .
mundane   (D) irrecoverable . . . inanimate   (E) economic . . . beneficial

_____ 6. Louisa has such an even __?__ , it is difficult to imagine her becoming angry.
(A) temperament   (B) interaction   (C) diversion   (D) singularity
(E) lethargy

_____ 7. Lush __?__ was destroyed by the __?__ emanating from the power plant.
(A) aggregation . . . coercion   (B) vegetation . . . radiation
(C) luxuriance . . . contamination   (D) species . . . collision
(E) civilization . . . contempt

_____ 8. Although the __?__ was minor, Lana __?__ to the police officer's request and went to the emergency room.
(A) reconciliation . . . aspired   (B) convulsion . . . conferred
(C) collision . . . acquiesced   (D) catastrophe . . . delineated
(E) assertion . . . ascribed

_____ 9. During the debate, Raphael clearly __?__ his team's position.
(A) diverted   (B) ejected   (C) deduced   (D) articulated   (E) exceeded

_____ 10. The orator spoke with __?__ as he tried to __?__ his listeners to avoid drugs.
A) prose . . . endure   (B) assertion . . . extract   (C) lassitude . . .
initiate   (D) luxuriance . . . agitate   (E) ardor . . . induce

Number correct _____ (total 10)

Number correct in Units 1-8 Test _____ (total 45)

Standardized Vocabulary Test

The following items test your comprehension of words studied in the second half of the book. As on most standardized vocabulary tests, test items are divided into the following categories: **antonyms, analogies,** and **sentence completion.**

Antonyms

Each test item below consists of a word in capital letters, followed by five lettered words or phrases. Choose the word or phrase that is most nearly opposite in meaning to the word in capital letters. Because some of the test items require you to distinguish fine shades of meaning, consider all the choices before deciding which is best.

_____ 1. SIMPLISTIC: (A) subsequent (B) complicated (C) enigmatic (D) shrouded (E) straightforward

_____ 2. BRAVADO: (A) distinction (B) obscurity (C) cowardice (D) swagger (E) melancholy

_____ 3. SYMPATHETIC: (A) civilized (B) receptive (C) abject (D) taciturn (E) pitiless

_____ 4. NAIVE: (A) solemn (B) simple (C) temperamental (D) sophisticated (E) intelligent

_____ 5. MELANCHOLY: (A) melodious (B) harmonious (C) estimable (D) depressed (E) cheerful

_____ 6. SECLUSION: (A) exposure (B) assertion (C) privation (D) profusion (E) isolation

_____ 7. SOLEMN: (A) methodical (B) serious (C) frivolous (D) exaggerated (E) foreboding

_____ 8. HALE: (A) peevish (B) frail (C) robust (D) pious (E) animated

_____ 9. MAUDLIN: (A) sentimental (B) unsentimental (C) explicit (D) vital (E) mushy

_____ 10. REPRESS: (A) impress (B) recur (C) depress (D) wrinkle (E) reveal

_____ 11. ALOOF: (A) elusive (B) aloft (C) social (D) costly (E) cool

_____ 12. CASUAL: (A) formal (B) friendly (C) responsible (D) inquisitive (E) solitary

_____ 13. TANTAMOUNT: (A) dissimilar (B) equal (C) paramount (D) profound (E) economical

_____ 14. RESERVED: (A) domestic (B) moderate (C) shy (D) devious (E) boisterous

_____ 15. GAUNT: (A) thin   (B) stout   (C) peevish   (D) hungry   (E) previous

_____ 16. TUMULT: (A) quietude   (B) agitation   (C) excess   (D) privation
(E) chaos

_____ 17. MUSTY: (A) fresh   (B) malodorous   (C) manifest   (D) old   (E) prime

_____ 18. ARCHAIC: (A) austere   (B) antiquated   (C) contemporary
(D) whimsical   (E) ideal

_____ 19. AUTHORITATIVE: (A) forceful   (B) vibrant   (C) submissive
(D) vindictive   (E) idealistic

_____ 20. SOLITARY: (A) exemplary   (B) solemn   (C) aloof   (D) delinquent
(E) accompanied

Number correct _____ (total 20)

Analogies

Each test item below consists of a pair of words or phrases, followed by five
lettered pairs of words or phrases. Select the lettered pair that best expresses a
relationship similar to that expressed in the original pair.

_____ 1. TIGHTROPE : TAUT ::   (A) diamond : hard   (B) cliché : unique
(C) misanthrope : loving   (D) neurosis : healthy   (E) acrobat : inanimate

_____ 2. EXERCISE : VITALITY ::   (A) confinement : emancipation
(B) freedom : seclusion   (C) laws : order   (D) sympathy : extortion
(E) laughter : anguish

_____ 3. AGITATOR : PROVOCATIVE ::   (A) mechanic : artistic   (B) leader :
authoritative   (C) waif : embodied   (D) delinquent : moderate
(E) cynic : sympathetic

_____ 4. POVERTY : PRIVATION ::   (A) toil : idealism   (B) duplicity :
demeanor   (C) aloofness : friendliness   (D) naiveté : innocence
(E) foresight : hindsight

_____ 5. BLOOD : CONGEAL ::   (A) water : freeze   (B) fog : reveal   (C) ice :
melt   (D) parachute : protect   (E) concrete : reinforce

_____ 6. APPREHENSION : WORRY ::   (A) induction : membership
(B) neurosis : well-being   (C) ignorance : stupidity   (D) foreboding :
hindsight   (E) sentiment : joy

_____ 7. DUPLICITY : HONESTY ::   (A) fragility : delicacy   (B) deterioration :
shriveling   (C) prevalence : lingering   (D) perturbation : peevishness
(E) agitation : tranquillity

_____ 8. ENGINEERING : VOCATION ::   (A) train : engineer   (B) vocation :
avocation   (C) stamp collecting : hobby   (D) hockey : rink
(E) training : police officer

_____ 9. INSIGHT : PERCEPTION ::   (A) intuition : hindsight   (B) rumination : meditation   (C) emanation : termination   (D) aspiration : declaration   (E) perturbation : virtue

_____ 10. MAGNETISM : ATTRACT ::   (A) rigor : rest   (B) insight : reveal   (C) duplicity : falter   (D) vindictiveness : cherish   (E) bravado : recur

_____ 11. MYSTERY : ENIGMATIC ::   (A) clue : misleading   (B) novel : romantic   (C) event : historic   (D) comedy : humorous   (E) journal : public

_____ 12. HINDSIGHT : FORESIGHT ::   (A) today : tomorrow   (B) past : future   (C) yesterday : today   (D) front : middle   (E) universe : world

_____ 13. MALE : PATERNALISTIC ::   (A) baby : infantile   (B) teen-ager : juvenile   (C) female : maternalistic   (D) man : adult   (E) girl : feminine

_____ 14. OBLITERATE : ERASER ::   (A) write : pencil   (B) interrelate : story   (C) emanate : cork   (D) escalate : slowdown   (E) duplicate : subtraction

_____ 15. MISANTHROPE : TRUST ::   (A) chef : food   (B) pessimist : hope   (C) reporter : newspaper   (D) teacher : student   (E) skeptic : doubt

Number correct _____ (total 15)

Sentence Completion

Each sentence below has one or two blanks, each blank indicating that something has been omitted. Beneath the sentence are five lettered words or sets of words. Choose the word or set of words that best fits the meaning of the sentence as a whole.

_____ 1. Margaret ___?___ a(an) ___?___ exercise program in order to prepare for the marathon race.
(A) devised . . . austere   (B) induced . . . solemn   (C) revitalized . . . whimsical   (D) solicited . . . vicarious   (E) expressed . . . idealistic

_____ 2. The speaker made a controversial ___?___ that appalled many people in the audience.
(A) assertion   (B) repression   (C) virtue   (D) intuition   (E) vindication

_____ 3. The use of so many ___?___ added to the ___?___ of the speech.
(A) clichés . . . dullness   (B) utterances . . . obliteration   (C) prerequisites . . . neurosis   (D) ideals . . . resonance   (E) virtues . . . deviousness

_____ 4. The ___?___ displayed by the host was ___?___ to his guests.
(A) anguish . . . pugnacious   (B) bravado . . . ruminating   (C) vitality . . . seamy   (D) hauteur . . . repulsive   (E) foreboding . . . reassuring

_____ 5. A fresh coat of paint __?__ the scuff marks on the wall.
(A) solicited   (B) redeemed   (C) obliterated   (D) comprised
(E) bisected

_____ 6. Cornell was known for his __?__ wisdom and his unusual __?__ for
remembering everything he read.
(A) solicitous . . . demeanor   (B) diabolical . . . advent   (C) provocative . . .
ebullience   (D) insightful . . . faculty   (E) unworldly . . . integrity

_____ 7. The soldiers __?__ on a dangerous mission that had been __?__ by their
superior officer.
(A) embarked . . . devised   (B) engaged . . . warranted   (C) faltered . . .
provoked   (D) escalated . . . issued   (E) deviated . . . duplicated

_____ 8. The __?__ forced his opinions on the people in a __?__ manner.
(A) waif . . . melancholy   (B) dictator . . . peremptory   (C) delinquent . . .
solicitous   (D) misanthrope . . . paternalistic   (E) aristocrat . . .
duplicitous

_____ 9. A scientist's time-consuming and __?__ research is easily __?__ in the
accuracy of his findings.
(A) sympathetic . . . interrelated   (B) macho . . . resolved   (C) simplistic
. . . faltered   (D) methodical . . . counterbalanced   (E) vital . . . negated

_____ 10. One of the __?__ for attending college is a high school diploma.
(A) sentiments   (B) objectives   (C) virtues   (D) perturbations
(E) prerequisites

Number correct _____ (total 10)

Number correct in Units 9-16 Test _____ (total 45)

SPELLING HANDBOOK

Knowing the meanings of words is of prime importance when it comes to using language correctly. However, another important skill is knowing how to spell the words you use. Good spelling goes hand-in-hand with vocabulary development.

Almost everyone has at least some problems with spelling. Some people have only a few problems; others have problems spelling many of the words they encounter. If you have trouble spelling, be encouraged to know that many others like yourself have learned to spell by following these suggestions.

1. **Proofread everything you write.** Everyone at one time or another makes errors caused by carelessness or haste. By reading through all that you write, you will be able to catch many of your errors.

2. **Learn to look at the letters in a word.** Spelling errors are errors in choosing or arranging the letters that compose a word. Learn to spell a word by examining various letter combinations contained in the different parts of the word. Then memorize these combinations for future use.

3. **Pronounce words carefully.** It may be that you misspell certain words because you do not pronounce them carefully. For example, if you write *probly* instead of *probably,* it is likely that you are mispronouncing the word. Learning how to pronounce words and memorizing certain letter combinations that create particular sounds will help you spell many of the words in our language.

4. **Keep a list of your own "spelling demons."** Although you may not think about it, most of the words you use you *do* spell correctly. It is usually a few specific words that give you the most trouble. Keep a list of the words you typically have trouble spelling. Concentrate on spelling them correctly, and you will show quick improvement.

5. **Memorize and apply the spelling rules given in this Spelling Handbook.** Make sure you understand these rules, or your memory work will be wasted. Practice using the rules so they will become automatic.

Words with Prefixes

The Addition of Prefixes

When a prefix is added to a word, the spelling of the word remains the same. (For information about word parts, see pages 6–12.)

in- + habit = inhabit   *un-* + related = unrelated
re- + present = represent   *fore-* + father = forefather

A prefix can be added to a root as well as to a word. A root is a word part that cannot stand alone; it must be joined to other parts to form a word. A root can be joined with many different prefixes to form words with different meanings. **However, the spelling of the root remains the same.**

di- + vert = divert   *per-* + sist = persist
in- + vert = invert   *con-* + sist = consist

Exercise Complete each sentence with two words from the list that have the same root.

accelerate   conjecture   gesticulating   inexplicable   interjection
aspired   decelerate   implicated   inspired   suggested

1. The actress's performance _____ many young drama students

   who _____ to play similar roles.

2. Marla _____ that instead of _____
   uncontrollably, we use words to convey our ideas.

3. When driving, _____ when approaching a stoplight

   and _____ when the light turns green.

4. Paul's _____ of supposed wisdom was based on

   pure _____ , not fact.

5. Although Mr. Mendel's participation in the scheme seemed

   _____ , the police _____ him.

   Number correct _____ (total 10)

The Prefix *ad-*

The prefix *ad-* changes in the following cases to create a double consonant.

ac- before *c*   *al-* before *l*   *ar-* before *r*
af- before *f*   *an-* before *n*   *as-* before *s*
ag- before *g*   *ap-* before *p*   *at-* before *t*

Examples:

ad- + celerate = accelerate   *ad-* + nounce = announce
ad- + range = arrange   *ad-* + tain = attain

Exercise Add the prefix *ad-* to each of the roots or base words below. Change the spelling of the prefix as appropriate.

1. *ad-* + vent = _____
2. *ad-* + locate = _____
3. *ad-* + plicable = _____
4. *ad-* + sert = _____
5. *ad-* + trition = _____
6. *ad-* + prehension = _____
7. *ad-* + gregation = _____
8. *ad-* + similation = _____
9. *ad-* + gression = _____
10. *ad-* + fluence = _____
11. *ad-* + culturation = _____
12. *ad-* + nexation = _____
13. *ad-* + ray = _____
14. *ad-* + company = _____
15. *ad-* + fect = _____

Number correct _____ (total 15)

The Prefix *com-*

The spelling of the prefix *com-* does not change when it is added to roots or words that begin with the letters *m*, *p*, or *b*.

com- + mon = common   com- + parable = comparable
com- + pound = compound   com- + bat = combat

The prefix *com-* changes to *con-* when added to roots or words that begin with the letters *c, d, g, j, n, q, s, t,* and *v*.

com- + dense = condense   com- + quest = conquest
com- + jecture = conjecture com- + spicuous = conspicuous

The prefix *com-* changes to *col-* when added to roots or words beginning with *l* to create a double consonant.

com- + lect = collect   com- + lide = collide

The prefix *com-* changes to *cor-* when added to roots or words beginning with *r* to create a double consonant.

com- + rupt = corrupt   com- + rect = correct

Exercise Add the prefix *com-* to each of the roots or base words below. Change the spelling of the prefix as appropriate.

1. *com-*+mute = _____

2. *com-*+template = _____

3. *com-*+prisal = _____

4. *com-*+serve = _____

5. *com-*+ference = _____

6. *com-*+sensus = _____

7. *com-*+respond = _____

8. *com-*+press = _____

9. *com-*+bine = _____

10. *com-*+lateral = _____

11. *com-*+fine = _____

12. *com-*+gest = _____

13. *com-*+gregate = _____

14. *com-*+temptuous = _____

15. *com-*+league = _____

16. *com-*+tour = _____

17. *com-*+plement = _____

18. *com-*+quistador = _____

19. *com-*+rugate = _____

20. *com-*+taminate = _____

Number correct _____ (total 20)

The Prefix *in-*

The spelling of the prefix *in-* does not change except in the following cases.
(a) The prefix *in-* changes to *im-* before *m, p,* or *b*.

in- + mediate = immediate   *in-*+ plication = implication
in- + mutable = immutable   *in-* + balance = imbalance

(b) The prefix *in-* changes to *il-* before *l* to create a double consonant.

in- + legal = illegal   *in-* + lustrate = illustrate

(c) The prefix *in-* changes to *ir-* before *r* to create a double consonant.

in- + regular = irregular   *in-* + rational = irrational

Exercise Add the prefix *in-* to each of the roots or base words below. Change the spelling of the prefix as appropriate.

1. *in-* + fer = _____

2. *in-* + tense = _____

3. *in-* + duce = _____

4. *in-* + press = _____

5. *in-* + merse = _____

6. *in-* + cipience = _____

7. *in-* + imitable = _____

8. *in-* + position = _____

9. *in-* + scription = _____

10. *in-* + validate = _____

11. *in-* + pose = _____

12. *in-* + centive = _____

13. *in-* + literate = _____

14. *in-* + hospitable = _____

15. *in-* + ertia = _____

16. *in-* + plicit = _____

17. *in-* + rigate = _____

18. *in-* + migrate = _____

19. *in-* + resistible = _____

20. *in-* + legible = _____   Number correct _____ (total 20)

Prefix ex-

The spelling of the prefix *ex-* does not change when joined to vowels or to the consonants *p*, *t*, *h*, or *c*.

ex- + it = exit   *ex-* + ternal = external
ex- + ample = example   *ex-* + hale = exhale
ex- + press = express   *ex-* + clamation = exclamation

Exception: *Ex-* becomes *ec-* before *c* in the word *eccentric*.
The prefix *ex-* changes to *ef-* before *f*.

ex- + fort = effort   *ex-* + fective = effective

The prefix *ex-* changes to *e-* before most other consonants.

ex- + mancipate = emancipate   *ex-* + rase = erase
ex- + lect = elect   *ex-* + vaporate = evaporate

No common English words begin with the letters *exs*. When the prefix *ex-* is joined to roots that begin with the letter *s*, the *s* is dropped.

ex- + spect = expect   ex- + sist = exist

Exercise Find the misspelled word in each group. Write the word correctly.

_____ 1. exceed
                 exrode
                 extol
                 expound

_____ 2. eject
                 explain
                 elate
                 eplode

_____ 3. explicable
                 evacuate
                 ellapse
                 effrontery

_____ 4. excommunicate
                 exhaust
                 eponent
                 eradicate

_____ 5. effervesce
                 extraneous
                 exmigrate
                 exemplary

Number correct _____ (total 5)

Words with Suffixes

Words Ending in *y*

When a suffix is added to a word ending in *y* preceded by a consonant, the *y* is usually changed to *i*.

envy + *-ous* = envious   rely + *-ance* = reliance
delicacy + *-es* = delicacies   primary + *-ly* = primarily

There are two exceptions:
(a) When *-ing* is added, the *y* does not change.

rely + *-ing* = relying   justify + *-ing* = justifying
envy + *-ing* = envying   defy + *-ing* = defying

(b) Some one-syllable words do not change the *y*.

dry + *-ness* = dryness   shy + *-ness* = shyness

When a suffix is added to a word ending in *y* preceded by a vowel, the *y* usually does not change.

array + *-ed* = arrayed   annoy + *-ing* = annoying
enjoy + *-able* = enjoyable   joy + *-ful* = joyful

Exceptions: day + *-ly* = daily   gay + *-ly* = gaily

Exercise A In these sentences, find each misspelled word and write the correct spelling on the line following the sentence.

1. Julie is trieing hard to make friends by rectifieing her quick temper.

   _____

2. The economy will determine whether or not our financial situation is envyable.

   _____

3. Lisa implyd that the delay in the baseball game was unfortunately typical.

   _____

4. The drama coach was the unifing force behind our successful performance.

   _____

5. The company produced many industryal products, all of which carried extensive warranties.

   _____

6. Joel's frustration with physics was due primaryly to his not understanding the basic theorys.

   _____

7. The Temmermans' gracious hospitality exemplifyed their generosity.

   _____

8. Chris was identifyed as the winner of the sportsmanship trophy.

   _____

   Number correct _____ (total 10)

Exercise B Add the suffixes indicated and write the new word.

1. entity + -es = _____

2. imply + -ed = _____

3. solitary + -ly = _____

4. modify + -ed = _____

5. heavy + -ly = _____

6. gray + -est = _____

7. plenty + -ful = _____

8. convey + -ance = _____

9. pray + -ing = _____

10. terrify + -ed = _____

11. spy + -es = _____

12. stingy + -ness = _____

13. diversify + -ing = _____

14. deny + -able = _____

15. policy + -es = _____

16. allay + -ed = _____

17. tenancy + -es = _____

18. comply + -ance = _____

19. satisfy + -ing = _____

20. controversy + -al = _____

21. testimony + -al = _____

22. charity + -es = _____

23. prey + -ed = _____

24. efficiency + -es = _____

25. duty + -ful = _____

26. accompany + -ment = _____

27. betray + -al = _____

28. extraordinary + -ly = _____

29. destroy + -ing = _____

30. voluntary + -ly = _____

Number correct _____ (total 30)

The Final Silent e

When a suffix beginning with a vowel is added to a word ending in a silent *e*, the *e* is usually dropped.

desolate + -ion = desolation   adventure + -ous = adventurous
expose + -ure = exposure   persevere + -ance = perseverance
reserve + -ed = reserved   peeve + -ish = peevish

When a suffix beginning with a consonant is added to a word ending in a silent *e*, the *e* is usually retained.

shame + -ful = shameful   entitle + -ment = entitlement
austere + -ly = austerely   adventure + -some = adventuresome
subtle + -ty = subtlety   exquisite + -ness = exquisiteness

Exceptions:

true + -ly = truly   whole + -ly = wholly
argue + -ment = argument   awe + -ful = awful

Exercise A In these sentences, find each misspelled word and write the correct spelling on the line following the sentence.

1. Myrna resolveed to work on the report until the committee was wholly satisfied.

   _____

2. The army officer mobilized his troops, ordering them to be extremly cautious.

   _____

3. Contaminateion of the lake enraged local residents.

   _____

4. Although the supermarket advertised low prices, we discovered that compareable prices could be achieveed by patronizeing our neighborhood market.

   _____

5. The mayor called for an allocateion of funds to curb the resurgeence of gang activity in the city.

   _____

6. The hermit lived a life marked by solitude and austereity.

   _____

7. The escalator moved in a hesitateing manner that made people nervous.

   _____

8. After the arguement, Darren felt embarrassed by his behavior.

   _____

9. A sense of forebodeing induced John to seek shelter.

   _____

10. Numerous procedures were discussed at the annual meeting of delegats.

   _____

11. To create a workable budget, the Yamamotos calculated their income conservativly.

   _____

12. Irreversible brain damage occurred because the brain had been depriveed of oxygen.

   _____

13. Every year Mr. Tibbs validates his parking permit and resigns himself to commutting in rush-hour traffic.

   _____

14. Dr. Skinner delicatly removed the splinter and proceeded to bandage my foot.

   _____

15. After peacful negotiations failed, opposeing factions collided in ruthless litigation.

   _____

Number correct _____ (total 20)

Exercise B Add the suffixes indicated and write the new word.

1. issue + -*ing* = _____

2. revenue + -*es* = _____

3. apprehensive + -*ness* = _____

4. universe + -*al* = _____

5. coerce + -*ed* = _____

6. implicate + -*ed* = _____

7. serenade + -*ing* = _____

8. projectile + -*es* = _____

9. spite + -*ful* = _____

10. induce + -*ment* = _____

11. fertile + -*ity* = _____

12. immerse + -*ion* = _____

13. inscribe + -*ing* = _____

14. dictate + -*or* = _____

15. globe + -*al* = _____

16. civilize + -*ed* = _____

17. mobile + -*ity* = _____

18. obstinate + -*ly* = _____

19. culture + -*al* = _____

20. intense + -*ity* = _____

21. coordinate + -*ed* = _____

22. requisite + -*ion* = _____

23. emancipate + -*ion* = _____

24. deteriorate + -*ing* = _____

25. appease + -*ment* = _____

26. calculate + -*ive* = _____

27. imitate + -*ion* = _____

28. reverse + -*ible* = _____

29. mediate + -*ion* = _____

30. vegetate + -*ing* = _____   Number correct _____ (total 30)

Doubling the Final Consonant

In words of more than one syllable, double the final consonant before adding a suffix beginning with a vowel only if the following conditions exist:

1. The word ends with a single consonant preceded by a single vowel.
2. The word is accented on the last syllable.

con fer′ + -ed = con ferred′   com mit′ + -ed = com mit′ ted
pro pel′ + -er = pro pel′ ler   per mit′ + -ing = per mit′ ting
re fer′ + -al = re fer′ ral   de ter′ + -ence = de ter′ rence

Note in the examples above that the syllable accented in the new word is the same syllable that was accented before adding the suffix.

If the newly formed word is accented on a different syllable, the final consonant is not doubled.

re fer′ + -ence = ref′ er ence   con fer′ + -ence = con′ fer ence

Exercise Each word below is divided into syllables. Determine which syllable in each word is accented and insert the accent mark. Look at each suffix indicated, noting if the accent moves to a different syllable with the addition of the suffix. Then write the new word, and if the accent moves, mark the accented syllable.

1. trans mit + -ed = _____ + -al = _____

2. re pel + -ing = _____ + -ent = _____

3. de ter + -ed = _____ + -ing = _____

4. re cur + -ed = _____ + -ence = _____

5. de liv er + -ed = _____ + -able = _____

6. dif fer + -ed = _____ + -ent = _____

7. pre fer + -ing = _____ + -ence = _____

8. in fer + -ed = _____ + -ence = _____

9. ben e fit + -ed = _____ + -ing = _____

10. com mit + -al = _____ + -ing = _____

11. gov ern + -ed = _____ + -ing = _____

12. re fer + -ed = _____ + -ence = _____

13. ed it + -ed = _____ + -or = _____

14. vis it + -ed = _____ + -or = _____

15. ex hib it + -ed = _____ + -or = _____

16. re mit + -ing = _____ + -ance = _____

17. im pel + -ed = _____ + -ing = _____

18. e quip + *-ed* = _____ + *-ing* = _____

19. in hib it + *-ed* = _____ + *-ing* = _____

20. a bet + *-ed* = _____ + *-ing* = _____

Number correct _____ (total 40)

Words Ending in *ize* or *ise*

The suffix *-ize* is added to words to form verbs meaning "to make or become."

tranquil + *-ize* = tranquilize (to make tranquil)

moral + *-ize* = moralize (to make moral)

The *-ise* ending is less common. It is usually part of the base word itself rather than a suffix.

surmise   paradise   advertise   precise

Exercise Decide whether *-ize* or *-ise* should be added to each word or letter group. Then write the complete word.

1. real	_____	11. central	_____
2. ideal	_____	12. critic	_____
3. desp	_____	13. human	_____
4. special	_____	14. organ	_____
5. immortal	_____	15. comprom	_____
6. surpr	_____	16. enterpr	_____
7. disgu	_____	17. idol	_____
8. telev	_____	18. author	_____
9. general	_____	19. superv	_____
10. merchand	_____	20. conc	_____

Number correct _____ (total 20)

The Suffix *-ion*

The suffix *-ion* changes verbs to nouns.

calculate + *-ion* = calculation   direct + *-ion* = direction

regulate + *-ion* = regulation   immerse + *-ion* = immersion

deplete + *-ion* = depletion   discuss + *-ion* = discussion

In the examples above, *-ion* is either added directly to the verb form or the final *e* is dropped before *-ion* is added.

Some verbs, when made into nouns, have irregular spellings.

induce + *-ion* = induction   embark + *-ion* = embarkation
ascribe + *-ion* = ascription   apprehend + *-ion* = apprehension

In the case of words that do not adhere to regular spelling patterns, you must memorize their spellings.

Exercise A Add *-ion* to each of the following words.

1. deteriorate _____   9. express _____

2. assert _____   10. react _____

3. contaminate _____   11. transact _____

4. deviate _____   12. delegate _____

5. postulate _____   13. dislocate _____

6. negotiate _____   14. mediate _____

7. remediate _____   15. decelerate _____

8. eject _____

Number correct _____ (total 15)

Exercise B Each of the following nouns is formed by adding a variation of the *-ion* suffix to a verb. Write the verb form of each. Use a dictionary if needed.

1. implication _____   9. condensation _____

2. augmentation _____   10. modification _____

3. seclusion _____   11. intensification _____

4. civilization _____   12. perturbation _____

5. fertilization _____   13. exposition _____

6. deduction _____   14. erosion _____

7. collision _____   15. acquisition _____

8. resolution _____

Number correct _____ (total 15)

214

Other Spelling Problems

Words with *ie* and *ei*

When the sound is long (ē), it is spelled *ie* except after *c*. If the vowel combination sounds like a long (ā), spell it *ei*.

i before e

belief	relieve	grief	achieve	yield
fierce	brief	thief	piece	

except after c

ceiling	conceive	deceit	deceive	receipt	perceive

or when sounded as *a*

neighbor   sleigh   reign

Exceptions:

either	financier	species	leisure
neither	weird	seize	

You can remember these words by combining them into the following sentence: *Neither financier seized either weird species of leisure.*

Exercise In these sentences, find each misspelled word and write the correct spelling on the line following.

1. The feirce storm swept over the vast fields of wheat.

   _____

2. Several species of birds use camouflage to decieve their enemies.

   _____

3. The man siezed the reins of the sleigh and hurried home.

   _____

4. Various nieghbors consoled the family during their grief.

   _____

5. The boss's wierd behavior weighed heavily on our minds.

   _____

6. Neither acheivement received the acclaim it deserved.

   _____

7. It is difficult to imagine a more decietful operation than the one perpetrated by the thief.

   _____

8. Sally's niece shreiked with delight when she saw her eight cousins.

   _____

9. The store issued a receipt cheifly to substantiate the large purchase we made.

_____

10. A breif but leisurely walk along the pier yielded a feeling of complete relaxation.

_____

Number correct _____ (total 10)

Words with the "Seed" Sound

Only one English word ends in *sede*:

supersede

Three words end in *ceed*:

exceed   proceed   succeed

All other words ending in the sound of *seed* are spelled *cede*:

accede   concede   precede   recede   secede

Exercise A In these sentences, find each misspelled word and write the correct spelling on the line following.

1. The preceding calamity suceded in testing our patience.

_____

2. The latest product claiming to correct receding hairlines superceded any previous preparations.

_____

3. Ms. Jackson acseded to the position of superintendent after she succeeded in receiving her doctorate degree.

_____

4. When the flood waters resede, we will proceed with the clean-up.

_____

5. Several associations conceded their wrongdoings and seceeded from the society.

_____

6. During the preceding performance, the audience was excedingly pleased.

_____

7. The moderator will intercede if the debaters excede their time limits.

_____

8. We hope you succeed with your plan to assede to the top.

_____

9. When the army conseded defeat, proceedings began for signing the treaty.

_____

10. Both governments agreed that the island would be ceeded to the country that interceded in the dispute.

_____

Exercise B Put a check by the five correctly spelled words below.

1. proceed	_____	6. accede	_____
2. precede	_____	7. supercede	_____
3. interseed	_____	8. seceed	_____
4. concede	_____	9. exseed	_____
5. receed	_____	10. succeed	_____

Number correct _____ (total 10)

The Letter c

When the letter _c_ has a _k_ sound, it is usually followed by the vowels _a, o, u,_ or by any consonant except _y_.

_ca_sually   _co_mmunity   _cu_riosity   ins_cr_iption

When the letter _c_ has an _s_ sound, it is usually followed by _e, i,_ or _y_.

elegan_ce_   impli_ci_t   bi_cy_cle

The Letter g

When the letter _g_ has a sound as in the word _go_, it is usually followed by the vowels _a, o, u,_ or by any consonant except _y_.

ele_ga_nt   ri_go_rous   en_gu_lfment   eni_gm_a

When the letter _g_ has a _j_ sound, it is usually followed by _e, i,_ or _y_.

_ge_nder   ri_gi_d   _gy_mnasium

Exceptions: _gi_ggle   _gi_ll   _gi_rl   _gi_ve

Exercise A Decide if the _c_ in each word below has a _k_ or an _s_ sound. Write _k_ or _s_ in the blank.

1. dissect	_____	9. policy	_____
2. capital	_____	10. domicile	_____
3. retroactively	_____	11. interact	_____
4. articulation	_____	12. descend	_____
5. rectify	_____	13. incipience	_____
6. incentive	_____	14. solicit	_____
7. correspond	_____	15. condense	_____
8. commute	_____	16. escalation	_____

17. solvency _____   19. incoherent _____

18. deduce _____   20. acquire _____

Number correct _____ (total 20)

Exercise B Decide if the *g* in each word below has a *j* sound or a sound as in the word *go*. Write *j* or *go* in the blank.

1. magnetic _____   11. forage _____

2. urgency _____   12. organize _____

3. litigate _____   13. integral _____

4. congestion _____   14. genetic _____

5. migrate _____   15. singular _____

6. burgeon _____   16. exceedingly _____

7. degradation _____   17. grimness _____

8. gaunt _____   18. assuage _____

9. polyglot _____   19. gyroscope _____

10. marginally _____   20. gesticulate _____

Number correct _____ (total 20)

Exercise C Find the missing letter or letters in each word.

1. reac __ ion   14. tac __ ic

2. deleg __ te   15. veg __ tate

3. c __ vilization   16. letharg __

4. heritage __   17. transc __ ndent

5. alterc __ tion   18. ac __ eleration

6. aug __ entation   19. provinc __

7. emig __ ate   20. amic __ ble

8. projec __ ile   21. disting __ ish

9. sugg __ stion   22. mag __ animous

10. c __ mprise   23. c __ teg __ ric __ l

11. solac __   24. ag __ reg __ te

12. g __ andeur   25. delic __ c __

13. neg __ tiate

Number correct _____ (total 25)

218

Spelling Review

Exercise A Add the prefix or suffix indicated and write the new word.

1. *ad-* + locate = _____

2. impress + *-ion* = _____

3. solitary + *-ly* = _____

4. reserve + *-ed* = _____

5. unify + *-ing* = _____

6. *ad-* + fluent = _____

7. *com-* + taminate = _____

8. *in-* + imitable = _____

9. *ex-* + rode = _____

10. universe + *-al* = _____

11. precede + *-ent* = _____

12. mobile + *-ize* = _____

13. *com-* + lide = _____

14. *ex-* + pose = _____

15. litigate + *-ion* = _____

16. *ad-* + venture = _____

17. manifest + *-ion* = _____

18. rely + *-ance* = _____

19. *in-* + merse = _____

20. *in-* + poverish = _____

Number correct _____ (total 20)

Exercise B In these sentences, find each misspelled word and write the correct spelling on the line following.

1. The jury anounced that the defendant was found guilty of coercion.

_____

2. Try various activitys until you find out where your talents lie.

_____

3. It was Tony's job to reppresent our class at the meeting.

_____

4. A slight modifycation in car design occured from year to year.

_____

5. As an expretion of our sincerest regrets, we furnished gifts to our neighbors.

_____

6. How much weight did you gain during the preseding year?

_____

7. The provinceial town was known for its rustic quaintness.

_____

8. Violet oppossed any deviation from her original plan.

_____

9. The severity of the drought had been underestimatd.

_____

10. Varyous pieces of the jigsaw puzzle were missing.

_____

11. Larry's confinment after surgery lasted two weeks.

_____

12. My friend regreted her negative comment and apologized.

_____

13. The annoing noise assaulted our senses.

_____

14. Anita deliberatly exluded several people from her list of invited guests.

_____

15. The financeer mobilised our assets and invested in stocks and bonds.

_____

16. Contrary to the dictator's reactionary ideas, some soldiers beleived in civil liberties.

_____

17. Jerome resolutly removeed his fingerprints from the refrigerator and counter.

_____

18. Suppression of Lucy's sentiments seemed inpossible.

_____

19. Joanna tryed to cancel the plane reserveations she had made.

_____

20. The movie was imteresting, entertaining, and ingenious.

_____

Number correct _____ (total 25) Number correct in Handbook _____ (total 385)

Commonly Misspelled Words

abbreviate
absence
accidentally
accommodate
accompanying
achievement
acknowledge
acquaintance
all right
altogether
amateur
analyze
annihilate
anonymous
apologize
appearance
appreciate
appropriate
arctic
argument
arrangement
ascent
assassinate
associate
attendance
audience
auxiliary
awkward
bachelor
bargain
beginning
believe
benefited
biscuit
bookkeeper
bulletin
bureau
business
cafeteria
calendar
calorie
campaign
cellophane
cemetery
changeable

characteristic
colonel
colossal
column
commission
committed
committee
competitive
complexion
compulsory
conscience
conscientious
conscious
consensus
contemptible
convenience
corps
correspondence
courageous
criticism
criticize
cylinder
dealt
decision
definitely
dependent
descent
description
despair
desperate
dictionary
different
dining
diphtheria
disappear
disappoint
disastrous
discipline
dissatisfied
efficient
eighth
eligible
eliminate
embarrass
eminent

emphasize
enthusiastic
equipped
especially
etiquette
exaggerate
excellent
exceptional
exhaust
exhilarate
existence
experience
familiar
fatigue
February
feminine
financial
foreign
forfeit
fragile
generally
genius
government
grammar
guarantee
gymnasium
handkerchief
height
hindrance
humorous
imaginary
immediately
implement
incidentally
inconvenience
incredible
indispensable
inevitable
infinite
influence
inoculation
intelligence
irrelevant
irresistible
knowledge

laboratory
legitimate
leisure
lieutenant
literacy
literature
luxurious
maintenance
maneuver
marriage
mathematics
medieval
miniature
minimum
mischievous
missile
misspell
mortgage
municipal
necessary
nickel
noticeable
nuclear
nuisance
obstacle
occasionally
occur
occurrence
opinion
optimistic
outrageous
pamphlet
parallel
parliament
particularly
pastime
permissible
perseverance
perspiration
persuade
picnicking
pleasant
pneumonia
possess
possibility

practice
preference
preparation
privilege
probably
professor
pronunciation
propeller
prophecy
psychology
quantity
questionnaire
realize
recognize
recommend
reference
referred
rehearse

reign
repetition
representative
restaurant
rhythm
ridiculous
sandwich
schedule
scissors
secretary
separate
sergeant
similar
sincerely
sophomore
souvenir
specifically
specimen

strategy
strictly
subtle
success
sufficient
surprise
syllable
sympathy
symptom
tariff
temperament
temperature
thorough
together
tomorrow
traffic
tragedy

transferred
truly
Tuesday
twelfth
tyranny
unanimous
undoubtedly
unnecessary
vacuum
vengeance
vicinity
village
villain
weird
wholly
writing

Commonly Confused Words

The following section lists words that are commonly confused and misused. Some of these words are homonyms, words that sound similar but have different meanings.   Study the words in this list and learn how to use them correctly.

accent (ak′ sent) n.—stress in speech or writing
ascent (ə sent′) n.—act of going up
assent (ə sent′) n.—consent; v.—to accept or agree

accept (ək sept′, ak-) v.—to agree to something or receive something willingly
except (ik sept′) v.—to omit or exclude; prep.—not including

adapt (ə dapt′) v.—to adjust, to make fitting or appropriate
adept (ə dept′) adj.—proficient
adopt (ə däpt′) v.—to choose as one's own, to accept

affect (ə fekt′) v.—to influence, to pretend
affect (af′ ekt) n.—feeling
effect (ə fekt′, i-) n.—result of an action
effect (ə fekt′, i-) v.—to accomplish or to produce a result

all ready adj.—completely prepared
already (ôl red′ ē) adv.—even now; before the given time

any way adj. (any) and n. (way)—in whatever manner
anyway (en′ ē wa′) adv.—regardless

appraise (ə prāz′) v.—to set a value on
apprise (ə prīz′) v.—to inform

bibliography (bib′ lē äg′ rə fē) n.—list of writings on a particular topic
biography (bī äg′ rə fē, bē-) n.—written history of a person's life

bizarre (bi zär′) adj.—odd
bazaar (bə zär′) n.—market, fair

coarse (kôrs) adj.—rough, crude
course (kôrs) n.—route, progression

costume (käs′ tσσm, -tyσσm) n.—special way of dressing
custom (kus′ təm) n.—usual practice or habit

decent (dē′ s'nt) adj.—proper
descent (di sent′) n.—fall, coming down
dissent (di sent′) n.—disagreement; v.—to disagree

desert (dez′ ərt) n.—arid region
desert (di zʉrt′) v.—to abandon
dessert (di zʉrt′) n.—sweet course served at the end of a meal

device (di vīs′) n.—a contrivance
devise (di vīz′) v.—to plan

elusive (ə lo͞o′ siv) adj.—hard to catch or understand
illusive (i lo͞o′ siv) adj.—misleading, unreal

emigrate (em′ ə grāt′) v.—to leave a country and take up residence elsewhere
immigrate (im′ ə grāt′) v.—to enter a country to take up residence

farther (fär′ *th*ər) adj.—more distant (refers to space)
further (fʉr′ *th*ər) adj.—additional (refers to time, quantity, or degree)

flair (fler) n.—natural ability, knack for style
flare (fler) v.—to flame; to erupt; n.—a blaze of light

lay (lā) v.—to set something down or place something
lie (lī) v.—to recline; to tell untruths; n.—an untruth

moral (môr′ əl, mär′-) n.,—lesson; ethic; adj.—relating to right and wrong
morale (mə ral′, mô-) n.—mental state of confidence, enthusiasm

personal (pʉr′ s'n əl) adj.—private
personnel (pʉr sə nel′) n.—a body of people, usually employed in an organization

precede (pri sēd′) v.—to go before
proceed (prə sēd′, prō-) v.—to advance; to continue

profit (präf′ it) v.—to gain earnings; n.—financial gain on investments
prophet (präf′ it) n.—predictor, fortuneteller

quiet (kwī′ ət) adj.—not noisy; n.—a sense of calm
quit (kwit) v.—to stop
quite (kwīt) adv.—very

step (step) n.—footfall; v.—to move the foot as in walking
steppe (step) n.—large, treeless plain

team (tēm) n.—group of people working together on a project
teem (tēm) v.—to swarm or abound

than (*th*an, *th*en; *unstressed th*en, *th*ən) conj.—word used in comparison
then (*th*en) adv.—at that time, next in order of time

thorough (*th*ʉr′ ō, -ə) adj.—complete
through (*th*ro͞o) prep.—by means of, from beginning to end; adv.—in one side and out the other

Glossary

A

abode (n.) place where one lives; home; p. 24.

absurdly (adv.) ridiculously; p. 13. *Related word*: absurdity; p. 21.

acculturation (n.) process of adjusting to a new culture or country; p. 35.

acquiesce (v.) to go along with; to consent; p. 13.

advent (n.) arrival; p. 161.

agitate (v.) to move violently; to disturb the feelings of; p. 79. *Related word*: agitation; p. 85.

aggregation (n.) accumulation; collection; p. 58. *Related word*: aggregate; p. 65.

aloof (adj.) detached; unconcerned; (adv.) apart; at a distance; p. 150. *Related word*: aloofness; p. 158.

alter (v.) to change; p. 24. *Related words*: alteration, altercation; p. 31.

ameliorate (v.) to make or become better; to improve; p. 35.

anguish (n.) great suffering, as from worry or grief; p. 106.

aphorism (n.) short statement of principle; saying giving a general truth or piece of wisdom; p. 150.

apprehensiveness (n.) worry; fearfulness; p. 117. *Related words*: apprehend, apprehension; p. 125.

archaism (n.) use or imitation of ancient or old-fashioned words or techniques; p. 171. *Related word*: archaic; p. 179.

ardor (n.) passion; enthusiasm; p. 79. *Related word*: ardent; p. 85.

aristocratic (adj.) of the upper class; p. 68. *Related words*: aristocracy, aristocrat; p. 75.

articulate (v.) to express oneself easily and clearly; (adj.) able to speak; p. 35. *Related word*: articulation; p. 42.

ascend (v.) to climb; to rise; p. 13. *Related words with the* cend *root*: ascent, descend, descendant, transcend; p. 21.

ascribe (v.) to attribute; to credit; p. 117. *Related word*: transcribe; p. 125.

aspect (n.) look or appearance; way in which an idea or problem may be regarded; p. 79.

aspiration (n.) strong ambition; inhalation of something into the lungs; p. 35. *Related words*: aspire, inspire; p. 42.

assertion (n.) statement; declaration; p. 68. *Related words*: assert, assertive; p. 75.

assimilate (v.) to become part of; to absorb; p. 58. *Related word*: assimilation; p. 65.

attainment (n.) something achieved; p. 35. *Related word*: attain; p. 42.

augment (v.) to enlarge; to increase; p. 58.

austere (adj.) very plain; forbidding; strict; stern; p. 150. *Related word*: austerity; p. 158.

authoritative (adj.) official; reliable because coming from an expert; p. 106. *Related word*: authoritarian; p. 114.

B

barbarian (n.) primitive or uncivilized person; (adj.) crude; p. 68. *Related word*: barbaric; p. 75.

beneficent (adj.) charitable; generous; p. 13. *Related words with the* bene *root*: benefactor, beneficiary, benefit, benevolent; p. 21.

bisect (v.) to divide into two equal parts; p. 150. *Related word*: dissect; p. 158.

bravado (n.) pretending to be brave when one is really afraid; swaggering conduct; p. 171. *Related word*: bravura; p. 179.

C

capital (adj.) excellent; punishable by death; chief in importance or influence; (n.) money; official seat of government; p. 161. *Related word*: capitalism; p. 168.

casual (adj.) indifferent; accidental; informal; p. 150. *Related words*: casually, casualty; p. 158.

catastrophic (adj.) tragic; disastrous; p. 79. *Related word*: catastrophe; p. 85.

category (n.) classification or grouping; division; p. 35. *Related words*: categorical, categorize; p. 42.

civilized (adj.) refined; having polite manners; p. 68. *Related words*: civil, civilian, civilization, uncivilized; p. 75.

cliché (n.) expression that has become stale from too much use; p. 171.

coerce (v.) to force; p. 13. *Related word*: coercion; p. 21.

collision (n.) crash; p. 58. *Related word*: collide; p. 65.

comparatively (adv.) by comparison; relatively; p. 58. *Related word*: comparable; p. 65.

component (n.) ingredient; (adj.) serving as one of the parts of the whole; p. 58. *Related words with the* pon/pos *root*: exponent, impose, opponent, repose; p. 65.

compose (v.) to make up; to constitute; to put together in proper form; to create a musical or literary work; p. 79.

condensation (n.) reduction of a gas to a liquid; condition of making dense or compact; p. 58. *Related word*: condense; p. 65.

conference (n.) meeting; discussion; p. 13. *Related word*: confer; p. 21.

congeal (v.) to solidify by cooling; to thicken; p. 171.

conjecture (n.) a guessing or predicting from incomplete evidence; a guess (would you care to make a *conjecture* about how much snow we will have this winter?) (v.) to guess; p. 58.

consensus (n.) general agreement; p. 35.

contamination (n.) pollution; p. 24. *Related word*: contaminate; p. 31.

contemplate (v.) to think about; to look at intently; p. 13. *Related word*: contemplation; p. 21.

contempt (n.) scorn; showing disrespect; p. 68. *Related word*: contemptuous; p. 75.

contour (n.) outline; (v.) to shape or mold; (adj.) made to conform to a shape; p. 128.

convulsive (adj.) characterized by violent shaking; spasmodic; uncontrollable; p. 79. *Related words*: convulsion, convoluted; p. 85.

correspondent (n.) person hired by a newspaper or magazine to furnish news articles from a distant place; letter writer; (adj.) matching; p. 13. *Related word*: correspond; p. 21.

counterbalance (n.) any force that balances another; (v.) to offset; p. 128.

counterpart (n.) person or thing that is the same as or looks much like another; p. 24.

cynical (adj.) doubting the sincerity of people's motives; sarcastic; p. 68. *Related word*: cynic; p. 75.

D

deduction (n.) reasoning from known facts to a logical conclusion; subtraction of money; p. 58. *Related word*: deduce; p. 65.

delineate (v.) to trace the outline of; to draw; to describe in words; p. 79. *Related word*: delineation; p. 85.

delinquency (n.) failure to do what is required; p. 128. *Related word*: delinquent; p. 134.

demeanor (n.) behavior; p. 150.

deportment (n.) conduct; behavior; p. 68. *Related word*: deportation; p. 75.

desolation (n.) ruination; loneliness; p. 161. *Related word*: desolate; p. 168.

deviousness (n.) deception; state of not being straightforward; p. 128. *Related words*: deviation, devious; p. 134.

devise (v.) to create; to plan; p. 128.

diabolical (adj.) devilish; very wicked; p. 117. *Related word*: diabolic; p. 125.

distinction (n.) difference; feature that differentiates; p. 13. *Related word*: distinctive; p. 21.

diversify (v.) to vary; p. 24. *Related words*: diverse, diversification, diversion, divert; p. 31.

domain (n.) rule; field of influence; ownership; territory under one government; p. 150. *Related word*: dominate; p. 158.

domestic (n.) servant; (adj.) having to do with home or housekeeping; native; p. 161. *Related words*: domesticity, domicile; p. 168.

dominate (v.) to rule or control; p. 13. *Related word*: dominant; p. 21.

dreary (adj.) gloomy; cheerless; depressing; p. 79.

duplicity (n.) deceit; underhandedness; p. 128. *Related words*: duplication, duplicitous; p. 134.

E

ebullience (n.) bubbling enthusiasm; exuberance; p. 171. *Related word*: ebullient; p. 179.

economic (adj.) having to do with the distribution and consumption of money or with business matters; p. 35. *Related word*: economist; p. 42.

eject (v.) to expel; to discharge; p. 58. *Related words with the* ject *root*: abject, dejection, ejection, interject, projectile; p. 65.

elegance (n.) luxury; dignified grace; p. 150. *Related word*: elegant; p. 158.

emanate (v.) to come forth; to emit; p. 171. *Related word*: emanation; p. 179.

emancipation (n.) freedom; release from bondage or slavery; p. 128. *Related word*: emancipate; p. 134.

embark (v.) to begin; to start a journey; p. 117.

embodiment (n.) formation of an idea or quality; incorporation; incarnation; p. 171. *Related word*: embody; p. 179.

enable (v.) to make possible; p. 13.

endeavor (v.) to make an earnest attempt; (n.) earnest attempt; p. 79.

endure (v.) to hold up under pain; to tolerate; to last; p. 79. *Related words*: durable, endurance; p. 85.

engaging (adj.) attractive; charming; interesting; p. 171. *Related words*: engage, engagement; p. 179.

enigmatic (adj.) mysterious; p. 150. *Related word*: enigma; p. 158.

escalate (v.) to expand step by step; to ascend; p. 128. *Related word*: escalation; p. 134.

ethnicity (n.) classification by nationality, language, culture, or history; p. 35. *Related word*: ethnic; p. 42.

exceed (v.) to be more than or greater than; to surpass; to excel; p. 79.

exemplify (v.) to represent; to show or illustrate by example; p. 150. *Related word*: exemplary; p. 158.

explicitly (adv.) precisely; definitely; clearly; p. 150. *Related word*: implicit; p. 158.

extortion (n.) demanding of too high a price; getting of money by force; p. 68. *Related word*: extort; p. 75.

extract (v.) to draw out by effort; to derive; (n.) concentrated form; excerpt; p. 68.

extrapolate (v.) to arrive at a conclusion based on known facts or observation; p. 58. *Related word*: extrapolation; p. 65.

F

faculty (n.) talent; aptitude; all of the teachers in a school; p. 128.

falter (v.) to stumble; to waver; to weaken; p. 106.

foreboding (adj.) characterized by apprehension; ominous; (n.) premonition; p. 117.

foresight (n.) power to see or know beforehand; p. 161. *Related words*: foresee, hindsight; p. 168.

fundamentally (adv.) basically; chiefly; p. 13.

G

gaunt (adj.) thin and bony; p. 161.

H

hale (adj.) vigorous and healthy; p. 161.

hauteur (n.) scornful pride; snobbery; p. 106. *Related words*: haughtiness, haughty; p. 114.

heritage (n.) something handed down from the past; history; p. 35. *Related word*: inheritance; p. 42.

I

idealism (n.) optimism; practice of forming ideals or living under their influence; p. 128. *Related word*: idealistic; p. 134.

immerse (v.) to plunge; to dip; to become completely involved; p. 58. *Related word*: immersion; p. 65.

impetuous (adj.) acting suddenly with little thought; rash; moving with great force; p. 24.

impose (v.) to place; to inflict; to take advantage of; p. 150. *Related word*: imposition; p. 158.

impress (v.) to affect strongly; to stamp; to fix in the mind; (n.) any mark, imprint, or stamp; p. 13. *Related word*: impression; p. 21.

inanimate (adj.) without life; dull; p. 79. *Related word*: animation; p. 85.

incipient (adj.) beginning; at an early stage; p. 58.

incoherent (adj.) not logically connected; not showing understandable speech or thought; not sticking together; p. 117. *Related word*: coherence; p. 125.

indifferent (adj.) impartial; uninterested; mediocre; p. 13. *Related word*: indifference; p. 21.

induce (v.) to persuade; to bring on; to cause; p. 117. *Related words*: inducement, induct; p. 125.

inequality (n.) lack of equality; difference in size, amount, rank; p. 35. *Related word*: equality; p. 42.

infuse (v.) to put into, as if by pouring; to instill; to impart; p. 79. *Related word*: infusion; p. 85.

initiate (v.) to begin; to introduce; to admit as a member; (n.) person who has been admitted or introduced; (adj.) brought in; introduced; p. 24. *Related words*: initial, initiation; p. 31.

inscribe (v.) to engrave; to write on; p. 150.

insight (n.) ability to see and understand clearly the inner nature of things; p. 106. *Related word*: insightful; p. 114.

integrity (n.) soundness; quality of completeness; honesty; p. 128. *Related word*: integral; p. 134.

interaction (n.) mutual influence or action; p. 24. *Related word*: interact; p. 31.

interpretation (n.) explanation; expression of a person's understanding; p. 35. *Related word*: interpret; p. 42.

interrelated (adj.) connected to one another; p. 106.

intuitive (adj.) knowing without the conscious use of reasoning; understanding in a way that is natural and immediate; p. 106. *Related word*: intuition; p. 114.

irrecoverable (adj.) unable to be regained; irretrievable; p. 24.

irreversible (adj.) not able to be changed back into an earlier form; p. 24. *Related word*: reversible; p. 31.

issue (v.) to discharge; to give out; to publish; (n.) outflow; offspring; publication; p. 117.

L

lassitude (n.) state of being tired and listless; p. 79.

lethal (adj.) deadly; capable of causing death; p. 24.

lethargy (n.) apathy; sluggishness; condition of drowsiness; p. 68. *Related word*: lethargic; p. 75.

lustrous (adj.) having luster; shining; p. 79. *Related word*: luster; p. 85.

luxuriance (n.) abundance; richness; p. 79.

lyric (adj.) poetic; musical; (n.) *usually pl.* words of a song; p. 68. *Related word*: lyricism; p. 75.

M

macho (adj.) masculine; virile; p. 171. *Related word*: machismo; p. 179.

magnetism (n.) power to attract; scientific principle concerning the use of magnets; p. 150. *Related word*: magnetic; p. 158.

magnitude (n.) importance, greatness of size or influence; p. 24. *Related word*: magnanimous; p. 31.

manifest (v.) to show plainly; to prove; (adj.) evident; obvious; p. 161. *Related word*: manifestation; p. 168.

maudlin (adj.) foolishly and tearfully or weakly sentimental; p. 171.

median (adj.) middle; intermediate; (n.) middle number, point, or line; p. 35. *Related word*: mediate; p. 42.

melancholy (adj.) gloomy; depressed; (n.) sadness; depression; p. 117.

methodical (adj.) characterized by method; orderly; systematic; p. 68.

millennium (n.) period of one thousand years; p. 24.

misanthrope (n.) one who hates or distrusts all people; p. 161.

mobilize (v.) to put into motion; to organize; to make ready; p. 35. *Related words:* immobilize, mobility; p. 42.

mode (n.) manner or way of acting or doing; current style; p. 128.

moderation (n.) keeping away from extremes; calmness; p. 79. *Related words:* immoderate, moderate, moderator; p. 85.

modify (v.) to change or alter; p. 24. *Related word*: modification; p. 31.

morality (n.) moral qualities or character; principles of right and wrong; ethics; p. 128.

mundane (adj.) commonplace; everyday; p. 35.

musty (adj.) having a stale, moldy smell or taste; p. 171.

N

naive (adj.) simple in an unaffected or foolish way; childlike; unsophisticated; p. 171. *Related word*: naiveté; p. 179.

neurosis (n.) excessive fear or worry; p. 128. *Related word*: neurotic; p. 134.

O

objective (n.) aim; goal; (adj.) real; actual; without bias; p. 106.

oblige (v.) to force to do something because the law or one's conscience demands it; to do a favor for; p. 13.

obliterate (v.) to erase; to destroy; p. 150. *Related word*: obliteration; p. 158.

obscure (adj.) dim; dark; unclear; indistinct; vague; not well known; (v.) to conceal; p. 58. *Related word*: obscurity; p. 65.

obstinately (adj.) stubbornly; p. 68.

omission (n.) leaving out; failure to include; p. 106. *Related word*: omit; p. 114.

P

paternalistic (adj.) fatherlike; controlling or exercising authority in a fatherlike way; p. 128. *Related word*: paternalism; p. 134.

peevish (adj.) irritable; p. 161. *Related word*: peeve; p. 168.

perception (n.) awareness; insight; p. 106. *Related word*: perceptive; p. 114.

peremptory (adj.) bossy; commanding; p. 117.

perseverance (n.) persistent effort; p. 161. *Related word*: persevere; p. 168.

perturbation (n.) disturbance; annoyance; p. 117. *Related word*: perturb; p. 125.

pious (adj.) devout; prayerful; p. 161. *Related word*: piety; p. 168.

plausible (adj.) believable; p. 13. *Related word*: implausible; p. 21.

plight (n.) predicament; condition; p. 13.

polyglot (adj.) speaking several different languages; (n.) one who speaks several different languages. p. 68.

postulate (v.) to claim to be true without proof; (n.) something assumed to be true; p. 58.

prerequisite (n.) something required beforehand; (adj.) essential; p. 128. *Related words:* requisite, requisition; p. 134.

prevail (v.) to win out; to succeed or gain advantage; to become stronger or more widespread; p. 128. *Related word*: prevalent; p. 134.

prime (adj.) most important; first; (n.) best part; number that can be evenly divided only by itself and one; most vigorous or successful stage; (v.) to prepare; p. 150. *Related words with the* prim *root*: primeval, primitive; p. 158.

privation (n.) loss or absence of some quality or condition; want; p. 106. *Related word*: deprivation; p. 114.

profound (adj.) intellectually deep; thorough; p. 150. *Related word*: profundity; p. 158.

prose (n.) nonpoetic language; ordinary form of language; p. 68. *Related word*: prosaic; p. 75.

provincial (adj.) narrow-minded; limited; of or belonging to a province; p. 68. *Related words*: province, provincialism; p. 75.

provocative (adj.) that arouses one to be excited, angry, curious; p. 106. *Related word*: provoke; p. 114.

pugnacious (adj.) eager and ready to fight; quarrelsome; p. 68. *Related word*: pugilist; p. 75.

R

radiation (n.) process of sending out rays of heat, light, etc.; p. 24. *Related word*: radiate; p. 31.

ramify (v.) to divide or spread out into branches; p. 106. *Related word*: ramification; p. 114.

reactionary (n.) one who resists change; (adj.) politically conservative; traditional; p. 150. *Related word*: reaction; p. 158.

recompense (n.) compensation; (v.) to repay; to make up for a loss or injury; p. 128.

reconcile (v.) to make or become friendly again; to make consistent; p. 58. *Related word*: reconciliation; p. 65.

rectify (v.) to correct; p. 35.

recur (v.) to occur again; p. 117. *Related word*: recurrence; p. 125.

redemption (n.) rescue from sin; making up for something; recovery; exchange; p. 171. *Related words*: redeem, redemptive; p. 179.

relatively (adv.) not absolutely; comparatively; p. 24.

repress (v.) to subdue; to force painful feelings into the unconscious; p. 128. *Related words with the* press *root*: compress, express, impress, repression, suppress; p. 134.

repulsive (adj.) causing strong dislike or disgust; p. 171. *Related word*: repulse; p. 179.

reserved (adj.) quiet; aloof; set apart; p. 161. *Related word*: reservation; p. 168.

resolution (n.) decision or determination; solution; p. 161. *Related words*: resolute, resolve; p. 168.

resonance (n.) quality of an echo or reverberation; p. 171. *Related words*: resonant, resonate, resounding; p. 179.

rigor (n.) severity; difficulty; exactitude; p. 150. *Related word*: rigorous; p. 158.

ruminate (v.) to meditate; to chew, as a cow does; p. 106. *Related word*: rumination; p. 114.

S

seamy (adj.) unpleasant; dirty; wretched; p. 68.

seclusion (n.) isolation; p. 117. *Related word*: seclude; p. 125.

segment (v.) to divide into parts; (n.) section; p. 35.

sentiment (n.) feeling; opinion; p. 161. *Related word*: sentimentality; p. 168.

serenity (n.) tranquility; peacefulness; p. 13. *Related word*: serenade; p. 21.

sheer (adj.) extremely steep; absolute; pure; very thin; fine; p. 171.

shrivel (v.) to shrink and become wrinkled or withered; p. 79.

shroud (v.) to hide; to cover; (n.) cloth used for burial; something that covers; p. 13.

simplistic (adj.) making complex problems seem too simple; oversimplified; p. 171.

simulate (v.) to pretend; to imitate; p. 58. *Related word*: simulation; p. 65.

singular (adj.) unique; separate; referring to only one in grammar; p. 13. *Related word*: singularity; p. 21.

sinister (adj.) evil or dishonest; threatening disaster; p. 24.

solar (adj.) produced by or coming from the sun; p. 58.

solemn (adj.) serious; formal; p. 117. *Related word*: solemnity; p. 125.

solicit (v.) to seek; to beg; p. 161. *Related word*: solicitous; p. 168.

soliloquize (v.) to talk to oneself, usually in a dramatic setting; p. 161. *Related word*: soliloquy; p. 168.

solitary (adj.) alone; p. 161. *Related word*: solitude; p. 168.

species (n.) distinct kind; biological classification; p. 24.

strive (v.) to try; to struggle; p. 128.

subsequently (adv.) afterward; later; p. 58.

sympathetic (adj.) showing an ability to share another person's feelings; p. 106. *Related word with* path *root*: pathos; p. 114.

synonymous (adj.) having the same meaning as; similar in meaning; p. 68.

T

tactic (n.) method or strategy; plan; p. 35. *Related word*: tactician; p. 42.

tamp (v.) to pack or pound down by a series of blows or taps; p. 106.

tantamount (adj.) equivalent to; p. 150.

taut (adj.) tightly stretched; strained; p. 106.

temperament (n.) disposition; frame of mind; p. 68. *Related words*: temper, temperamental; p. 75.

toil (v.) to work hard; (n.) hard work or effort; p. 79.

transition (n.) passing from one stage, activity, place, etc., to another; p. 117. *Related words*: transfuse, transgress, transitory; p. 125.

traverse (v.) to pass over, across, through; to move back and forth; p. 79.

tumult (n.) noisy commotion; p. 161. *Related word*: tumultuous; p. 168.

U

unify (v.) to blend or unite; p. 35. *Related word*: unification; p. 42.

universal (adj.) occurring everywhere; affecting all; p. 24. *Related word*: universe; p. 31.

unspeakably (adv.) hard to describe or speak about because so great or so bad; inexpressibly; indescribably; p. 171.

unworldliness (n.) unsophistication; not being concerned with the things of the world; spirituality; p. 171. *Related word*: unworldly; p. 179.

utter (adj.) complete; absolute; p. 106. *Related words*: utterly, utterance; p. 114.

V

vegetation (n.) plant life; p. 24. *Related word*: vegetate; p. 31.

vicariously (adv.) as a substitute; p. 117. *Related word*: vicarious; p. 125.

vindictive (adj.) vengeful; spiteful; p. 117. *Related word*: vindication; p. 125.

virtue (n.) goodness; general or specific moral excellence; p. 106. *Related word*: virtuous; p. 114.

vitality (n.) mental or physical energy; vigor; power to live; p. 106. *Related words*: revitalize, vital, vitalize; p. 114.

vocation (n.) professional occupation or activity that one feels called to; p. 117. *Related word*: vocational; p. 125.

vociferous (adj.) loud; insistent; p. 35.

volatile (adj.) explosive; unpredictable; p. 58.

W

waif (n.) homeless child; stray animal; p. 171.

warranty (n.) justification; guarantee; p. 117. *Related word*: warrant; p. 125.

whimsical (adj.) fanciful; unpredictable; having odd notions; p. 117. *Related word*: whimsy; p. 125.

wince (v.) to draw back slightly, usually twisting the face, as in pain; p. 161.

Pronunciation Key

Symbol	Key Words
a	ask, fat, parrot
ā	ape, date, play
ä	ah, car, father
e	elf, ten, berry
ē	even, meet, money
i	is, hit, mirror
ī	ice, bite, high
ō	open, tone, go
ô	all, horn, law
o͞o	ooze, tool, crew
o͝o	look, pull, moor
yo͞o	use, cute, few
yo͝o	united, cure, globule
oi	oil, point, toy
ou	out, crowd, plow
u	up, cut, color
ʉr	urn, fur, deter
ə	a in ago
	e in agent
	i in sanity
	o in comply
	u in focus
ər	perhaps, murder

Symbol	Key Words
b	bed, fable, dub
d	dip, beadle, had
f	fall, after, off
g	get, haggle, dog
h	he, ahead, hotel
j	joy, agile, badge
k	kill, tackle, bake
l	let, yellow, ball
m	met, camel, trim
n	not, flannel, ton
p	put, apple, tap
r	red, port, dear
s	sell, castle, pass
t	top, cattle, hat
v	vat, hovel, have
w	will, always, swear
y	yet, onion, yard
z	zebra, dazzle, haze
ch	chin, catcher, arch
sh	she, cushion, dash
th	thin, nothing, truth
th	then, father, lathe
zh	azure, leisure
ŋ	ring, anger, drink
′	able (a′ b'l)
′ ′	expedition (ek′ spə dish′ ən)

Pronunciation key and some glossary entries reprinted from *Webster's New World Dictionary,* Student Edition. Copyright © 1981, 1976 by Simon & Schuster. Used by permission.

Inventory Test

These are all the target words in the book. Why not see how many you think you already know . . . or don't know?

- If you're sure *you know the word, mark the* **Y** *("yes") circle.*
- If you think you *might* know it, mark the **?** *(question mark) circle.*
- If you have *no idea* what it means, mark the **N** *("no") circle.*

Y	?	N		Y	?	N		Y	?	N	
○	○	○	abode	○	○	○	component	○	○	○	enable
○	○	○	absurdly	○	○	○	compose	○	○	○	endeavor
○	○	○	acculturation	○	○	○	condensation	○	○	○	endure
○	○	○	acquiesce	○	○	○	conference	○	○	○	engaging
○	○	○	advent	○	○	○	congeal	○	○	○	enigmatic
○	○	○	aggregation	○	○	○	conjecture	○	○	○	escalate
○	○	○	agitate	○	○	○	consensus	○	○	○	ethnicity
○	○	○	aloof	○	○	○	contamination	○	○	○	exceed
○	○	○	alter	○	○	○	contemplate	○	○	○	exemplify
○	○	○	ameliorate	○	○	○	contempt	○	○	○	explicitly
○	○	○	anguish	○	○	○	contour	○	○	○	extortion
○	○	○	aphorism	○	○	○	convulsive	○	○	○	extract
○	○	○	apprehensiveness	○	○	○	correspondent	○	○	○	extrapolate
○	○	○	archaism	○	○	○	counterbalance	○	○	○	faculty
○	○	○	ardor	○	○	○	counterpart	○	○	○	falter
○	○	○	aristocratic	○	○	○	cynical	○	○	○	foreboding
○	○	○	articulate	○	○	○	deduction	○	○	○	foresight
○	○	○	ascend	○	○	○	delineate	○	○	○	fundamentally
○	○	○	ascribe	○	○	○	delinquency	○	○	○	gaunt
○	○	○	aspect	○	○	○	demeanor	○	○	○	hale
○	○	○	aspiration					○	○	○	hauteur
○	○	○	assertion				*You're making progress.*	○	○	○	heritage
○	○	○	assimilate	○	○	○	deportment	○	○	○	idealism
○	○	○	attainment	○	○	○	desolation	○	○	○	immerse
○	○	○	augment	○	○	○	deviousness	○	○	○	impetuous
○	○	○	austere	○	○	○	devise	○	○	○	impose
○	○	○	authoritative	○	○	○	diabolical	○	○	○	impress
○	○	○	barbarian	○	○	○	distinction	○	○	○	inanimate
○	○	○	beneficent	○	○	○	diversity	○	○	○	incipient
○	○	○	bisect	○	○	○	domain	○	○	○	incoherent
○	○	○	bravado	○	○	○	domestic	○	○	○	indifferent
○	○	○	capital	○	○	○	dominate	○	○	○	induce
○	○	○	casual	○	○	○	dreary	○	○	○	inequality
○	○	○	catastrophic	○	○	○	duplicity	○	○	○	infuse
○	○	○	category	○	○	○	ebullience	○	○	○	initiate
○	○	○	civilized	○	○	○	economic	○	○	○	inscribe
○	○	○	cliché	○	○	○	eject	○	○	○	insight
○	○	○	coerce	○	○	○	elegance	○	○	○	integrity
○	○	○	collision	○	○	○	emanate	○	○	○	interaction
○	○	○	comparatively	○	○	○	emancipation	○	○	○	interpretation
			That's the first 40.	○	○	○	embark				*Take a break!*
				○	○	○	embodiment				

Y	?	N		Y	?	N		Y	?	N	
O	O	O	interrelated	O	O	O	perseverance	O	O	O	simplistic
O	O	O	intuitive	O	O	O	perturbation	O	O	O	simulate
O	O	O	irrecoverable	O	O	O	pious	O	O	O	singular
O	O	O	irreversible	O	O	O	plausible	O	O	O	sinister
O	O	O	issue	O	O	O	plight	O	O	O	solar
O	O	O	lassitude	O	O	O	polyglot	O	O	O	solemn
O	O	O	lethal	O	O	O	postulate	O	O	O	solicit
O	O	O	lethargy	O	O	O	prerequisite	O	O	O	soliloquize
O	O	O	lustrous	O	O	O	prevail	O	O	O	solitary
O	O	O	luxuriance	O	O	O	prime	O	O	O	species
O	O	O	lyric	O	O	O	privation	O	O	O	strive
O	O	O	macho	O	O	O	profound	O	O	O	subsequently
O	O	O	magnetism	O	O	O	prose	O	O	O	sympathetic
O	O	O	magnitude	O	O	O	provincial	O	O	O	synonymous
O	O	O	manifest	O	O	O	provocative	O	O	O	tactic
O	O	O	maudlin	O	O	O	pugnacious	O	O	O	tamp
O	O	O	median	O	O	O	radiation	O	O	O	tantamount
O	O	O	melancholy	O	O	O	ramify	O	O	O	taut
O	O	O	methodical	O	O	O	reactionary	O	O	O	temperament
O	O	O	millennium	O	O	O	recompense	O	O	O	toil
O	O	O	misanthrope	O	O	O	reconcile				*Only 20 more.*
O	O	O	mobilize	O	O	O	rectify	O	O	O	transition
O	O	O	mode	O	O	O	recur	O	O	O	traverse
O	O	O	moderation	O	O	O	redemption	O	O	O	tumult
O	O	O	modify	O	O	O	relatively	O	O	O	unify
O	O	O	morality	O	O	O	repress	O	O	O	universal
O	O	O	mundane	O	O	O	repulsive	O	O	O	unspeakably
O	O	O	musty	O	O	O	reserved	O	O	O	unworldliness
			Half the alphabet.	O	O	O	resolution	O	O	O	utter
O	O	O	naive	O	O	O	resonance	O	O	O	vegetation
O	O	O	neurosis	O	O	O	rigor	O	O	O	vicariously
O	O	O	objective	O	O	O	ruminate	O	O	O	vindictive
O	O	O	oblige	O	O	O	seamy	O	O	O	virtue
O	O	O	obliterate	O	O	O	seclusion	O	O	O	vitality
O	O	O	obscure	O	O	O	segment	O	O	O	vocation
O	O	O	obstinately				*This list will end soon.*	O	O	O	vociferous
O	O	O	omission	O	O	O	sentiment	O	O	O	volatile
O	O	O	paternalistic	O	O	O	serenity	O	O	O	waif
O	O	O	peevish	O	O	O	sheer	O	O	O	warranty
O	O	O	perception	O	O	O	shrivel	O	O	O	whimsical
O	O	O	peremptory	O	O	O	shroud	O	O	O	wince

Congratulations!

That was 240 words. How many of them *don't* you know? Highlight any words you marked **N**, and pay special attention to them as you work through the book. You'll soon know them all!

Strategies for Discovering Word Meaning

Use What You Already Know

There are many ways to get information about what an unfamiliar word might mean.

- It may contain a familiar **whole word**.
- It may be a **compound** of familiar words put together.
- You may recognize the **root**.
- You may recognize a **prefix** or **suffix**.
- There may be **context clues** to the meaning.

Try Everything

When you see an unfamiliar word, use every trick you can think of. You may be surprised to discover how useful what you already know can be. Take a look at how this can work with the word *enfeeblement* in the sentence, "She resented her enfeeblement."

	THOUGHT PROCESS	
enfeeblement	Since *resent* means "to feel hurt about," *enfeeblement* seems to be something bad.	**a context clue**
en • feeble • ment	I see *feeble* in there. Doesn't it mean "weak"?	**a whole word**
en • feeblement	Hmm . . . *en-* like in *endear, enlarge, enrage.* So it means something like "to make" or "to cause."	**a familiar prefix**
enfeeble • ment	That ending is common . . . *enjoy, enjoyment . . . measure, measurement.* It creates nouns.	**a familiar suffix**
	Noun. Feeble. To make. . . . So, she resented being made weak!	

Try It Yourself

_____ 1. disinclination (think about *disfavor, incline* and *admiration*)
     a. desire   b. ability   c. unwillingness

_____ 2. optimum (think about *optimism* and *maximum*)
     a. best amount   b. hopelessness   c. least possible

_____ 3. promptitude (think about *prompt* and *solitude*)
     a. guarantee   b. quickness   c. carelessness

_____ 4. rejuvenate (think about *redo, juvenile* and *originate*)
     a. to punish   b. to make young again   c. to teach again

_____ 5. somnolent (think about *insomnia* and *fraudulent*)
     a. sleepy   b. gloomy   c. partial

UNIT 1 Test Yourself

Part A Applying Meaning

Write the letter of the best answer.

_____ 1. A child's <u>serenity</u> is most often seen when he or she is
     a. crying.   b. running.   c. sleeping.   d. learning to walk.

_____ 2. Which of the following is employed as a <u>correspondent</u>?
     a. a clown   b. a teacher   c. a movie actor   d. a newspaper reporter

_____ 3. A person trying to <u>ascend</u> a mountain is attempting to
     a. climb it.   b. avoid it.   c. get down from it.   d. tunnel through it.

_____ 4. If one <u>contemplates</u> an action, that action tends to be
     a. hurried.   b. dangerous.   c. instinctive.   d. well thought out.

_____ 5. An example of an <u>indifferent</u> reaction to a comment would be a
     a. gasp.   b. shrug.   c. giggle.   d. nod.

_____ 6. If you are <u>obliged</u> to do something, you are likely to think of it as a
     a. duty.   b. treat.   c. danger.   d. goal.

_____ 7. Which of the following is most likely to be used to <u>coerce</u> someone?
     a. a bribe   b. a weapon   c. a plea   d. an argument

_____ 8. If a suggestion is made and you <u>acquiesce</u>, you are likely to
     a. nod.   b. groan.   c. shake your head.   d. express confusion.

Part B Matching Definitions

Match each word on the left with its definition on the right. Write the letter of the
definition in the blank.

_____ 9. absurdly   a. to cover or hide

_____ 10. plight   b. ridiculously

_____ 11. distinction   c. to rule or control

_____ 12. enable   d. believable

_____ 13. shroud   e. basically; essentially

_____ 14. dominate   f. a discussion; meeting

_____ 15. singular   g. to make possible; give power to

_____ 16. impress   h. remarkable; uncommon; unusual

_____ 17. plausible   i. to fix firmly on the mind

_____ 18. fundamentally   j. charitable; generous; doing good

_____ 19. beneficent   k. a condition or state, usually bad; predicament

_____ 20. conference   l. that which makes a difference; special recognition

---

UNIT 2   Test Yourself

Part A   Synonyms

Write the letter of the word that is closest in meaning to the capitalized word.

_____ 1. MODIFY: (A) describe   (B) decrease (C) adapt   (D) repeat

_____ 2. ABODE: (A) clay   (B) home   (C) livestock   (D) permanence

_____ 3. IMPETUOUS: (A) outraged (B) calm   (C) impulsive (D) risky

_____ 4. LETHAL: (A) lazy   (B) dignified (C) upsetting (D) deadly

_____ 5. SINISTER: (A) poor   (B) evil   (C) bitter   (D) rapid

_____ 6. IRREVERSIBLE: (A) unlimited (B) unusual (C) unusable (D) unchangeable

_____ 7. MAGNITUDE: (A) size   (B) glory   (C) beauty   (D) forgiveness

_____ 8. ALTER: (A) change   (B) start   (C) climb   (D) say

_____ 9. INITIATE: (A) acquire   (B) confuse (C) abandon (D) begin

_____ 10. IRRECOVERABLE: (A) lost   (B) open   (C) damaged (D) certain

_____ 11. DIVERSIFY: (A) shorten   (B) eliminate (C) vary   (D) lengthen

_____ 12. CONTAMINATION: (A) criticism   (B) pollution (C) destruction (D) delay

Part B   Applying Meaning

Write the letter of the best answer.

_____ 13. A baseball pitcher's <u>counterpart</u> would be
a. the coach.   b. the diamond.   c. the batter.   d. the opposing pitcher.

_____ 14. _Relatively_ is usually used to mean
a. "somewhat."   b. "extremely."   c. "occasionally."   d. "typically."

_____ 15. Any <u>interaction</u> results in effects that are
a. balanced.   b. widespread.   c. harmful.   d. shared to some degree.

_____ 16. Which of the following is a source of <u>radiation</u>?
a. the moon   b. the sun   c. gold   d. wind

_____ 17. A <u>millennium</u> is a period of
a. 10 years.   b. 100 years.   c. 1,000 years.   d. 1,000,000 years.

_____ 18. Which of the following is a pair of the same <u>species</u>?
a. eagle/hawk   b. snake/frog   c. man/woman   d. bull/stallion

_____ 19. A type of <u>vegetation</u> commonly found in yards is
a. grass.   b. a worm.   c. a fence.   d. a swing set.

_____ 20. An example of a <u>universal</u> law is
a. a speed limit.   b. a federal law.   c. a building code.   d. the law of gravity.

Score Yourself!   _The answers are on page 248._   Number correct: _____   Part A: _____   Part B: _____

Part A   Recognizing Meaning

Write the letter of the word or phrase that is closest in meaning to the word or words in italics.

_____ 1. to *ameliorate* the conditions
    a. ignore   c. improve
    b. change   d. overcome

_____ 2. to *articulate* a plan
    a. express   c. discuss
    b. discourage   d. take pride in

_____ 3. my own *aspiration*
    a. belief   c. responsibility
    b. ability   d. ambition

_____ 4. to describe this *attainment*
    a. event   c. competition
    b. punishment   d. achievement

_____ 5. an interesting *interpretation*
    a. experience   c. change
    b. explanation   d. argument

_____ 6. to determine the *median*
    a. truth   c. normal cost
    b. highest point   d. middle number

_____ 7. to *mobilize* voters
    a. educate   c. fool
    b. organize   d. appeal to

_____ 8. a *mundane* job
    a. difficult   c. volunteer
    b. low-paying   d. commonplace

_____ 9. to *rectify* the situation
    a. correct   c. ignore
    b. respond to   d. worsen

_____ 10. *segments* of oranges and grapefruits
    a. juices   c. sections
    b. supplies   d. orchards

_____ 11. a dangerous *tactic*
    a. spike   c. desire
    b. force   d. method

_____ 12. could not *unify* them
    a. unite   c. locate
    b. understand   d. inform

Part B   Matching Definitions

Match each word on the left with its definition on the right. Write the letter of the definition in the blank.

_____ 13. ethnicity   a. loud and uncontrolled

_____ 14. economic   b. an opinion held by all or most

_____ 15. heritage   c. racial or cultural status or character

_____ 16. vociferous   d. difference in size, rank, or status

_____ 17. category   e. something handed down from the past

_____ 18. acculturation   f. having to do with managing income and expenses

_____ 19. inequality   g. a group or division in a system of classification

_____ 20. consensus   h. the process of adjusting to a new culture and adopting its practices

---

Score Yourself!   *The answers are on page 248.*   Number correct: _____   Part A: _____   Part B: _____

UNIT 5   Test Yourself

Part A   Applying Meaning
Write the letter of the best answer.

_____ 1. An <u>aggregation</u> of cattle is a
a. herd.   b. corral.   c. Texas longhorn.   d. rancher.

_____ 2. <u>Solar</u> energy comes from
a. oil.   b. wind.   c. sunlight.   d. electricity.

_____ 3. <u>Condensation</u> appears as
a. ice.   b. a gas.   c. a gel.   d. moisture.

_____ 4. If you <u>extrapolate</u> an answer, you base it on
a. chance.   b. a dim memory.   c. complete facts.   d. a reasoned guess.

_____ 5. A <u>deduction</u> requires the use of
a. logic.   b. mathematics.   c. physical strength.   d. courage.

_____ 6. Something that <u>obscures</u> vision is
a. light.   b. fog.   c. corrective lenses.   d. a magnifying glass.

_____ 7. The need to <u>reconcile</u> facts or ideas occurs when they
a. are hidden.   b. are mistaken.   c. disagree.   d. rely on guesswork.

_____ 8. If Joe is described as a <u>comparatively</u> tall boy, he is taller than
a. few boys.   b. most boys.   c. all boys.   d. exactly one other boy.

_____ 9. <u>Postulating</u> a fact is most similar to
a. denying it.   b. proving it.   c. assuming it.   d. trying to hide it.

_____ 10. Race car drivers are protected from being <u>ejected</u> during car crashes by
a. bumpers.   b. air bags.   c. helmets.   d. seat belts.

Part B   Synonyms
Write the letter of the word that is closest in meaning to the capitalized word.

_____ 11. ASSIMILATE: (A) copy   (B) absorb   (C) observe   (D) destroy

_____ 12. CONJECTURE: (A) union   (B) insult   (C) guess   (D) connection

_____ 13. IMMERSE: (A) submerge   (B) protect   (C) disappear   (D) complicate

_____ 14. AUGMENT: (A) discuss   (B) honor   (C) frighten   (D) increase

_____ 15. COMPONENT: (A) enemy   (B) ingredient   (C) flattery   (D) partnership

_____ 16. SIMULATE: (A) divide   (B) signal   (C) prod   (D) imitate

_____ 17. VOLATILE: (A) happy   (B) determined   (C) explosive   (D) unbalanced

_____ 18. SUBSEQUENTLY: (A) during   (B) before   (C) afterward   (D) underneath

_____ 19. COLLISION: (A) crash   (B) secretiveness   (C) combination   (D) knowledge

_____ 20. INCIPIENT: (A) dangerous   (B) beginning   (C) accidental   (D) meaningless

Score Yourself!   The answers are on page 248.   Number correct: _____   Part A: _____   Part B: _____

UNIT 6 Test Yourself

Part A Recognizing Meaning

Write the letter of the word or phrase that is closest in meaning to the word or words in italics.

_____ 1. *lyric* forms of expression
a. musical c. unusual
b. agreeable d. elevated

_____ 2. to make this *assertion*
a. effort c. declaration
b. mistake d. disturbance

_____ 3. her *methodical* behavior
a. normal c. illegal
b. orderly d. unusual

_____ 4. to show *contempt*
a. fear c. pride
b. scorn d. jealousy

_____ 5. to suffer from *lethargy*
a. shyness c. sluggishness
b. dizziness d. overconfidence

_____ 6. his *deportment*
a. behavior c. beliefs
b. intelligence d. appearance

_____ 7. to ask *obstinately*
a. quickly c. foolishly
b. stubbornly d. occasionally

_____ 8. on *seamy* streets
a. neat c. unlit
b. crowded d. unpleasant

_____ 9. a *provincial* attitude
a. thoughtful c. religious
b. responsible d. narrow-minded

_____ 10. a bad *temperament*
a. fever c. natural attitude
b. habit d. reason for action

_____ 11. their *aristocratic* friends
a. snobbish c. insincere
b. upper-class d. intelligent

_____ 12. among the *barbarians*
a. workers c. attackers
b. crude people d. poets or singers

Part B Matching Definitions

Match each word on the left with its definition on the right. Write the letter of the definition in the blank.

_____ 13. extract a. eager and ready to fight

_____ 14. prose b. the act of getting something by force

_____ 15. cynical c. educated and polite

_____ 16. pugnacious d. speaking several languages

_____ 17. civilized e. to draw out by effort

_____ 18. polyglot f. non-poetic language

_____ 19. extortion g. having the same meaning as another

_____ 20. synonymous h. doubtful of people's sincerity

UNIT 7   Test Yourself

Part A   Recognizing Meaning

Write the letter of the word or phrase that is closest in meaning to the word or words in italics.

_____ 1. to *exceed* the budget
   a. go beyond   c. estimate
   b. agree to   d. describe

_____ 2. to *infuse* courage
   a. need   c. put in
   b. admire   d. demonstrate

_____ 3. to *shrivel* with age
   a. forget   c. wrinkle
   b. struggle   d. come to accept

_____ 4. to *compose* herself
   a. adorn   c. describe
   b. calm   d. inspire

_____ 5. a *catastrophic* event
   a. disastrous   c. disturbing
   b. casual   d. fascinating

_____ 6. to *endure* the meeting
   a. require   c. strictly limit
   b. tolerate   d. participate in

_____ 7. to display *moderation*
   a. energy   c. new techniques
   b. great skill   d. proper restraint

_____ 8. its *convulsive* movement
   a. unexpected   c. long-lasting
   b. remarkable   d. violently disturbed

Part B   Synonyms

Write the letter of the word that is closest in meaning to the capitalized word.

_____ 9. LUXURIANCE: (A) abundance   (B) fortune   (C) enjoyment   (D) need

_____ 10. DELINEATE: (A) lengthen   (B) reject   (C) describe   (D) deliver

_____ 11. TOIL: (A) idea   (B) goal   (C) labor   (D) success

_____ 12. DREARY: (A) gloomy   (B) exhausting   (C) dim   (D) continual

_____ 13. ASPECT: (A) result   (B) possession   (C) belief   (D) appearance

_____ 14. LUSTROUS: (A) bright   (B) unusual   (C) costly   (D) frightening

_____ 15. ARDOR: (A) terror   (B) passion   (C) joy   (D) reluctance

_____ 16. LASSITUDE: (A) regret   (B) wisdom   (C) outlook   (D) weariness

_____ 17. INANIMATE: (A) lifeless   (B) unhappy   (C) silent   (D) unconcerned

_____ 18. ENDEAVOR: (A) try   (B) repeat   (C) move   (D) appreciate

_____ 19. AGITATE: (A) grow   (B) shake   (C) consent   (D) flow

_____ 20. TRAVERSE: (A) beg   (B) drag   (C) send   (D) cross

---

Score Yourself!   *The answers are on page 248.*   Number correct: _____   Part A: _____   Part B: _____

UNIT 9 Test Yourself

Part A Synonyms
Write the letter of the word that is closest in meaning to the capitalized word.

_____ 1. UTTER: (A) possible (B) complete (C) partial (D) dangerous

_____ 2. HAUTEUR: (A) beauty (B) sorrow (C) arrogance (D) embarrassment

_____ 3. RUMINATE: (A) ponder (B) recall (C) complain (D) propose

_____ 4. VITALITY: (A) necessity (B) friendliness (C) dignity (D) liveliness

_____ 5. ANGUISH: (A) fury (B) laziness (C) misery (D) sensitivity

_____ 6. VIRTUE: (A) reality (B) goodness (C) belief (D) concern

_____ 7. FALTER: (A) waver (B) tumble (C) continue (D) retreat

_____ 8. TAUT: (A) sudden (B) strange (C) tight (D) smart

_____ 9. OBJECTIVE: (A) criticism (B) lesson (C) method (D) goal

_____ 10. PERCEPTION: (A) talent (B) completeness (C) awareness (D) welcome

Part B Matching Definitions
Match each word on the left with its definition on the right. Write the letter of the definition in the blank.

_____ 11. tamp   a. to divide or spread out into branches

_____ 12. ramify   b. able to share another's feelings

_____ 13. insight   c. the ability to see into a situation; sensitivity

_____ 14. omission   d. to pack or pound down with taps or blows

_____ 15. privation   e. connected to one another

_____ 16. sympathetic   f. a leaving out or failing to include

_____ 17. authoritative   g. reliable due to coming from an expert

_____ 18. intuitive   h. causing excitement, anger, or curiosity

_____ 19. provocative   i. the absence of a needed quality or condition

_____ 20. interrelated   j. knowing without the conscious use of reasoning

UNIT 10 Test Yourself

Part A Recognizing Meaning

Write the letter of the word or phrase that is closest in meaning to the word or words in italics.

_____ 1. a *solemn* look
    a. grave   c. frantic
    b. lonely   d. surprising

_____ 2. to *induce* coughing
    a. stop   c. cause
    b. prevent   d. reduce

_____ 3. it will *recur*
    a. begin   c. cause regret
    b. go backward d. happen again

_____ 4. a short *transition*
    a. journey   c. change
    b. repetition   d. communication

_____ 5. her *whimsical* story
    a. boring   c. puzzling
    b. fanciful   d. alarming

_____ 6. their *diabolical* plans
    a. similar   c. sly
    b. wicked   d. unstoppable

_____ 7. my chosen *vocation*
    a. purchase   c. occupation
    b. enjoyment   d. means of travel

_____ 8. a sense of *foreboding*
    a. dread   c. strong dislike
    b. eagerness   d. mild disapproval

_____ 9. to cause *perturbation*
    a. loneliness   c. great upset
    c. resentment d. quick awareness

_____ 10. to *issue* from a window
    a. differ   c. look out
    b. be seen   d. come out

_____ 11. a rather *melancholy* song
    a. sad   c. amusing
    b. irritating   d. old-fashioned

_____ 12. to remain in *seclusion*
    a. poverty   c. ignorance
    b. isolation   d. serious danger

Part B Applying Meaning

Write the letter of the best answer.

_____ 13. A woman can experience romance <u>vicariously</u> through
    a. being in love.   b. flirting.   c. romantic movies.   d. breaking a man's heart.

_____ 14. <u>Peremptory</u> orders are those one cannot
    a. obey.   b. refuse to follow.   c. acknowledge.   d. clearly understand.

_____ 15. A <u>vindictive</u> action is motivated by
    a. spite.   b. mercy.   c. regret.   d. curiosity.

_____ 16. A poem that is <u>ascribed</u> to you is one that you are believed to have
    a. read.   b. written.   c. copied.   c. inspired.

_____ 17. A traveler <u>embarks</u> when he or she
    a. packs.   b. plans the trip.   c. begins the trip.   d. returns home.

_____ 18. Your statements will be <u>incoherent</u> if you
    a. mumble.   b. shout.   c. write them down.   d. apologize for them.

_____ 19. Someone might show <u>apprehensiveness</u> by
    a. blushing.   b. trembling.   c. applauding.   d. yawning.

_____ 20. A punishment without <u>warranty</u> is one that is
    a. brief.   b. very harsh.   c. not deserved.   d. not effective.

Score Yourself!   *The answers are on page 248.*   Number correct: _____   Part A: _____   Part B: _____

UNIT 11 Test Yourself

Part A   Matching Definitions

Match each word on the left with its definition on the right. Write the letter of the definition in the blank.

_____ 1. devise   a. deceitfulness

_____ 2. repress   b. a mental or emotional disorder

_____ 3. neurosis   c. to create; plan

_____ 4. idealism   d. to keep down or put down; subdue

_____ 5. emancipation   e. principles of right and wrong

_____ 6. duplicity   f. failure to do what is required

_____ 7. morality   g. something required beforehand

_____ 8. counterbalance   h. the practice of living according to standards of perfection

_____ 9. delinquency   i. the act of setting free; release

_____ 10. prerequisite   j. any force that balances another

Part B   Synonyms

Write the letter of the word that is closest in meaning to the capitalized word.

_____ 11. ESCALATE: (A) move   (B) avoid   (C) resemble   (D) increase

_____ 12. PREVAIL: (A) help   (B) triumph   (C) suppose   (D) hinder

_____ 13. FAULTY: (A) ability   (B) meeting   (C) part   (D) concept

_____ 14. CONTOUR: (A) shape   (B) adventure (C) volume   (D) surface

_____ 15. INTEGRITY: (A) talent   (B) mixture   (C) soundness   (D) sympathy

_____ 16. RECOMPENSE: (A) balance   (B) approval   (C) cost   (D) repayment

_____ 17. DEVIOUSNESS: (A) difference (B) sneakiness (C) separation (D) wit

_____ 18. STRIVE: (A) walk   (B) desire   (C) exist   (D) struggle

_____ 19. PATERNALISTIC: (A) partial   (B) pitiful   (C) fatherlike (D) strong

_____ 20. MODE: (A) trait   (B) method   (C) invention   (D) center

---

Score Yourself!   *The answers are on page 248.*   Number correct: _____   Part A: _____   Part B: _____

244

UNIT 13 Test Yourself

Part A Recognizing Meaning

Write the letter of the word or phrase that is closest in meaning to the word or words in italics.

_____ 1. the student's *demeanor*
   a. main goal   c. behavior
   b. intelligence d. intentions

_____ 2. to *obliterate* a building
   a. damage   c. add to
   b. construct   d. totally destroy

_____ 3. his *austere* appearance
   a. stern   c. unusual
   b. very neat   d. old-fashioned

_____ 4. the *domain* of biology
   a. rules   c. importance
   b. study   d. field of thought

_____ 5. her *enigmatic* reply
   a. short   c. alarming
   b. puzzling   d. cautious

_____ 6. a very *casual* statement
   a. witty   c. uninterested
   b. reasonable   d. inspirational

_____ 7. to require *rigor*
   a. patience   c. energy
   b. formality   d. logical exactness

_____ 8. *explicitly* said
   a. definitely   c. enthusiastically
   b. cleverly   d. disapprovingly

_____ 9. the *magnetism* between them
   a. similarity   c. understanding
   b. attraction   d. huge problem

_____ 10. to *bisect* the line
   a. draw   c. run into
   b. double   d. divide in two

Part B Matching Definitions

Match each word on the left with its definition on the right. Write the letter of the definition in the blank.

_____ 11. elegance

_____ 12. impose

_____ 13. aloof

_____ 14. profound

_____ 15. aphorism

_____ 16. prime

_____ 17. tantamount

_____ 18. exemplify

_____ 19. inscribe

_____ 20. reactionary

a. apart in distance, interest, or feeling

b. graceful and dignified beauty

c. to write on; engrave

d. as much as; equivalent

e. to put (a burden or penalty) on

f. very scholarly or intellectual; deep

g. to show by example; represent.

h. a short statement of a general truth or bit of wisdom

i. highly traditional; resistant to change; conservative

j. most important or best; in math, having no divisor but one and the number itself

---

UNIT 14 Test Yourself

Part A   Synonyms

Write the letter of the word that is closest in meaning to the capitalized word.

_____ 1. GAUNT: (A) tall   (B) bony   (C) sickly   (D) irritable

_____ 2. SOLICIT: (A) request   (B) purchase   (C) abandon   (D) represent

_____ 3. MANIFEST: (A) show   (B) observe   (C) object   (D) appeal

_____ 4. WINCE: (A) lift   (B) succeed   (C) flinch   (D) escape

_____ 5. ADVENT: (A) prediction   (B) arrival   (C) reception   (D) journey

_____ 6. SENTIMENT: (A) statement   (B) departure   (C) awareness   (D) feeling

_____ 7. DESOLATION: (A) answer   (B) deceit   (C) loneliness   (D) quietness

_____ 8. HALE: (A) plump   (B) hesitant   (C) honest   (D) vigorous

_____ 9. TUMULT: (A) growth   (B) commotion   (C) blunder   (D) difficulty

_____ 10. CAPITAL: (A) first-rate   (B) noticeable   (C) bossy   (D) central

_____ 11. PEEVISH: (A) fretful   (B) ignorant   (C) self-centered (D) unhealthy

_____ 12. RESERVED: (A) lonely   (B) withdrawn   (C) changeable   (D) uncooperative

Part B   Applying Meaning

Write the letter of the best answer.

_____ 13. A person who works as a <u>domestic</u> might be a
a. farmer.   b. maid.   c. detective.   d. mail carrier.

_____ 14. One would expect a <u>misanthrope</u> to be
a. cheerful.   b. wise.   c. unfriendly.   d. disorganized.

_____ 15. Someone with <u>foresight</u> is probably skilled at
a. planning.   b. communication.   c. storytelling.   d. relationships.

_____ 16. A person who <u>soliloquizes</u> speaks as if he or she is
a. alone.   b. important.   c. severely burdened.   d. rejoicing.

_____ 17. A person could express <u>resolution</u> by saying,
a. *"I can't."*   b. *"I won't."*   c. *"I hope."*   d. *"I will."*

_____ 18. A <u>solitary</u> house is
a. large.   b. alone.   c. empty.   d. in bad repair.

_____ 19. What is important to a truly <u>pious</u> person?
a. wealth   b. romance   c. religion   d. privacy

_____ 20. You show <u>perseverance</u> when you refuse to
a. give up.   b. apologize.   c. complain.   d. accept change.

Score Yourself!   *The answers are on page 248.*   Number correct: _____   Part A: _____   Part B: _____

UNIT 15 Test Yourself

Part A Recognizing Meaning

Write the letter of the word or phrase that is closest in meaning to the word or words in italics.

_____ 1. a *repulsive* idea
    a. hostile   c. foolish
    b. disgusting   d. disturbing

_____ 2. to *congeal* over time
    a. change   c. become clear
    b. disappear   d. become solid

_____ 3. a display of *ebullience*
    a. deep pride   c. stubbornness
    b. selfishness   d. great enthusiasm

_____ 4. to *emanate* from her
    a. stay away   c. set free
    b. come forth   d. bring out

_____ 5. a sense of *sheer* happiness
    a. absolute   c. brief
    b. unusual   d. lasting

_____ 6. *unspeakably* violent
    a. silently   c. indescribably
    b. secretively   d. not realistically

_____ 7. to write *engaging* stories
    a. pleasing   c. romantic
    b. detailed   d. inspirational

_____ 8. his *naive* reaction
    a. cheerful   c. unsophisticated
    b. hot-tempered   d. formally polite

_____ 9. their *macho* pride
    a. foolish   c. masculine
    b. deeply felt   d. clearly shown

_____ 10. her show of *bravado*
    a. aggression   c. disorderliness
    b. amazing   d. pretended
       courage   bravery

Part B Matching Definitions

Match each word on the left with its definition on the right. Write the letter of the definition in the blank.

_____ 11. cliché

_____ 12. waif

_____ 13. archaism

_____ 14. musty

_____ 15. embodiment

_____ 16. resonance

_____ 17. simplistic

_____ 18. maudlin

_____ 19. redemption

_____ 20. unworldliness

a. having a stale, moldy smell or taste

b. representation in physical form

c. foolishly or weakly sentimental

d. unrealistically and overly simplified

e. the use of something characteristic of an earlier time

f. not caring much for material goods; spirituality

g. an expression that has lost freshness from overuse

h. salvation; rescue; a setting free

i. a homeless or neglected person, especially a child

j. the quality of being rich in sound; echoing quality

Score Yourself!   *The answers are on page 248.*   Number correct: _____   Part A: _____   Part B: _____

Score Yourself!

Unit 1	Unit 2	Unit 3	Unit 5	Unit 6	Unit 7
Part A	*Part A*	*Part A*	*Part A*	*Part A*	*Part A*
1. c	1. C	1. c	1. a	1. a	1. a
2. d	2. B	2. a	2. c	2. c	2. c
3. a	3. C	3. d	3. d	3. b	3. c
4. d	4. D	4. d	4. c	4. b	4. b
5. b	5. B	5. b	5. a	5. c	5. a
6. a	6. D	6. d	6. b	6. a	6. b
7. b	7. A	7. b	7. c	7. b	7. d
8. a	8. A	8. d	8. b	8. d	8. d
Part B	9. D	9. a	9. c	9. d	*Part B*
9. b	10. A	10. c	10. d	10. c	9. A
10. k	11. C	11. d	*Part B*	11. b	10. C
11. l	12. B	12. a	11. B	12. b	11. C
12. g	*Part B*	*Part B*	12. C	*Part B*	12. A
13. a	13. d	13. c	13. A	13. e	13. D
14. c	14. a	14. f	14. D	14. f	14. A
15. h	15. d	15. e	15. B	15. h	15. B
16. i	16. b	16. a	16. D	16. a	16. D
17. d	17. c	17. g	17. C	17. c	17. A
18. e	18. c	18. h	18. C	18. d	18. A
19. j	19. a	19. d	19. A	19. b	19. B
20. f	20. d	20. b	20. B	20. g	20. D

Unit 9	Unit 10	Unit 11	Unit 13	Unit 14	Unit 15
Part A	*Part A*	*Part A*	*Part A*	*Part A*	*Part A*
1. B	1. a	1. c	1. c	1. B	1. b
2. C	2. c	2. d	2. d	2. A	2. d
3. A	3. d	3. b	3. a	3. A	3. d
4. D	4. c	4. h	4. d	4. C	4. b
5. C	5. b	5. i	5. b	5. B	5. a
6. B	6. b	6. a	6. c	6. D	6. c
7. A	7. c	7. e	7. b	7. C	7. a
8. C	8. a	8. j	8. a	8. D	8. c
9. D	9. c	9. f	9. b	9. B	9. c
10. C	10. d	10. g	10. d	10. A	10. d
Part B	11. a	*Part B*	*Part B*	11. A	*Part B*
11. d	12. b	11. D	11. b	12. B	11. g
12. a	*Part B*	12. B	12. e	*Part B*	12. i
13. c	13. c	13. A	13. a	13. b	13. e
14. f	14. b	14. A	14. f	14. c	14. a
15. i	15. a	15. C	15. h	15. a	15. b
16. b	16. b	16. D	16. j	16. a	16. j
17. g	17. c	17. B	17. d	17. d	17. d
18. j	18. a	18. D	18. g	18. b	18. c
19. h	19. b	19. C	19. c	19. c	19. h
20. e	20. c	20. B	20. i	20. a	20. f

Acknowledgments

- Houghton Mifflin Company: For an excerpt from *Silent Spring* by Rachel Carson; copyright © 1962 by Rachel L. Carson.
- Farrar, Straus & Giroux, Inc.: For a selection from *The Chicanos* by Matt S. Meier and Feliciano Rivera; copyright © 1972 by Matt S. Meier and Feliciano Rivera, reprinted with the permission of Hill and Wang (a division of Farrar, Straus & Giroux, Inc.).
- Harper & Row, Publishers, Inc.: For an excerpt (pp. 13–16) of *The Physics of the Earth* by T. F. Gaskell (Funk & Wagnells); copyright © 1970 by T. F. Gaskell.
- Little, Brown and Company: For an excerpt from *Ship of Fools* by Katherine Anne Porter; copyright © 1962.
- Airmont Unabridged Classics Paperbacks: For an excerpt from *Frankenstein* by Mary Shelley.
- Summit Books, a division of Simon & Schuster, Inc.: For an excerpt from *Her Mother's Daughter* by Marilyn French; copyright © 1987 by Belles-Lettres, Inc.
- The Bobbs-Merrill Co., Inc.: For an excerpt from *Moby Dick* by Herman Melville, edited by Charles Feidelson, Jr.; copyright © 1964.
- Granada Publishing Ltd. and McGraw-Hill, Inc.: For an excerpt from *The Female Eunuch* by Germaine Greer; copyright © 1971.
- W. H. Freeman and Company, Publishers: For excerpts from "Gauss" by Ian Stewart; copyright © 1977 by Scientific American, Inc., all rights reserved.
- Houghton Mifflin Company: For an excerpt from *Wuthering Heights* by Emily Brontë, edited with an introduction and notes by V. S. Pritchett, Riverside Editions B2; copyright © 1965 by V. S. Pritchett.
- Henry Holt and Company, Inc.: For specified excerpts from pp. 213–215 of "Stallone and Stahr," from *When the Lights Go Down* by Pauline Kael; copyright © 1980 by Pauline Kael.

Every effort has been made to trace the ownership of all copyrighted material and to obtain permission.

Cover Art

Relativity, 1953, M.C. Escher. National Gallery of Art, Washington, D.C., Gift of C.V.S. Roosevelt.

Photographs

The Bettmann Archive: 27, 109, 131; Danny Lyon/Magnum Photos, Inc.: 37; California Institute of Technology, Mt. Palomar Observatory: 61; Photofest: 81, 174.

Illustrations

Tom Dunnington: 16; David Cunningham: 70; Suzanne Snider: 153; Diana Magnuson: 164.

Personal Vocabulary Log

Use the following pages to keep track of the unfamiliar words you encounter in your reading. Write brief definitions and pronunciations for each word. This will make the words part of your permanent vocabulary.

Personal Vocabulary Log

Personal Vocabulary Log

Personal Vocabulary Log

Personal Vocabulary Log

Personal Vocabulary Log

Personal Vocabulary Log

Personal Vocabulary Log

Personal Vocabulary Log

Personal Vocabulary Log